CURRENT ISSUES IN CRIMINAL JUSTICE
(VOL. 10)

MEDIA, PROCESS, AND THE SOCIAL CONSTRUCTION OF CRIME

GARLAND REFERENCE LIBRARY
OF THE HUMANITIES
(VOL. 1690)

CURRENT ISSUES IN CRIMINAL JUSTICE

GENERAL EDITORS: FRANK P. WILLIAMS III AND MARILYN D. MCSHANE

STRANGER VIOLENCE
A Theoretical Inquiry
by Marc Riedel

CRIMES OF STYLE
Urban Graffiti and the Politics of Criminality
by Jeff Ferrell

UNDERSTANDING CORPORATE CRIMINALITY
edited by Michael B. Blankenship

POLITICAL CRIME IN CONTEMPORARY AMERICA
A Critical Approach
edited by Kenneth D. Tunnell

THE MANAGEMENT OF CORRECTIONAL INSTITUTIONS
by Marilyn D. McShane and Frank P. Williams III

INNOVATIVE TRENDS AND SPECIALIZED STRATEGIES IN COMMUNITY-BASED CORRECTIONS
edited by Charles B. Fields

THE WINDS OF INJUSTICE
American Indians and the U.S. Government
by Laurence Armand French

ALTERED STATES OF MIND
Critical Observations of the Drug War
edited by Peter Kraska

CONTROLLING STATE CRIME:
An Introduction
edited by Jeffrey Ian Ross

MEDIA, PROCESS, AND THE SOCIAL CONSTRUCTION OF CRIME
Studies in Newsmaking Criminology
edited by Gregg Barak

MEDIA, PROCESS, AND THE SOCIAL CONSTRUCTION OF CRIME

Studies in Newsmaking Criminology

Edited by
Gregg Barak

GARLAND PUBLISHING, Inc.
New York & London / 1994

Library of Congress Cataloging-in-Publication Data

Media, process, and the social construction of crime : studies in
newsmaking criminology / edited by Gregg Barak.
    p. cm. — (Current issues in criminal justice ; vol. 10)
(Garland reference library of the humanities ; vol. 1690)
    Includes bibliographical references.
    ISBN 0-8153-1259-8 (hardcover)—
    ISBN 0-8153-1855-3 (paperback)
    1. Crime in mass media. 2. Mass media and criminal justice.
3. Crime and the press. I. Barak, Gregg. II. Series.
III. Series: Garland reference library of the humanities. Current
issues in criminal justice ; v. 10.
P96.C74M43 1994
364—dc20   93-39423
                                            CIP

Paperback cover design by Karin Badger.

Printed on acid-free, 250-year-life paper
Manufactured in the United States of America

To Maya and Charlotte

Contents

Series Foreword

One of the most pervasive forms of social control in our society is the mass media. The public learns from television, newspapers, magazines, movies, and books what is happening in the world and "how to" interpret it. The problem, however, is that full or complete interpretations of reality are not presented. In short, reality itself, clear and unadorned, is not to be found in the information provided by the media. Instead, media presentations consist of those various viewpoints that succeed in capturing the minds and imaginations of the masses, or in terms of the 1992 presidential campaign, that successfully put the winning "spin" on information.

Crime information represents some of the most potent imagery the media can present. As Gregg Barak and the contributors to this volume argue, crime information is "spun" with the effect that it reinforces particular forms of social control. They do not, however, argue that the depiction of crime, criminals, and victims has remained the same over time. On the contrary, their examination of the historical presentation of crime and justice news reveals that it is subject to and inseparable from political, economic, and social struggle. Thus, it is always possible that the media can be a forum to help promote new understandings of crime and social control, if only those with the most knowledge on the subject—criminologists—were ever to develop their collective public voice.

Accordingly, Barak and others believe that criminologists should participate in the various media presentations of crime and justice. By bringing their knowledge to bear on media presentations, criminologists can help make some news more representative and less distorted of the social reality of crime. At the same time, criminologists can serve as the best possible sources for educating both the media and the public about the nature of crime and justice in society. Barak also believes that criminologists should not confine their writings to academic audiences nor their teachings to the classroom. In addition, they should engage journalists and media analysts wherever and whenever possible, as a means of influencing public discourse as well as public policy.

We, Barak, and the contributors to this volume believe that criminologists can do a whole lot more than they have historically done to educate themselves, the public, and the media about the social construction and reconstruction of crime. With this in mind, the various contributions here shed much needed light on the ways in which the mass media produce news, and on the practical ways in which criminologists can go about the business of crime news production.

Marilyn McShane
Frank Williams

Preface

In the tradition of such classic studies on crime and the media as Cohen and Young's *The Manufacture of News: Social Problems, Deviance, and the Mass Media* (1973) and Ericson et al. *Visualizing Deviance: A Study of News Organization* (1987), or more recent studies such as Ericson et al. *Representing Order: Crime, Law, and Justice in the News Media* (1991), Surette's *Media, Crime and Criminal Justice: Images and Realities* (1992), and Benedict's *Virgin or Vamp: How the Press Covers Sex Crimes* (1992), this anthology explores the news construction of crime and justice by a politically and culturally constituted media. Like those works that precede this one, similar conclusions are reached about the prevalent biases to be found in the portrayals of crime, law, and justice. However, unlike its predecessors, this study also moves beyond explication and criticism to suggest how oppositional discourse can work to expose biased media images and to replace them with demystified images of crime and justice based on reason rather than emotion.

Pertaining to media biases and the production of news stories about crime and justice, newsmaking criminologists distinguish themselves from those weakly founded condemnatory judgments of media pundits and others because they ground their analyses and critiques on scientific assessments. As students of mass media, social construction, and criminal history, newsmaking criminologists appreciate that some trends have changed in the selection and presentation of newsworthy criminality over the past 150 years, such as the tendency to define criminals as outside the community. However, other trends have remained constant, such as the appeal of and to sensationalist crime coverage. Newsmaking criminologists ask questions about how the inherent selectivity, summation, and simplification of news production influences the context of what becomes newsworthy crime and deviance. They ask questions about the relationship between changes in media biases and changes in the wider social order. They also ask questions about the various stereotypical profiles that are used to construct images of criminals and victims. Newsmaking criminologists want to know how historical and social changes in race, class, and gender relations have affected the news media's portrayals of crime, criminals, and victims. Have the crimes of the rich and powerful, for example, been understated or has their representation been proportional to their occurrences or social harm? Similarly, have the crimes of the poor and powerless— particularly those involving racial minorities—been exaggerated or have these been accurate depictions of the social reality of crime?

Additionally, does the media focus on stories where the victims are white and where the perpetrators are public figures? Are black-on-white crimes the media's preferred crime stories? Are black male rapists and white female rape victims, respectively, the media's favorite subjects for crime news coverage? For example, does the socially stereotypical and racially charged rape of middle-class and virginal white women by dangerous and lower-class black men still dwarf the coverage of the more common everyday occurrences of the rape of black and white working-class women by men of every class and race? In order to move beyond the various myths, opinions, and stereotypes of the relationship of the media and crime, newsmaking criminology examines the determination of newsworthiness as well as the commodification of information about crime and justice. An investigation of these social relations becomes a prerequisite for understanding the cultural perception of crime. In particular, the authors in this volume focus their collective attention on the selection and presentation of newsworthy crime. They attempt to develop not only an understanding of the historical and contemporary coverage of media crime, but to explain the relationship of that coverage in the context of changing and conflicting views of individuals, property, and the public/private domains. Moreover, the readings in this anthology examine the processes and interactions of the day-to-day operations of video and print journalism in an attempt to explain how these two media both contribute to and reflect the dominant cultural ideologies about crime and crime control. Finally, while the readings in this book emphasize the scrutiny of two news media distribution systems, they also explore the other mass media distribution systems.

A complete analysis of the social construction of crime requires that all media forms which contribute to the public perception of crime be fully investigated, including radio, films, television, crime docu-dramas, and "true crime" books. *Studies in Newsmaking Criminology* focuses, however, mostly on the systemic and routine distribution of newsworthy crime found daily on television and in the newspaper. It is the belief that because of their repetitive nature these two spheres of mass media are the most important. These two systems of mass communication involve relatively greater frequency, intensity and duration of circulation than do the other spheres whose contributions are more subtle and indirect. Nevertheless, attention is paid to the interplay between the news media and other mass-communicated portrayals of crime and justice, and to the importance of how the two reinforce and/or frame the cultural fabric that is sewn into the official reality of crime. Also appreciated is the historical importance of tabloid print journalism, and more recently, the emerging convergence between news media and entertainment media as evidenced by the formation of video info-tainment.

In an earlier article, "Newsmaking Criminology: Reflections on the Media, Crime, and Intellectuals," reprinted here, I introduced a criminological practice that I called "newsmaking criminology." I was referring to the conscious efforts and activities of criminologists to interpret, influence, or shape the presentation of "newsworthy" items about crime and justice. Initially, my concern was with the role that criminologists could play in the production and distribution of newsworthy crime stories. I was sounding a call for criminologists to actively participate in the mass-consumed ideology of crime and justice. I was asking criminologists to break away from their obsessive dialogue with themselves in esoteric journals and to go public with their knowledge and understanding of crime and deviance. I was specifically asking criminologists to engage reporters, editors, and producers in a twofold mission. On the one hand, I invited them to expose journalistic conventions and societal biases as these have shaped the coverage (selection and presentation) of "crime stories." On the other hand, I felt that it was important for them (us) to permeate the mass-mediated popular discourse on crime and justice with alternative views, based more on scientific research than on moralistic treatises of crime and deviance. I was particularly interested in whether or not it was possible for criminologists to help (un)confound society's understanding of "crime and punishment." I was also interested in whether it was possible for criminologists to substitute structural and historical analyses of criminality and victimization in place of the more traditional and ahistorical analyses of "good" and "bad" people.

In this book, which is an extension of those initial thoughts, the boundaries of newsmaking criminology are considerably expanded. While I still believe it is important for criminologists to confront the production of news crime by placing our own "journalistic spins" on crime and justice, we need not confine our expertise to facilitating the production of newsworthy crime stories. In addition, we should stake a claim to the scientific study of newsmaking crime and crime control and its relationship with the ongoing development of criminal justice policy in particular and of public consciousness concerning law and order in general.

The implicit assumptions driving this work are two: first, that the social construction of crime and deviance is part of the ideological and political socialization involved in the cultural legitimation of law and order—the end result being conformity and enhanced social control. And second, that conversely the social deconstruction and reinterpretation of crime and deviance is part of an alternative or oppositional discourse capable of challenging the prevailing legal order and of producing social change in the cultural consciousness of crime and its control. Newsmaking criminologists also understand that, dialectically speaking, social movements and ideas, over time, influence mass media depictions, and then, over time again, mass media depictions influence social thought and action. In sum, neither is overly deterministic but both are subject to the interaction with the other. Finally, by acknowledging the causal relationship between the two, we are simultaneously striving to influence its course at various points.

Armed with this kind of knowledge, criminologists are in an ideal position not only to make sense of "newsworthy" crime, but to help educate both the crime-consuming public and the crime-producing reporters and editors to the consequences of news words and pictures, especially when many of these can be viewed as harmful to victims, defendants, and society at large. If this book helps to move the discipline of criminology into a more active role in understanding and influencing the mass distribution of media images of crime and justice, then it will have accomplished its primary objective.

G.B.
Ann Arbor, March 1993

Acknowledgments

I would like first to acknowledge the contributors for their willingness to participate in this project. A venture such as this involves a certain kind of trust between contributors and the editor and also a certain degree of risk as authors deliver their manuscripts to an unknown collection of unknown quality. For these reasons I thank the contributing authors.

Others who have contributed to the larger project of newsmaking criminology have included various media people and journalists that I have known and talked with over the past ten years, most of whom worked in Illinois, Alabama, or Georgia. Academicians who have helped in this project have included: Francis Cullen, Walter Dekeseredy, Dragan Milovanovic, Hal Pepinsky, and Tony Platt. There are also colleagues both at Eastern Michigan University and elsewhere who provided me with feedback on this anthology and its organization as well as its introduction. From EMU there are three persons whom I wish to thank: Mark Lanier, Liza Cerroni-Long, and Stuart Henry. I especially want to thank Stuart, once again, for what I call "our dangling theoretical conversation." Three other persons had critical input into the final version of the introduction to this anthology: Bob Bohm, Coramae Richey Mann, and Ray Surette.

Three more people made this book possible. First, there were the editors of this series, Marilyn McShane and Frank Williams, who had the faith and good sense to proceed with this project with very little evidence up front. Second, there was my graduate student, Karen Schaumann. Once again, without Karen's work on this anthology as with my other most recent anthology, *Varieties of Criminology*, it would not have reached the publisher's desk in such a timely fashion. Karen not only brought the manuscripts and disks into publishing uniformity, but she also assisted me in the editing process.

Gregg Barak
April 1993

PART I

Introduction

CHAPTER 1

Media, Society, and Criminology

Gregg Barak

Understanding the construction of newsmaking requires an examination of the conscious and unconscious processes involved in the mass dissemination of symbolic consumer goods. Commonly referred to as information or as ideas, these symbolic bites or commodities of news production and the pictures of social reality that they create are inseparable from their cultural history. Media images or characterizations of crime and crime control in the United States are constituted within the core of the social, political, and psychological makeup of American society. Mass news representations in the "information age" have become the most significant communication by which the average person comes to know the world outside his or her immediate experience. As for the cultural visions of crime projected by the mass media, or the selections and presentations by the news media on criminal justice, these representations are viewed as the principal vehicle by which the average person comes to know crime and justice in America.

Crime stories produced by the news media in this country reveal as much about the American experience and U.S. values as they do about crime and the administration of justice. As for the importance of the media's role in the social construction of crime and criminal justice, Surette (1992: 6) maintains that an improved comprehension of "the underlying dynamics of a society can be gained by examining the points of contact between society's primary information system—the mass media—and its primary system for legitimizing values and enforcing norms—the criminal justice system." Moving back and forth between these two systems of social control are morality plays or struggles between bad guys and good guys. While "the tendency to make moral evaluations is of course not limited to thinking about crime," it does seem that crime is a "focal point for the human need to hold positive and negative attitudes toward social objects" (Claster, 1992: ix).

Throughout society there are both individuals and groups of people with a wide range of perceptions about crime and justice. These perceptions are influenced by the different ways in which the interplay between criminals, apprehenders, and victims are socially and ethically perceived by ordinary citizens, criminal justice policy makers, those responsible for carrying out legal norms, criminologists, and the press. The mass communication of these perceptions construct a cultural awareness of crime, of victim/offender encounters, and of the administration of justice.

The cultural formation of moral evaluations does not randomly occur. They are not the unadulterated by-products of logic and facts. Moreover, cultural evaluations are not the offspring of some kind of all-powerful elite of the "Left" or "Right." Nor are the moral or social panics associated with urgent societal problems the exclusive territory of moral or social entrepreneurs. Whether the subject is civil disturbances like the L.A. riots that erupted in response to the Rodney King beating verdict in the spring of 1992, everyday activities like rape and domestic violence that are commonly committed by both strangers and intimates, or homeless victims of the AIDS epidemic who are dying in the streets, what emerges in the construction of social and criminal crises is the tendency for the political parameters of discussion to become rather fixed by a limited public discourse. As Watney (1987) demonstrates in *Policing Desire: Pornography, AIDS, and the Media*, there is an important need for analysts of media to deconstruct culturally taken-for-granted factuality. In his study, Watney did precisely that by showing how the British government and media based their approach to the AIDS crisis on an agenda of sexual uniformity and conformity, fueled by a not-so-subtle homophobia.

In contrasting nineteenth-century rural America with our emerging twenty-first century urban society, one should appreciate that while the one-dimensional or limited public discourse on "right" and "wrong" remains a constant theme, both its content and form change according to various developments in the political economy, technology, and society at large. As Claster suggests, it was only natural that the cowboy melodrama of the nineteenth-century dime novel was replaced by the twentieth-century fiction and nonfiction of cops-and-robbers. After all, "the urban milieu is more in tune with the experiences and moral expressions of the modern public, among whom struggles between innocent crime victims or 'untouchable' lawmen on the one hand and muggers or political terrorists or vice lords on the other are more popular than fights between good cowboys in shining white hats and bad cowboys in greasy black ones" (Claster, 1992: 3). Contemporary cultural fascination or preoccupation with certain kinds of anomalic violent crime, for example, like that involving serial killers, is reflected in the "True Crime" sections of popular bookstores and is not disconnected from the minds and imaginations of news media audiences that are nurtured on a constant diet of an unsafe world where subhuman criminals apparently run rampant. As these types of statistically rare and gruesome crimes are merged in the public (mass) mind with the crimes of fiction, a distorted view of crime (and justice) is perpetuated. At the same time, these mixed perceptions of real and make-believe criminals produced by the mass media not only "provide modern audiences with an outlet for their needs to participate vicariously in the struggle between good and evil forces," but with "accounts of real struggles between the established moral order and threats to subvert it" that satisfy those same needs (Claster, 1992: 3). Numerous films, docu-dramas, and prime time television shows such as "America's Most Wanted," "Top Cops," "American Detective," and "Unsolved Mysteries" testify to this mass media construction of law, order, and justice.

As implied so far, the consideration or examination of the interrelationships between media, society, and criminology is essentially a complex and dynamic enterprise. It involves the interaction of journalists, sources, and audiences that coexist within a diverse and eclectic cultural and social system. Serious study also involves attention to the developing political economy and the socio-historical experience of news production that exist within the larger organization of mass media and technological arrangement.

A formulaic expression of media, process, and the perception of crime may be thought of as: PERCEPTION OF CRIME=MEDIA × (CULTURE + POLITICAL ECONOMY) OVER TIME. See figure 1.1 for a conceptual or integrated model of crime news construction. The model suggests that how we define the cultural production of crime as a "social problem" and how we regard victims, offenders, and agents of crime control emerges out of the social interactions between ordinary people, journalists, and sources of information within the structural and political-economic contexts of active processes of news construction and crime management.

More specifically for our purposes, newsmaking criminology—or the study of and interaction with crime and justice news construction—consists of a scrutiny of the dynamism between the production of crime news stories and the wider social order. It further entails an appreciation that crime news, like other news, emerges from struggles that are ultimately resolved, at least momentarily, by the prevailing but not necessarily dominant relations of power. Like news in general, crime news is chiefly a reflection of "the exercise of power over the interpretation of reality" (Gans, 1980: 81). Generally like students of news media, students of newsmaking criminology are concerned with the degree of distortion and bias in the news, or with the distance between the social reality of crime and the newsmaking reality of crime. Like other analysts of the news media, newsmaking criminologists are similarly interested in seeing that the news media "tell it like it is," and better yet, "like it could be" or "like it should be," based on an informed scientific view of crime and justice.

Newsmaking criminologists can distinguish themselves from other analysts of the media because they possess a much wider knowledge of the social, political, economic, and cultural complexities of crime and justice. As experts on law and order,

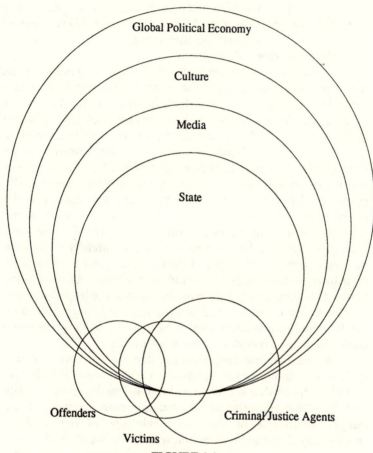

FIGURE 1.1
Media, Process, and the Perception of Crime

newsmaking criminologists are in a better position than other analysts of media to assess the "newsworthiness" of crime news, to deconstruct the selection and presentation of crime news, and to help reconstruct an alternative crime news. These areas of inquiry and activity, taken together, constitute the praxis of what I call "Newsmaking Criminology."

The studies in this book on news media in general and on newsmaking crime in particular move well beyond those one-dimensional interpretations which maintain either that crime news is a reflection of the interests, preferences, and needs of political, class, and cultural elites, or that crime news is a reflection of the demands, interests, and needs of an homogenized mass audience. Dialectically, our analyses recognize that crime news ultimately reflects the socially constructed perspectives of both the privileged elites and the popular masses. Moreover, our analyses are no less concerned with the policy implications of the construction of crime news than they are with the news media's representation of criminal behavior per se, especially in terms of how these constructions help to reproduce or reduce crime and violence in the United States. Our focus, then, concerns the various contradictions and tensions involved in the subjective and organizational production of crime news, and in the implicit and explicit crime control policies advocated by the news media.

As part of the larger criminological enterprise, newsmaking criminologists investigate a variety of social relations, including those that encompass the mass media more broadly and those that comprise the news media more narrowly. For a deeper awareness of the social relations of newsmaking criminology, I articulate them below as including three dynamic and interrelated processes of news construction: (1) media reflection, cultural diversity, and crime news; (2) mass media, public order, and symbolic deviance; and (3) social control, news media, and political change. Before turning to this analysis of news media and crime, it makes sense to establish some kind of working definition of "what constitutes news."

News

Gans (1980: xi), in his classic study of "CBS Evening News," "NBC Nightly News," *Newsweek*, and *Time*, referred to the national news in the U.S. simply as "what this society tells itself about itself." He argued in much detail that "news is about the economic, political, social, and cultural hierarchies" found within society and, that for the most part, the news "reports on those at or near the top of the hierarchies and on those, particularly at the bottom, who threaten them, to an audience, most of whom are located in the vast middle range between top and bottom" (Gans, 1980: 284). Perhaps more accurately, Gans (1980: 80) defined news as "information which is transmitted from sources to audiences, with journalists—who are both employees of bureaucratic commercial organizations and members of a profession—summarizing, refining, and altering what becomes available to them from sources in order to make the information suitable for their audiences."

Gans (1980: 52) conceptualized actual news stories by dividing them into two types: "One type is called disorder news, which reports threats to various kinds of order, as well as measures taken to restore order. The second type deals with the routine activities, as well as the periodic selection of new officials, both through election and appointment." Both types of news stories, despite differences, help to reproduce the dominant social order.

This work is about disorder news of which Gans identified four major categories: natural, technological, social, and moral. Our preoccupation is with news stories that fit the categories of social and moral disorder. The social disorder news stories deal with activities which disturb the public peace. These news stories may include the deterioration of valued institutions such as the nuclear two-parent family. They usually involve violence or the threat of violence against life or physical property. As for the moral disorder news story, it typically reports transgressions of laws and mores which do not necessarily endanger the social order, such as homosexual marriages.

Media Reflection, Cultural Diversity,
and Crime News

In *Media Performance*, McQuail (1992: 162–63) argues that "the degree of correspondence between the diversity of the society and the diversity of media content is the key to assessing . . . whether or not the media give a biased or a true reflection of society." It has been shown that despite the expanding media pluralism (many channels) in this and other societies, message pluralism (diversity of content) has not grown accordingly (Gormley, 1980; Gerbner et al, 1982). This is generally the case for media coverage of political, racial, ethnic, class, or sexual diversity. Instead of reflecting the increasingly greater diversity, the media has continued to provide homogenized, mainstream, and uniform versions of reality that tend to avoid fundamental controversy. What accounts for this consistency in the lack of diversity of news media is a reliance on shared journalistic routines, on the same news sources, and on the interaction between fundamental news values and society's core values. Put another way, since the news media compete for the same audiences and reflect the narrow topical and selection criteria of significance and relevance to the concerns of their audiences and their media organizations alike, it is not surprising that what constitutes "news" does not necessarily conform with reality.

Distortions abound with the portrayals of issues related to race, ethnicity, gender, and class in the news media. Blacks, Hispanics, and other "minorities" such as Asians and Middle-Easterners are generally under-represented in the "good news." However, when it comes to "bad news," which is often thought to be more newsworthy than "good news," blacks and other ethnic minorities are more likely to be identified in negative contexts (e.g., crime), even when they are cast as victims (Hartman and Husband, 1974; van Dijk, 1991). The same kinds of patterns exist with the depictions of women in the news. For example, the economic role of women is usually underestimated. The media typically reports on women of lower status, in subordinate positions to men, or in some statistically uncommon negative role like mistress or prostitute, while other roles, which are no less common in real life, are neglected (Miller, 1975; Blackwood and Smith, 1983). When it comes to class, occupation, and social status, the same kinds of news reporting prevail. Here, "media portrayals accentuate higher skilled, better paid and higher status occupations, both in terms of frequency and often in direction of valuation. Routine or normal working class jobs are rarely seen, except for service roles" (McQuail, 1992: 166).

As for portrayals of crime, distortions also exist (Davis, 1952; Fishman, 1978; Graber, 1980; Fedler and Jordan, 1982). The news media consistently underplay petty, nonviolent and white-collar offenses while they overplay interpersonal, violent, and sexual crimes. Invariably, media portrayals of criminals tend to be one-dimensional reflections of the crimes commonly committed by the poor and the powerless and not those crimes commonly committed by the rich and powerful (Barak, 1988; Munro-Bjorklund, 1991). By contrast, with respect to news media images of the criminal justice system in general and to crime fighters in particular, distortions persist that are contradictory in nature. For example, while the docu-dramas and news tabloid shows repeatedly represent the police as gallant warriors fighting the forces of evil, on the one side, mainstream news constructions, on the other side, often personify the agents of crime control as negatively ineffective and incompetent. Nevertheless, the outcome or "the cumulative effect of these portraits is support for more police, more prisons, and more money for the criminal justice system" (Surette, 1992: 249).

While the reflections of the media on cultural diversity are generally poor, they are not uniformly poor. For example, on some topics such as national politics, sports, big business, and popular entertainment, the media "perform quite well in faithfully reflecting what is going on in the world" (McQuail, 1992: 169). When it comes to "crimes news" in particular, the performance of the news media is generally but not uniformly poor. From the perspective of newsmaking criminology, it is my contention that criminologists should be engaged in research endeavors and news media presentations that will facilitate the mass dissemination of a more accurate picture of crime and social control. In the tradition of the women's movement's efforts in the areas of wife battering and sexual assault, newsmaking criminologists also should symbolically "take back the night." In other words, in response to inaccurate media portrayals of crime and justice, newsmaking criminologists should interject their own characterizations and images of crime and justice for the purpose of redefining these social stories. In doing so, newsmaking criminologists strive to change mass-communicated perceptions of crime and justice. Specifically, newsmaking criminologists work to alter the counterproductive news discourse on deviance, to reconstruct images of crime and justice, and to replace the dominant models of social control with models based on a scientific understanding of the phenomenon in question that might actually help reduce it.

Mass Media, Public Order, and Symbolic Deviance

When it comes to reporting crime news there is journalistic tension between those objective norms that call for images that reflect actual crime in amount and type, and those organizational norms that recognize that crime stories are a commodity whose audience or market value "may be higher than its value according to other criteria: relevance, accuracy, concern about effect, real significance" (McQuail, 1992: 253). In newsmaking practice, however, crime reporting is shaped more by the way the system of law enforcement and crime control works than by either official or unofficial crime statistics or by audience demand (Chibnall, 1977; Fishman, 1980; Surette, 1992). The lessons learned from news stories about successful and unsuccessful "crime fighting" tend to reinforce and thus support the dominant power relations in society as individuals rather than social relations are always depicted as the problem. Such lessons are also consistent with more general media stories that cultivate a mainstream set of outlooks, assumptions, and beliefs about behavior (Gerbner et al., 1982; Signorielli and Morgan, 1989).

The model of the media as a process that contributes to social conformity and consensus is thought to work through the symbolic rewarding and punishing of good and bad deeds. Symbolic rewarding is accomplished primarily by identifying heroes, villains, and neutral characters and associating them with specific traits, beliefs, or kinds of behavior. Symbolic punishment is achieved through labeling or stigmatizing certain activities or traits as antisocial, deviant or undesirable. Sometimes this rewarding and punishing is done explicitly, sometimes it is accomplished by way of unspoken assumptions, or by the framing of news accounts. The essentially ideological construction of symbolic deviance occurs against the backdrop of a taken-for-granted normality of existing social arrangements: "Whatever is normal requires no explanation or justification, while whatever seems to challenge normality is suspect" (McQuail, 1992: 257). The outcome of this process of symbolic policing is the resolution of short-term conflicts and the restoration of public order for the primary benefit of the status quo.

This is not to suggest that the media are fixed and stagnant; on the contrary, by their very nature media are active and subject to changing norms and values. The mass media also have a dialectical relationship with their object matter. For example, although there is still great concern over the racism and sexism found in fictional and nonfictional media accounts of criminals and victims, there has been a shift in media presentation away from a strongly normative control of marginals and towards one of increasing ambivalence, tolerance, and even solidarity with minorities and other "deviant" groups such as single parents, homosexuals, the mentally ill, and the homeless (Berry, 1988; Campbell and Reeves, 1989; Barak, 1991a). Sometimes the media follow social trends and the dictates of their audiences; sometimes they are out in front of their audiences, creating social trends.

Examples of mass media following the trends in economic and social development include two of the most successful prime time television situation comedies of the early 1990s, "Roseanne" and "Murphy Brown." Both shows reflect different responses to the breakdown of the traditional nuclear family under the stress of advanced capitalism and fulfil the respective needs of their changing demographic audiences. In very distinct, yet related ways, these shows also reflect the way gender relations are changing in American society. In the first sitcom, a white working-class nuclear family barely "makes ends meet" through the relatively shared economic obligations and responsibilities of mother and father. In the second sitcom, as Rapping (1992) has discussed, the unmarried and independent Murphy Brown represents the triumph of decades of work by feminists, inside and outside the media industry, to change the way gender issues, at least as they pertain to white, middle-class women, are understood and portrayed.

A good example of the news media taking the lead on a controversial issue was the way the American press positively framed President Clinton's attempted lifting of the ban against homosexuals serving in the U.S. armed services in early 1993. While polls showed that the American people were evenly divided on the issue, the overwhelming perspective shared by news editorials across the country favored the lifting of the ban on civil rights and anti-discrimination grounds ("Mac-Neil/Lehrer News Hour," 1/29/93). The news media, for the most part, by asserting these values were refusing to acknowledge other competing values. For example, they simply dismissed as illegitimate or homophobic the arguments that lifting the ban would result in an undisciplined and morally dejected military. Instead, the press very neatly framed the issue as a matter of one's sexual *conduct* rather than one's sexual *orientation*.

Social Control, News Media, and Political Change

Both functional and critical theories of communication associate the working of mass media with social order:

> The first attributes to mass media the "function" (or hidden purpose) of securing the continuity of a given social order, maintaining control, establishing a broad

> consensus of values, integrating activities, anchoring individuals and groups in society. . . . Critical theory has often involved a view of mass media as controlled by powerful class elites which impose their dominant meanings on the many and use the media to marginalize and delegitimize opposition. (McQuail, 1992: 237)

The dialectical view employed here recognizes the interactive and contradictory processes inherent in the "functional" and "critical" relations of mass communications. It also assumes that people as individuals and groups are actively struggling throughout society, with very uneven degrees of success and failure, to create through the mass media their own social order out of the materials made available to them from the political economy. As McQuail (1992: 237) correctly points out, "whatever the choice of theory, no evaluation can be made without first determining *whose* order might be sustained or disrupted by mass media: that of society, of ruling elites or [of] what individuals choose to construct for themselves."

Clearly the mass and news media are both intricately connected to the maintenance of public order. But, nevertheless, in the process of social control the news media in particular can be viewed as exhibiting value or normative contradictions that may facilitate both order and change. For example, during the Vietnam War, as Lefever (1976), Gitlin (1980), and Paletz and Entman (1981) have shown, and contrary to popular and critical belief, the press did not undermine the patriotic cause, but actually shifted its coverage over a ten-year period reflecting the changing political momentum. What transpired was that the news media helped to frame opposition to the war as respectable only after the war had lost its legitimacy with not only the anti-war activists and demonstrators, but with a section of the established elite as well.

By comparison, during the Gulf War of 1991, the news media experienced *angst* about its manipulation by the government. In fact, the press took a lot of heat from media critics as they were characterized as lapdogs for the Pentagon (MacArthur, 1992). Faced with the kind of censorship that the press received, their role primarily became one of cheerleading and propagandizing for the forces of good against the evils of

Saddam Hussein. And, while critics decried the media's unexplicated attachment to the "national interest" and to the values of "patriotism," news media pundits of all political persuasions were shedding buckets of tears in print and on the air about the repressive censors at the Pentagon. The point is simply that the press' constricted views reveal multiple and even contradictory roles, including that of an alleged: "lapdog" on behalf of the powers that be, "watchdog" on behalf of the citizens that be, and "neuterdog" on behalf of the value-neutral journalists that be. Therefore, the news media should be correctly understood as multi- rather than one-dimensional.

Similarly, when it pertains to civil disturbance, domestic unrest, and localized violence, media performance has varied according to the nature of the case and local conditions. Generally, however, there seem to be at least two widely shared perspectives, both inside and outside the media: "first, that media *ought* to report such happenings fully and fairly, because of the public 'need to know'; secondly, that their reporting should not itself contribute to illegal behaviour" (McQuail, 1992: 244). Of course, these roles sometimes come into conflict with each other.

On close observation, it appears that the news media have reacted both to the conventional norms of media performance and to what is viewed as in the "public interest." On the one hand, when legitimacy has been claimed for civil disturbance and when the aim was to redress some known and considerable grievance, or where a deep political division was present, the news media have tended to distance themselves from authorities. Those cases, for example, have included antiwar protests, major strikes, and political and civil rights demonstrations. On the other hand, when those more illegitimate forms of civil disturbance (i.e., responses to alleged police misbehavior or unfair jury verdicts) have occurred involving violent rioting or crimes against property, the news media have been more likely, within and without the boundaries of "truth" and "balance," to side with the existing forces of law and order (McQuail, 1992).

Finally, despite their sometimes adversarial role, the news media typically follow rather than lead the masses or elites in social or political change. Moreover, the mass media generally subscribe to the cultural norms of solidarity and social identity. In the words of McQuail (1992: 273), "there is a latent power to advance collective ends and humanitarian goals, but it is very sporadically and selectively exercised." In part, this is a result of the fact that the news media are not primary social actors. In part, this also is due to two of the fundamentals of newsmaking: "one is the primacy of media organizational goals, another the fact that media are generally instruments, not instigators, of other social forces" (McQuail, 1992: 273).

The relationship between news media and social solidarity refers to the capacity of the mass media, in general, to promote "pro-social" or "positive" values, to symbolically sympathize or empathize with individuals or groups in trouble or need, as well as to the "public recognition of shared risks, sorrows and hardships, which reminds people of their common humanity" (McQuail, 1992: 263). The "pro-social" values are also part of the domain of social control, bringing us full circle to the question of policing versus changing the symbolic environment. The news media in particular are capable of making their audiences feel intimate with the wider community, society, or "global village" as it were, thereby aiding audiences in their ability to share in or experience the collective life of humankind.

Both the categories of media formats and the social problems in which the collective expression of empathy appear are varied and numerous. Media formats include: news background; documentary and docu-drama; realistic fiction such as T.V. soap operas; editorial comments; letters to newspapers; appeals for support; fund-raising efforts and media campaigns on behalf of groups; advertising in the media; and attention to talk shows. With respect to social problems, the list is practically endless, but it also includes a "social desirability" factor that is reflected in the distribution of emphatic attention by the media (McQuail, 1992). Some of the more identifiable problems that receive sympathetic attention are: all kinds of illness and disability; homelessness and poverty; old age; racial and sexual discrimination; and victimization through child abuse and neglect. Some of the less identifiable problems that can still receive sympathetic attention include: drug addiction; juvenile delinquency; conditions of criminalization; and dehumanizing prison conditions.

Between the "more" or "less" identifiable problems lies the arena in which newsmaking criminologists can draw fundamental relations that constitute all social problems. By seizing and redefining the empathy or affective factor within the processes of newsmaking, criminologists can not only assist the press in their quest to provide the most accurate information about crime and justice, about criminals and victims, and about what works and does not work in the struggle to reduce crime and punishment, but they can also inform and alter public attitudes and understanding of law and order. Concomitantly, newsmaking criminologists can deconstruct and reconstruct the perceptions of crime and justice, and provide the necessary public service of assisting to demystify both the causes of crime and the obstacles to social and economic justice.

Constructed and Reconstructed Crime News

In *Rape and Criminal Justice*, LaFree (1989) thoroughly examined the social construction of sexual assault from the perspective of those who must respond formally to the claim that a rape has occurred. Among his findings are some very useful analogies for the study of crime news construction. As LaFree (1989: 236) underscores, for example, "legal agents, no less than other human beings, must actively construct their own perceptual world. This world is always at least one step away from the world 'as it really is'." He continues that "the distance between perception and reality is likely to be especially great in the case of the criminal-selection process, because legal [or media] agents most often respond to events that they did not actually observe." Finally, Lafree (1989: 237) concludes:

> From the very beginning of legal [and media] processing, officials [and media reporters, editors, producers] must depend on interpretations, stereotypes, definitions, and accounts at least one step removed from the actual events they describe. In fact, it is these accounts, colored in turn by the typifications of the agents themselves, that are the

reality of criminal [and media] processing—not the events
on which those presentations are based. Hence, beginning
with the victim herself, those who interpret and process
cases are often as concerned about how the case will be
interpreted by others as they are with what "really"
happened.

The sociology of "social construction" in relation to issues
of deviance and control has been represented historically by
three prominent theoretical traditions: "symbolic interactionism" (Blumer, 1939), "labelling" (Becker, 1963), and
"postmodernism" (Milovanovic, 1992). Presently, in the study of
crime and justice there is an emerging theoretical model—
Constitutive Criminology—that combines insights from the two
older traditions and from a more recently developed synthesis of
postmodernism and cultural Marxism. I believe that constitutive
criminology, as articulated by Henry and Milovanovic, yields an
ideal theoretical venue from which to study newsmaking
criminology. They represent the world of constitutive
criminology as that which is:

concerned with identifying the ways in which the
interrelationships between human agents and their social
world constitute crime, victims, and control as realities. It
is oriented to how we may deconstruct these realities, and
to how we may reconstruct less harmful alternatives.
Simultaneously, it is concerned with how emergent
socially constructed realities themselves constitute human
agents with the implication that, if crime is to be replaced,
this necessarily must involve a deconstruction and
reconstruction of the human subject. (Henry and
Milovanovic, in press: 1)

Moreover, the constitutive version of criminology that both
incorporates postmodernism and Marxism involves grasping
both discourse and practice in order to retain the coexistence and
mutual determination of practices and discourses, structure, and
agency (Hunt, 1990). Unlike many Marxist critics who recognize
only the negative side of postmodernism, grounded in its basic
nihilistic and relativistic tendencies, Henry and Milovanovic also
recognize the positive change-oriented side, grounded in the
possibilities of critical opposition, transpraxis, and reconstitutive

effects. Constitutive criminology, in other words, works toward the development of a "replacement discourse." As Henry and Milovanovic (in press: 34) explain, replacement discourse captures "the fluid nature of criminal violations and the legal processing of such infractions . . . [It also envelops] not just the declarations of policy but the ways its practitioners and policy makers distinguish their reality from the totality" of offenders, victims, criminal justice agencies, and the wider political economies. Finally, it requires "a 'bringing back in' of the under-emphasized, informal, unofficial, and marginalized practices (the unspoken) that are part of the totality of power that passes for crime control" (Henry and Milovanovic, in press: 35). In the end, they conclude that "only with such a comprehension of the totality and the contribution of these excluded parts to the reality-making process, is it possible to provide an alternative understanding of the phenomena of crime and crime control in our society. Only from such an understanding of the total constitutive process is it possible to generate a replacement discourse that begins the deconstruction of crime and crime control, the correction of corrections and the ultimate criminal justice policy that denies itself" (Henry and Milovanovic, in press: 35). As newsmaking criminology also calls for an examination of the conscious and unconscious cultural totality involved in the mass dissemination of crime news, it shares in common with constitutive criminology the desire to deconstruct and reconstruct crime and crime control.

Obviously, neither newsmaking nor constitutive criminology suggests, let alone argues, that without the social construction of crime and justice the reality of crime and its administration of criminal justice would not exist. What these criminologies do argue is that mass media realities of crime, and societal reaction to various crimes, criminals, and victims, reinforce paradigms or models for addressing crime and crime control as though they were some kind of independent contagious social problem unrelated to cultural production and mass media. A primary objective of newsmaking criminology, then, is to expose the underlying cultural and political-economic nature of the crime problem, and to draw the necessary connections between this nature and the way in which crime is defined as a particular type of individual pathology or social problem. In the process, newsmaking criminologists seek to "overthrow" the mainstream discourses, views, points of perception, and policies associated with crime and justice, replacing them with alternative conceptions and practices such as those which are part of an emerging "criminology of peacemaking." Peacemaking criminology refers to those proposals and programs that foster mediation, conflict resolution, reconciliation, and community. It is a criminology that "seeks to alleviate suffering and thereby reduce crime . . . that is based necessarily on human transformation in the achievement of peace and justice . . . [and that] takes place as we change our social, economic, and political structure" (Pepinsky and Quinney, 1991: ix).

The need to change our mass-mediated understanding of crime and justice is strongly supported by the available research on media, crime, and criminal justice. Recognizing the tremendous influence that the mass media have on the development of beliefs and attitudes, and on the subsequent development of policies of criminal justice, Surette (1990: 3) underscores that "these policies determine what behaviors we criminalize, what crimes we tolerate, how we treat criminals, and how we fight crime. . . . " As the mass media create a social reality of crime for their audiences, they also shape their audiences' perceptions about crime and the larger world. In fact, the research of Gerbner et al. (1978; 1979; 1980) demonstrates an association between television viewing and what they call a "mean world view." This view is characterized by "mistrust, cynicism, alienation, and perceptions of higher than average levels of threat and crime in society" (Surette, 1990: 8). The work of Barrile (1980) has likewise revealed an association between television viewing and a "retributive justice perspective" that supports authorities and favors punitive policies such as harsher punishments and the death penalty. Marks (1987) provides further evidence of the effects of television exposure on the increased fear of crime and perceived vulnerability, and on the adoption of self-protective anticrime behaviors. All of this "translates into attitudes regarding who can employ violence against whom, who are appropriate victims of crime, and who are likely to be criminals" (Surette, 1990: 8).

Bad Crime News/Good Crime News: The Dialectics of Mass Media

Discourse, whether written, spoken, or visualized, that is expressed in dualities, black and white dichotomies without shades of gray, oversimplified and without too much or any context, are reflective of Western culture and our folklore tradition. Both the news media and the public find themselves trapped, seemingly forever, in morality plays of "good" versus "evil." Accordingly, the deconstruction and reconstruction of crime news involves the development of what Henry and Milovanovic have called a "replacement discourse" that understands that both the production of crime news and its performance evaluation, in terms of how well it explains and demystifies reality, requires that newsmaking criminologists and others transcend dualistic-type analyses of mass media or crime news. As an illustration, an examination of the shifting trends in crime news media reveal that there are actually some "worst" crime news, some "bad" crime news, and some "good" crime news.

Worst News

While the medium may still be the message, *the* medium is still television. With respect to crime and justice, the news medium's media are the "reality" and tabloid news series. Coming into their own during Bush's tenure as president, the number of shows in this genre "have multiplied and garnered audiences at a terrifying rate" (Rapping, 1992: 35). By 1992 there were ten of these shows, mostly low-budget syndication deals, occupying the prime time (family) viewing hours from 7 to 9 P.M. Among the best known are probably "Hard Copy" and "America's Most Wanted": "both feature a confusing mix of 'live footage' and dramatic re-creations of 'actual events.' And they both present a world view that . . . flirts dangerously with certain aspects of fascist ideology" (Rapping, 1992: 35). Concerning the social construction of crime, this is probably the worst news; especially, if one believes in communications theory which argues that attitudes and beliefs develop gradually in response to significant trends in media representation. Making these shows particularly dangerous is the absence of commentary by informed criminologists and other students of justice and social control.

Making these shows socially dangerous is the fact that serious commentary by media analysts or by political and cultural elites is conspicuously absent. It is somehow taken-for-fact by media pundits and commentators that these programs "address themselves to an audience assumed, implicitly, to be incredibly illiterate, gullible, and 'outside the loop' of serious social discourse" (Rapping, 1992: 35). In short, these television tabloids, obsessed with serial murderers, sexual abusers, scandals that have no political relevance, weird religious rites, and the occult, present themselves as "outside" the cultural and political mainstream. In reality, however, the high ratings of these shows reveal that they are integral to the cultural and ideological production of social control and crime.

For example, these shows mix in news stories about important members of the cultural and political world caught in scandal and intrigue; men and women who also may serve as positive role models and leaders of democratic institutions, together with news stories about degenerates and nut cases. This interesting mixture of "high lives" and "low lives" for the mass consumption of "mid lives" helps to fuel political cynicism and apathy, if not outright despair. As Rapping (1992: 36) argues, the meaning of these re-created "real-life crimes" is perfectly clear:

> Whether pushing a simple law-and-order line or conjuring up worlds of supernatural occult phenomena or wholesale degeneracy and corruption, they all, in their own weird ways, have a common underlying message: The world is out of control; we are at the mercy of irrational forces, of deranged, sex- and drug-crazed criminals, of heroes and leaders who are degenerate, corrupt, and powerless against their own inner demons and outer temptations—Call the Police!

Of course, while such portrayals of urban America may capture an important dimension of criminality, they fail miserably to communicate any sense of the causes of crime, and they mistakenly imply that the resolution of criminality and related social problems remains within the reach of law enforcement.

By contrast, the previously unfocused, unprecedented, and short-lived attention paid by the news media to violence by local police forces in the context of their routine operations, brought about by the repeated replay of the video of the Rodney King beating, is related to the fact that then-Attorney General Dick Thornburgh and his staff, a year after the beating, still had no clear answer to the query: Are there any local, regional, or national patterns of police misconduct or brutality? Not only does the federal government not know the answer to this question for L.A., it does not know the answer for any police organizations across the nation. In particular, the Bureau of Justice Statistics within the Justice Department, which collects all kinds of data on crime and law enforcement, does not collect statistics on police violence in American society. Conspicuously absent from the annual publication of the Bureau's 700-plus-page *Sourcebook of Criminal Justice Statistics* are any data on the number of civilians shot by the police, times police use deadly force, citizen complaints against the police, officers disciplined by departments and the nature of their offenses, or police prosecuted for local crimes. Quietly and privately, however, some of these data have been collected. For example, the FBI maintains records of the number of complaints filed yearly against its agents. There are also the National Center for Health Statistics' poorly kept data on the number of persons killed by the police use of deadly force (Roberg and Kuykendall, 1993). In short, since the government does not widely disseminate records of police misbehavior for public consumption, its agencies and the reporting media cannot tell us either how common or uncommon police brutality and violence is or in what cities it is most prevalent. Consequently, neither criminologists nor the public can study or compare how the police are doing in different localities across the country, establishing, if you will, a "quality of police" index for rating cities.

Without this kind of rudimentary knowledge of police behavior, nobody has any answers, and so the news media asks no questions, rarely even addressing anecdotal evidence that it stumbles upon. And, in the absence of a newsmaking reality nothing can be done about a (significant or insignificant) "social problem" but to forget about it until the next time urban America erupts in response to real or imagined police oppression. As Chevigny (1992: 371) has written, because "we have no systematic knowledge on the national level—either of the prevalence of police violence or what can be done about it— we simply don't recognize it as a persistent problem. The systematic ignorance of the federal government works very well to keep police violence off the national agenda." Meanwhile, it appears that camcorders and videotapes of police misbehavior in the hands of citizen sources will periodically circulate images locally and nationally through the electronic news media reminding society of this police problem. Of course, these relatively rare crime news stories by amateur reporters are no match for the everyday reporting of the news media generally and of the prime time television fare of "reality" and tabloid news journalism.

With respect to the dearth of police violence stories, there are no government sources or newsmaking criminologists with the data to make sense of or to provide perspective for these media representations. Without context for explaining complex behavior, both the mass and news media tend to revert to their simplistic "good" versus "bad" cop scenarios, rather than to analyses that examine the social, institutional, organizational, and environmental interactions of police/citizen, police/criminal, and police/victim encounters. The end results are that much about police work remains unknown, or at least, hidden from mass consumption. And, therefore, much about police behavior that might change remains in place.

Bad News

When it comes to the social reconstruction of crime, there is an obvious need for newsmaking criminologists to confront, challenge, and expose the "worst" crime news. Equally important is the need to confront "bad" crime news that figures so prominently in reproducing the very language, discourse, and thinking about crime and justice that needs replacement. What distinguishes the "worst" crime news from the "bad" crime news is that the former is more subtle and unconscious, the latter much more overt and recognizable by both experts and lay people.

Benedict's (1992) ethnomethodological, historical, and critical analysis of how the press covers sex crimes is very instructive. Author, journalist, communications professor, rape authority, and social critic, Benedict (1992: 251) argues that the coverage of sex crimes has been steadily declining since the early eighties:

> All in all, rape as a societal problem has lost interest for the public and the press, and the press is reverting to its pre-1970 focus on sex crimes as individual, bizarre, or sensational case histories—witness the furor over the celebrity rape case against William Kennedy Smith. Along with the loss of interest has come a loss of understanding.

Benedict's book is based on a detailed examination of four very specific and prominent sex-crime cases: the 1979 Greta and John Rideout marital rape case in Oregon; the 1983 pool table gang rape of a woman in a New Bedford, Massachusetts, bar; the 1986 sex-related killing of Jennifer Levin by Robert Chambers in New York; and the 1989 gang rape and beating of the Central Park jogger in New York. In chronological order, these four cases raise questions about marriage, ethnicity, class, and race. All of them should have raised questions of gender, but for the most part the media coverage was silent on the subject. This news media omission reveals much about power/gender relations, about cultural attitudes, and about how public opinion and the press regard sex, women, and violent crime.

According to Benedict and others, the news media portrayals of these sex crimes generally reflected journalism's predominantly male and white constituency, especially in relationship to crime coverage; the still prevalent stereotypes associated with both rape and sex; the absence of any recognition or reference to misogyny in American society; and the tendency of the press to prefer individual to societal or cultural explanations of crime. As Benedict (1992: 246) concludes that "these reporters and editors were willing to go to sociologists, psychologists, and community leaders to talk about class and race hatred but not about the hatred of women revealed the extent to which they considered racism a subject for news stories, but saw sexism as fit only for columns and editorials. It also revealed that . . . these reporters and editors seemed more able to admit to their racism than their sexism—they were apparently more comfortable talking about the sick socialization of blacks in urban ghettos than the sick socialization everyone gets at schools, fraternities, and in society at large." Benedict further argues that the extent to which the press would not research and explain gang rape or cover the rape of the jogger as a gender-based crime exposed both the racism of coverage and the backlash against feminism in the United States during the 1980s.

Besides, even those news stories that bothered to examine "the mind of the rapist" were grounded in a familiar combination of individual pathology and such myths as rape is sex or rape is motivated by lust. More fundamentally, the press' lack of understanding of the crime of rape was revealed by their inability to describe even the gruesome, bloody, comatose, near-death, jogger's rape in nonsexual terms. Rather than talking in terms of the boys *grabbing* or even *touching* the jogger's breasts and legs, news accounts used such terms as *fondling* and sexually *exploring*. Instead of substituting such terms as *having sex with* for the rape, implying consent on the part of the victim, why not use the term *penetrate* or why not the more realistic terms used by defendant Kharey Wise in his description of his "running" buddies' acts that night which appeared in the *City Sun*: "Steve and Kevin both f—ed her. Ramon was holding her too and he was grabbing her tits and Antron was laughing and playing with her leg" [6/21–27/89, p. 6]. The latter phraseology refers to the acts of rapacious behavior, the former phraseology refers to the acts of making love.

The common "spin" that kept these sex crime news stories alive was the press' ability to once again revert to its formulaic presentation of the "good" and "bad" morality play. Found on the "stage" here are the images of two Western puritanical classics found "in the story of Eve as temptress and corruptor (the 'vamp'), and in the later Victorian ideal of woman as pure and uninterested in sex (the 'virgin')" (Benedict, 1992: 18). Combined with these antiquated and unrealistic thematic representations of women as either whores or Madonnas, are the postmodern habits of media journalism. Whatever the gauge, women fare badly at the hands of the mass media. Taken in its totality, the portrayals of sex, crime, and rape both in myth and in news media construction serve to reinforce negative images of women and of social justice. Benedict (1992: 23) sums up the print media's coverage of rape as follows:

> Pushed into subordinate roles of sex objects, wives, mothers, or crime victims, they have little opportunity to be portrayed as self-determining individuals. When a reporter sits down to write a story about any woman, therefore, let alone a woman who has been victimized in a sex crime, he or she has an enormous burden of assumptions, habits, and clichés to carry to the story. Not only are conventional images of women limited, but our very language promotes those images. It is not surprising, therefore, that the public and the press tend to combine the bias in our language, the traditional images of women, and rape myths into a shared narrative about sex crimes that goes like this:
>
>> The "Vamp" version: The woman, by her looks, behavior or generally loose morality, drove the man to such extremes of lust that he was compelled to commit the crime. The "Virgin" version: The man, a depraved and perverted monster, sullied the innocent victim, who is now a martyr to the flaws of society.

Sex crime victims tend to be squeezed into one of two images: either a wanton female who provoked the assailant with her sexuality or a pure and innocent victim attacked by monsters. As Benedict (1992: 24) explains:

> Both of these narratives are destructive to the victims of rape and to public understanding of the subject. The vamp version is destructive because it blames the victim of the crime instead of the perpetrator. The virgin version is destructive because it perpetuates the idea that women can only be Madonnas or whores, paints women

dishonestly, and relies on portraying the suspects as inhuman monsters.

Benedict (1992: 24) continues that her "research has shown that reporters tend to impose these shared narratives—which are nothing but a set of mental and verbal clichés—on the sex crimes they cover like a cookie-cutter on dough, forcing the crimes into prescribed shapes, regardless of the specifics of the case or their own beliefs. They do this through their choice of vocabulary, the slant of their leads, and the material they choose to leave out or put in, and they often do it unconsciously."

Finally in terms of replacement discourse, Benedict (1992: 266) reminds us that the stigmatization of women by the coverage of sex crime victims in general and of victims of rape in particular will only be eliminated when these victims are taken seriously without having to hide behind the narratives of innocence and virginity, and when the mainstream news media assert in their representations "the role of women and the way men are trained to see them as objects of prey," as demonstrated in the jogger case.

Other examples of bad news include the intermittent, limited and one-sided coverage of terrorism or the pervasive and yet shallow coverage of the domestic and international war on drugs. With respect to terrorism, media attention has focused on selective terrorist acts—selected not only in terms of countries emphasized and neglected, but also in terms of the various forms of terrorism committed. Typically discussed or portrayed are "retail" terrorist acts, acts committed by groups or individuals against agents or symbolic representatives of an enemy state. Typically ignored are "wholesale" acts of terrorism, those waged by state-supported networks against independence or national revolutionary movements (Chomsky and Herman, 1979; Herman, 1982).

The shallow and one-dimensional portrayals of the "war" on drugs by the news media and others, and the "moralistic rhetoric about drugs and drug traffickers which is a fundamental part of this 'war' has distorted the realities of the situation and complicated any attempt to find realistic solutions to the drug problems" in the United States (Johns and Borreo, 1991: 79). The point being that the bad news coverage of crime and justice in general, or of terrorism and drugs and drug trafficking in particular, have become holy wars, almost like religious crusades. "In the ensuing fervor, the [two main] factors underlying the problems of drug use and trafficking are obscured," namely "the effects of economic exploitation and inequality" and a social reality "that is so unbearable and stressful that most people spend a great deal of their time trying to escape it," rather than change it (Johns and Borreo, 1991: 79).

Good News

In relation to the Central Park rape, Lichter, Lichter, and Amundson (1989) offer a different interpretation of the overall media coverage of crime in New York City. While they corroborate many of the findings of Benedict, especially as related to gender, the two analyses reach mixed conclusions with regard to the issues of race, class, and crime. With respect to gender, Lichter et al. agree with Benedict that lost in these news reports was the fact that this attack by a group of "wilding" teenagers was essentially a crime against women. Lichter and her associates' spin on local crime news reporting on the gang beating and rape makes the argument that both print and broadcast news media have improved their historically biased and racially stereotyped images of criminals and victims. The media controversy surrounding the general reporting of crime, and interracial crime in particular, provided Lichter et al. of the Center for Media and Public Affairs with fertile ground to examine this complex newsmaking crime.

Set against the background of such racially charged "crimes" as Howard Beach, Tawana Brawley, and Bernhard Goetz, their content analysis determined that news media framed the Central Park rape case, first and foremost, by what the police called it, a "crime of opportunity." The attack also was portrayed as one of randomness, apparently lacking any purpose or meaning beyond the immediate gratification of its perpetrators. Amid the charges of racism and sensationalism that were raised and debated by media reports of the Central Park rape, Lichter et al. (1989) analyzed the topics, themes, and language of local media coverage between April 20 and May 4,

1989. In all, they studied 406 news items from the evening newscasts of six New York television stations and from the city's four daily newspapers and one black weekly.

Consistent with most studies on the mass media, their content analysis revealed that news is not uniformly reported. It is not a mirror on reality but more like a prism "whose refracted images are formed not only by events but by the choices and perspectives of journalists and news organizations" (Lichter et al., 1989: 15). In other words, although the news prism is essentially the same, journalists and news organizations do differ as the Lichter et al. study revealed about issues of race. By comparison, the variation or difference in mainstream news coverage of crime and justice was of less significance or consequence to matter. As these researchers concluded about the reporting of the rape, it was "split between a populist tabloid approach (emotional language, focus on public outrage, and calls for "law and order" measures) and concerns about social responsibility (the frequent denial that race was relevant to crime) (Lichter et al., 1989: 2). At the same time, however, as Lichter et al. (1989: 2) point out, "the media missed an opportunity to confront racial undertones that well up in cases of interracial violence, even when no overt racial motive is present."

In summary, the news media does not cover systemically all forms and expressions of crime and victimization. It emphasizes some crimes and ignores other crimes. It sympathizes with some victims while blaming other victims. At the same time, with respect to those crimes covered by the news media, the performances vary in both quality and quantity. Some of that coverage has been characterized above as "worst," some as "bad," and some as "good." These distinctions refer not only to the distance between "objective" realities of crime and justice and their portrayals in the mass media, but to the distortions between the crimes covered and the degree to which they are explained relative to the criminological knowledge base. Finally, the production of crime news represents the commodification of both conscious and unconscious interests (Tunnell, 1992). To understand the forces or variables responsible for this mediated social construction of crime, newsmaking criminologists and others must unravel the intersection of gender, race, and class in the context of a changing political economy.

Conclusion

In the trilogy, *Visualizing Deviance* (1987), *Negotiating Control* (1989), and *Representing Order* (1991), Ericson, Baranek, and Chan report their findings from what is probably the most intensive and comprehensive study of news media and crime to date. Paying attention to how news content varies by media and markets, their focus of comparison has been on both "quality" and "tabloid" news outlets in newspapers, television, and radio concentrated in the Toronto and overlapping regional markets. In their third volume, subtitled *Crime, Law, and Justice in the News Media*, the researchers underscore the importance of crime news not only as it represents a force of order, control, and change in society, but in terms of how predominant such items are in news production in general. They found that crime news constituted slightly less than one-half of all news coverage in newspapers and tabloid television, more than one-half of all news coverage in quality television, and about two-thirds of all news coverage on radio. Their percentages are significantly higher than those reported in other studies included and cited in this volume. Whatever the exact figures, and they do vary, their conclusions are valid.

As Ericson et al. correctly explain, the media obsession with stories of crime, law, and justice has become a primary cultural device for defining acceptable behavior, identity, and reality, and as a result it is often difficult, if not impossible, to separate the perception of crime and the reaction to crime: "conceptions of deviance and control not only define the central object and character of news stories, but are woven into the methodology of journalists, influencing their choices from assignment, through the selection and use of sources, to the final composition of the story." In turn, news of deviance and control represents order through constituting an active discourse: "as an active *agency* of social control, stability, and change, news representations provide people with preferred versions and visions of social order, on the basis of which they take action" (Ericson et al., 1991: 239). Herein lies the opportunities for newsmaking criminologists and others to use their research, presentations, books, and other communications to redirect the prevailing discourse on crime and justice. Means for engaging in this kind of criminological practice are laid out in various generic cookbooks on "how to be interviewed" by the media. In chapter ten of this anthology, Cecil Greek not only highlights this literature and discusses how criminologists can respond to interviews, but he also establishes some realistic expectations and guidelines for what is possible.

Nothing can be more important than the mass content of crime and justice news. The omission of certain types of criminality is equally if not more important than the types of criminality included. By analogy, just as it is critical that there be a vigorous investigative journalism like that set in motion by the Watergate scandal some two decades ago, today there also needs to be an investigative criminology (Surette, 1993). For example, an AP story that broke in March 1993 revealed that the U.S. spied on blacks for seventy-five years, including the use of U2 spy planes to gather information on civil rights demonstrators throughout the 1960s. This type of state criminality or these criminal and civil violations by the U.S. government of individuals' fundamental rights need to be uncovered and exposed. Stories of these kinds of governmental actions need to be discovered by journalists and criminologists and communicated to the general public. People need to know that their government is capable of using not only the FBI, the CIA, and the police to investigate its citizens, but the military as well when threats, real or imagined, are perceived by our political leaders. As the Army's top spy in the mid-1960s said in an interview: "Blacks were using the uncertainty of the Vietnam period and taking advantage of it. You couldn't expect people to be rational and look at this in a cool way. We were trying to fight a war at the same time where the home base was being eroded" [*Ann Arbor News*, 1993: A12].

Besides the preoccupation with certain kinds of crimes, criminals, victims, law enforcement practices, and justice policies to the exclusion of other crimes and policies of social control, the news discourse surrounds itself with very subtle "explanations" that appear in enclosed forms that do not enhance causal understanding:

> When an explanation can be read into the news, it "is more likely to be tacitly evoked by cues in the text or by the powerful master labels such as 'violent' and 'criminal' which carry unambiguous connotations and meld together disparate phenomena and their meanings. . . . They are deployed stereotypically. The stereotypes are blended with imputations of motives, whether noble or blameworthy. The imputations of motives, in turn, carry excuses and justifications for behaviour. (Ericson et al., 1991: 269)

Concomitantly, what is important from the perspective of an emerging newsmaking criminology is the relatively little attention paid to causal explanation in crime news discourse. Graber (1980: 70) reported that in her sample only 4 percent of the crime-news stories discussed "causes" of crime. In the politics of knowledge and explanation, what is excluded from news discourse is, of course, as important as what is included. Not only missing from crime news coverage are the systematic, organizational, and institutional explanations of crime and violence, but the sustained coverage of white-collar, corporate, and state crimes that lend themselves readily to these kinds of analyses.

In other words, lost in all of the crime and justice media hype surrounding the individual exploits of relatively powerless criminals are the far more serious institutional exploits of the crimes of the powerful. Barely represented, let alone misrepresented, in the news of the late eighties and early nineties were such activities as the S & L thefts, the involvement of the B.C.C.I. in drug-money laundering, and George Bush's millions in agricultural credits to Saddam Hussein via Banca Nationale del Lavoro. Coverage did occur, however, when some of these acts were attached to the faces of such famous persons as Charles Keating, Neil Bush, or Clark Clifford. Nevertheless, serious analysis of these crimes did not precede or follow these news presentations.

Caught up in such imperatives of news production as the need for dramatic structuring, crime news is oversimplified and reduced to subtle and not so subtle forms of stereotyping that socially construct criminals and victims alike. In this manner, "crime" news discourse explains away more than it explains: "it 'explains away' deviance as part of the process of reaffirming reality and representing order. In the process, it 'erases' considerations of structure and political economy that may deconstruct reality and thereby destabilize our sense of order" (Ericson et al., 1991: 269). This, of course, brings us back to the need for, and the question of, a "replacement discourse."

As I have argued in the context of domestic violence and sexual assault (Barak, 1986) or in the context of race, multiculturalism, and crime (Barak, 1991b), greater diversity and representation in criminal justice administration or in criminological theory without radical transformation of the dominant cultural discourses, ideological constructions, and political economies will fall short of the ultimate goal of a replacement discourse for crime and justice news as we have known it. But falling short of such a transformation, changes in diversity and representation can, at least, provide opportunities for the development of other voices and alternative views to those of the constituted mainstream. In this way, resistance to socialization and cooptation can occur, and the seeds for deconstructing and reconstructing crime and justice can be planted. As we argue throughout this book, an untapped source for nurturing the growth of a replacement discourse lies in the development of a newsmaking criminology.

Chapter Overview of Studies in Newsmaking Criminology

Following the rest of the Introduction, this book is divided into two sections: Constructing Crime News and Reconstructing Crime News. Constructing Crime News consists of chapters two through eight and Reconstructing Crime News consists of chapters nine, ten, and eleven.

In chapter two, "Crime News in the Old West," Werner J. Einstadter provides a content analysis and case study of newspaper journalism and social control in a Montana town in the late nineteenth century. His historical study relates the importance of how the depiction of more or less crime in the news can be used "as a means to control and direct the social polity." This was more the condition when there were smaller communities, fewer sources of information dissemination, and the absence of electronic media. When the frontier West was in need of profitable business-type settlement, crime news was underreported, local crimes were de-emphasized, and crime was portrayed primarily as an outsider phenomenon. Combining a Kai Erikson-type analysis of rural America with that of a developing political economy, these emerging communities were defining their boundaries as well as their cultural identities. But these communities did so in reaction to specific historical conditions; their "products" reflected the emerging interests or struggles for political and economic power. Newspapers were engaged in the business of doing more than merely reporting the news. They were also in the business of partisanship and social control. "Newspapers played active roles in community building and through their management of crime news were instrumental in the type of order and control resources that were eventually developed and adopted essentially to protect economic interests." Einstadter concludes that the newspaper acted as a catalyst in the process "by continually placing before its readers the picture of an almost idyllic social and cultural space [that] aided in the coalescing of the people. Moreover, by picturing crime or evil largely as an outside event or the result of those foreign or marginal to the community, it could readily solidify the people in pointing to the threat, and thereby create a definition of where the cultural boundaries should be." At the same time, this newspaper's lack of internal crime during a relatively violent period in frontier history would hopefully act to attract new businesses and community social types from the civilized East that would facilitate economic development in the "wild" West.

In chapter three, "Communal Violence and the Media: Lynchings and Their News Coverage by *The New York Times* between 1882 and 1930," Ira M. Wasserman and Steven Stack provide an historical examination of the national media coverage of lynching behavior in the United States. While most studies in newsmaking criminology consider individual crimes, Wasserman and Stack's study underscores the importance of giving consideration to "communal crimes" or to when local communities become the perpetrators of criminal acts. Using logistic regression to estimate coefficients in their model of "degree of coverage," they considered 3,403 lynching incidents in testing their hypotheses that various factors such as historic time, geography, race, intensity of incident, and provocative behavior determine national coverage. While a number of the tested factors support their various hypotheses, the most important factors were historic time and race. Geography also was influential in the national coverage of a communal crime during the period prior to the development of television when print was still the dominant means of mass communication. Undoubtedly, the advent and development of television as the primary instrument of mass media has changed the national coverage of crime news, individual or communal.

In chapter four, "Crime in the News Media: A Refined Understanding of How Crimes Become News," Steven Chermak presents data on the prevalence of crime in the news while he examines the newsmaking process as primarily an organizational phenomenon that produces a limited picture of both crime and victims because of selected criteria and decision-making. Chermak's chapter reflects the combined methodologies of ethnographic and content analysis research. His ethnographic portion involved the observation and study of the selection, production, and editing decisions of both a newspaper and television station in a large midwestern city. His content analysis examined more than 2,700 crime news stories, including data collected from television stations in Albany, New York, Cleveland, and Dallas as well as from six newspapers scattered from coast-to-coast. Chermak argues that the news media select "a limited number of stories from the large pool of crimes that are available." In order to "refine our understanding of the crime news process" and to make sense out of how reporters and news media organizations conceptualize and determine "newsworthiness," he develops a typology on the different kinds of crime stories that sheds light on those "factors that influence whether a crime becomes news."

In chapter five, "Predator Criminals as Media Icons," Ray Surette renders a picture of the contemporary mass media portrayal of predatory criminality; a depiction where innocent and helpless victims are randomly selected by seemingly incomprehensible and uncontrollable criminals. Grounded in the historical development of media in general and news media in particular, he maintains that the modern mass media have raised the specter of the predator criminal from a minor character reflected in Western classic literature to an icon image that drives both public consciousness and public policy regarding crime and justice. As with other icons, Surette argues that "they represent a largely unquestioned set of beliefs about the world—a constructed reality that—as the aphorism 'perception is reality' suggests—has the ability to shape the actual world to fit the media image. In the world of crime and justice, the icon of predator crime pushes life to imitate art." His explanation for the dominance of the predator criminal as media icon moves beyond its mass popularity to the very foundations of basic cultural values and characteristics. Finally, in the context of social policy and crime, Surette discusses the effects of the criminal predator as media icon and ultimately concludes that the "continuing disparity between the media constructed reality of crime and justice and the non-media reality of crime and justice results in the public receiving an unnecessarily distorted image that supports only one anti-crime policy approach, an expanded and enhanced punitive criminal justice system. An approach lacking evidence of success."

In chapter six, "University Professor or Sadistic Killer? A Content Analysis of the Newspaper Coverage of a Murder Case," Harry L. Marsh examines "the possible deleterious effects newspaper coverage might have on the defendant in a murder trial." His study of the newspaper coverage of an average (noncelebrity) murder is conducted in the context of the relationship between media portrayals of offenders and alleged offenders. Marsh is primarily concerned with the "possible effect of newspaper coverage on the reader's perception of the defendant's guilt or innocence," and with the introduction of "prejudicial factors" or items of information that either come to the attention of jurors before trial, unconfronted and unexamined, or specific items of news that never make their way into evidence at the trial.

Marsh's findings support several tentative conclusions. The most significant conclusions were that newspaper crime coverage of this murder "tended to be prejudicial toward the accused" both before and after the trial. Even after the defendant was acquitted by a jury, "the post-trial coverage left a cloud of doubt on the innocence" of the freed man. Finally, in the name of fairness rather than censorship, Marsh recommends that the news media report only legally factual information. News media agencies and personnel "should refrain, as much as possible, from reporting opinions and untested observations, whether it be theirs or that of others."

In chapter seven, "Murder and Mayhem in *USA Today*: A Quantitative Analysis of the National Reporting of States' News," Robert A. Jerin and Charles B. Fields studied the crime news content that appeared in the *Across the USA: News from Every State* section for 1990 from the nation's premier daily newspaper. Out of a total of more than 26,000 news summaries that were coded, more than 4,200 were crime-related. Among the most interesting findings was the fact that "during periods of decreasing crime rates it seems that, at least in some instances, crime reporting has increased." Similarly, "none of the states with the five highest crime rates are included in the top five rankings of murder and rape." In general, reporting patterns found in regional newspapers were reproduced in *USA Today*, such as the lack of a relationship between official crime statistics or state populations and the amount of crime coverage. Jerin and Fields also found, just as in regional and local newspapers, that the crime committed has less to do with its coverage than such other factors as the circumstances surrounding the crime, the public stature of the offender or victim, and the notoriety of the individuals involved. As their study revealed, "it seems that the accuracy of the reporting of criminal acts" is always "compromised by the 'newsworthiness' of the incident."

In chapter eight, "Patrolling the Facts: Media, Cops, and Crime," Renée Goldsmith Kasinsky examines how the role of the police, the news media, and the interaction between these two organizations as a "textual mediated reality" is established. Generally, she looks at the whole question involving legitimacy, power, and control and the roles that the police and media play in the cultural production of crime news. Specifically, she explores "the culture and ideology of police in general as well as the police organization, and the influence of 'news texts' and sourcing." Utilizing a complex model of the media that integrates a neo-Gramscian theory of hegemony, a propaganda or dominant ideological perspective, and a framework of symbolic interactionism, Kasinsky reviews and juxtaposes the texts taken from the *Boston Globe*, the *Los Angeles Times*, and the *New York Times* coverage of the Charles and Carol Stuart murder case in Boston and the Rodney King beating in Los Angeles. She concludes that there is a distinct possibility for the role of the news media to become a major watchdog institution over police activities. Rather than merely maintaining their own legitimacy with the public or "patrolling the facts" through "carefully selected images of crime and police, the media could begin to take their critical, investigative role more seriously. They could begin to police the police."

In chapter nine, "Newsmaking Criminology: Reflections on the Media, Intellectuals, and Crime," Barak indicts the fields of criminology and criminal justice for not considering the ways in which they could use mass communications for the purposes of informing, interpreting, and altering ideologically constructed images of crime and punishment. Beginning with an analysis of the relationships among the developing political economy of the mass media, intellectuals, and conceptions of crime and justice, this chapter introduces one criminological practice—namely the conscious effort of criminologists and others to participate in the presentation of "newsworthy" items about crime and justice—capable of taking advantage of the available opportunities in the production of crime news. Barak concludes "that the role of a newsmaking criminologist is possible because journalists' values and practices are not fixed rigidly but are rather fluid. The newsmaking process involves not only the ongoing negotiations and conflicts among newsroom personnel at all levels but also the interaction of newspeople with newsmaking sources, both elite and nonelite."

In chapter ten, "Becoming a Media Criminologist: Is 'Newsmaking Criminology' Possible?," Cecil E. Greek tests my proposition that criminologists can use their expertise to better inform and thereby provide more realistic images of crime and the criminal justice system, based on his extensive interaction with news media in Oklahoma City and Tampa. First, Greek makes comparisons of newspaper interviews, remote television interviews, live "on air" interviews, and live television and radio talk shows. Second, he details the various problems that he encountered in each of these media-type situations. Third, in the context of whether an adequate communication of criminological knowledge and research is possible in terms of the various media formats, Greek reviews the literature by professional media consultants whose goals include helping people get their messages across the various media outlets. Greek concludes that although "it is extremely difficult to communicate the complexities of social scientific research" through these various media formats, criminologists should "seek permanent ongoing relationships with the press." In particular, "criminologists should strive to become consultants with the ability to provide input over story editing, whom to interview, or even which stories to cover."

In chapter eleven, "Newsmaking Criminology as Replacement Discourse," Stuart Henry argues that in order for criminologists and others to transcend their "passive constitution of such socially, and publicly consumed, crime truths, it is necessary for criminologists to actively intercede in the constitutive process" of newsmaking. Henry rounds out our discussion on reconstructing crime news by identifying the strengths and weaknesses of four possible styles of criminological intercession. He calls these: disputing data; reconstructive description; media manipulation; and challenging journalism. Each of these styles "relies upon expressed journalistic interest in a particular facet of crime and its reportage." As Henry concludes, the development of a replacement discourse requires a "bringing back in" of the underemphasized, informal, unofficial, and marginalized practices and discourses. In short, it necessitates a consciousness of the unspoken as a part of the totality of the criminological enterprise. In this way, voices of repression and marginality are given genuine expression, and the possibility exists for completing the cycle from deconstruction to reconstruction.

REFERENCES

Associated Press. 1993. "Report: Army Spied on Blacks 75 Years." *Ann Arbor News*, March 23, A1 and A12.

Barak, G. 1991a. *Gimme Shelter: A Social History of Homelessness in Contemporary America*. New York: Praeger.

———. 1991b. "Cultural Literacy and a Multicultural Inquiry into the Study of Crime and Justice." *Journal of Criminal Justice Education*, 2, 2: 173–192.

———. 1988. "Newsmaking Criminology: Reflections on the Media, Intellectuals, and Crime." *Justice Quarterly*, 5, 4: 565–587.

———. 1986. "Feminist Connections and the Movement against Domestic Violence: Beyond Criminal Justice Reform." *Journal of Crime and Justice*, 9: 139–162.

Barrile, L. 1980. *Television and Attitudes about Crime*. Ph.D. Diss., Sociology, Boston College.

Becker, H. 1963. *Outsiders: Studies in the Sociology of Deviance*. New York: Free Press.

Benedict, H. 1992. *Virgin or Vamp: How the Press Covers Sex Crimes*. New York: Oxford University Press.

Berry, G.L. 1988. "Multicultural Role Portrayals on Television as a Social Psychological Issue," in S. Oskamp (ed.), *Television as a Social Issue*, pp. 88–102. Newbury Park, CA: Sage.

Blackwood, R. E. and J. A. Smith. 1983. "The Content of News Photos: Roles Portrayed by Men and Women." *Journalism Quarterly*, 60: 710–714.

Blumer, H. 1939. "The Crowd, the Public and the Mass," in A.M. Lee (ed.), *New Outline of the Principles of Sociology*, pp. 185–189. New York: Barnes and Noble.

Campbell, R. and J. L. Reeves. 1989. "Covering the Homeless: The Joyce Brown Story." *Critical Studies in Mass Communications*, 6: 21–42.

Chevigny, P. 1992. "Let's Make It a Federal Case." *The Nation*, March 23: 370–372.

Chibnall, S. 1977. *Law and Order News*. London: Tavistock.

Chomsky, N. and E. S. Herman. 1979. *The Washington Connection and Third World Fascism*. Boston: South End Press.

Claster, D. S. 1992. *Bad Guys and Good Guys: Moral Polarization and Crime*. Westport, CT: Greenwood Press.

Davis, F. J. 1952. "Crime News in Colorado Newspapers." *American Journal of Sociology*, 57: 225–230.

Ericson, R. V., P. M. Baranek, and J. B. L. Chan. 1991. *Representing Order: Crime, Law, and Justice in the News Media*. Toronto: University of Toronto Press.

————. 1989. *Negotiating Control: A Study of News Sources*. Toronto: University of Toronto Press.

————. 1987. *Visualizing Deviance: A Study of News Organization*. Toronto: University of Toronto Press.

Fedler, F. and D. Jordan. 1982. "How Emphasis on People Affects Coverage of Crime." *Journalism Quarterly*, 59: 474–478.

Fishman, M. 1980. *Manufacturing the News*. Austin, TX: University of Texas Press.

————. 1978. "Crime Waves as Ideology." *Social Problems*, 25, 5: 530–543.

Gans, H. J. 1980. *Deciding What's News: A Study of CBS Evening News, NBC Nightly News, Newsweek and Time*. New York: Vintage Books.

Gerbner, G., N. Signorielli and M. Morgan. 1982. "Charting the Mainstream: Television's Contributions to Political Orientation." *Journal of Communication*, 32, 2: 100–127.

————. 1980. "The Mainstreaming of America: Violence Profile No. 11." *Journal of Communication*, 30, 1:10–29.

————. 1979. "The Demonstration of Power: Violence Profile No. 10." *Journal of Communication*, 29, 4: 176–207.

————. 1978. "Cultural Indicators: Violence Profile No. 9." *Journal of Communications*, 28, 4.

Gitlin, T. 1980. *The Whole World Is Watching*. Berkeley: University of California Press.

Gormley, W. T. 1980. "An Evaluation of the FCC's Cross Ownership Policy." *Policy Analysis*, 6: 61–83.

Graber, D. A. 1980. *Crime News and the Public*. New York: Praeger.

Hartman, P. and C. Husband. 1974. *Racism and Mass Media*. London: Davis Poynter.

Henry, S. and D. Milovanovic. In press. "The Constitution of Constitutive Criminology: A Postmodern Approach to Criminological Theory," in D. Nelken (ed.), *The Futures of Criminology*. London: Sage Publications.

Herman, E. S. 1982. *The Real Terror Network: Terrorism in Fact and Propaganda*. Boston: South End Press.

Hunt, A. 1990. "The Big Fear: Law Confronts Postmodernism." *McGill Law Journal*, 35: 507–540.

Johns, C. and J. Borreo. 1991. "The War on Drugs: Nothing Succeeds Like Failure," in G. Barak (ed.) *Crimes by the Capitalist State: An Introduction to State Criminality*. Albany, NY: State University of New York Press.

LaFree, G. D. 1989. *Rape and Criminal Justice: The Social Construction of Sexual Assault*. Belmont, CA: Wadsworth Publishing Company.

LeFever, E. W. 1976. *Television and National Defense: An Analysis of News*. Washington, D.C.: Brookings Institution.

Lichter, L. S., S. R. Lichter, and D. Amundson. 1989. "The New York News Media and the Central Park Rape." New York: Center for Media and Public Affairs.

MacArthur, J. R. 1992. *Second Front: Censorship and Propaganda in the Gulf War*. New York: Hill and Wang.

McQuail, D. 1992. *Media Performance: Mass Communication and the Public Interest*. London: Sage Publications.

Marks, A. 1987. *Television Exposure, Fear of Crime and Concern about Serious Illness*. Ph.D. Diss., Evanston, IL: Northwestern University.

Miller, S. H. 1975. "The Content of News Photos: Women and Men's Roles." *Journalism Quarterly*, 52: 70–75.

Milovanovic, D. 1992. *Postmodern Law and Disorder: Psychoanalytic Semiotics, Chaos and Juridic Exegeses*. Liverpool, England: Deborah Charles Publications.

Munro-Bjorklund, V. 1991. "Popular Cultural Images of Criminals and Convicts since Attica." *Social Justice*, 18, 3: 48–70.

Paletz, D. and R. Entman. 1981. *Media, Power, Politics*. New York: Free Press.

Pepinsky, H. and R. Quinney (eds.). 1991. *Criminology as Peacemaking*. Bloomington: Indiana University Press.

Rapping, E. 1992. "Tabloid TV and Social Reality." *The Progressive*, August: 35–37.

Roberg, R. and J. Kuykendall. 1993. *Police and Society*. Belmont, CA: Wadsworth Publishing Company.

Signorielli, N. and M. Morgan (eds.). 1989. *Cultivation Analysis*. Newbury Park, CA: Sage Publications.

Surette, R. 1993. Personal communication with the author.

———. 1992. *Media, Crime, and Criminal Justice: Images and Realities*. Pacific Grove, CA: Brooks/Cole Publishing Company.

———. (ed.). 1990. *The Media and Criminal Justice Policy: Recent Research and Social Effects*. Springfield, IL: Charles C. Thomas.

Tunnell, K. 1992. "Film at Eleven: Recent Developments in the Commodification of Crime." *Sociological Spectrum* 12: 293–313.

van Dijk, T. 1991. *Racism and the Press*. London: Routledge.

Watney, S. 1987. *Policing Desire: Pornography, AIDS, and the Media*. Minneapolis: University of Minnesota Press.

PART II

Constructing Crime News

CHAPTER 2

Crime News in the Old West*

Werner J. Einstadter

Modern communities not only have had to deal with the objective consequences of crime, but they also been have involved in a persistent struggle with its publicity. While the immediacy of TV coverage of crime events is of recent origin, the impact of which we are still trying to discern, the treatment of crime by other forms of mass media is not. Although crime chroniclers have existed for many centuries, the advent of newspapers gave the publicity of crime a special dimension beyond the mere telling of the event; it allowed the persuasion of readers. The depiction of crime, like the recounting of other social events, could be used as a means to control and direct the social polity. This was particularly true when the sources of information dissemination were few and communities were small or in their developing phase. Such was the case for many of the early communities on the American frontier. While historians have relied on newspaper accounts to a considerable degree in the recounting of the wildness of the West (Miller and Snell, 1963), little attention has been paid to the role newspapers have played in the actual formation of communities and in particular how crime news was used or managed during the frontier period. This chapter is a case study of one northwestern newspaper's use of crime news during the latter phases of the American frontier.

While the American frontier was regionally diverse, a concern with crime and violence served as a common denominator.[1] Not that all crime was similar or that the

49

frequency of violence was uniform, but as communities began to take shape with any sort of permanence as a goal, a precondition for their stability was a modicum level of order. How this level of order was perceived as well as how it was to be achieved differed. For some burgeoning frontier communities order was achieved through the absorption of some forms of crime and deviance (Dykstra, 1968); while in others vigilante committees enforced order without law (Dimsdale, 1866; Gard, 1949); in still others law was used at the expense of procedure (Shirley, 1957). Much depended on the type of community, e.g., agricultural communities, cattle towns, or mining settlements (Sundholm, 1978), as well as its people. Recourse to violence as a means of resolving conflict was common, particularly since the frontier culture seemed to glorify it (Bensman, 1971).

With the founding of practically every community or semblance of one, newspapers quickly became integral parts of community life. While in their own way these early publications at times attempted to deal generally with the problems of law and order, often their journalistic viewpoints were not well received and resulted in rousing the public or specific segments of it to violent action. For example, it was not uncommon for newspaper offices to be burned and editors threatened and beaten (Myers, 1967). On the other hand, neither did editors nor publishers follow strict codes of ethics, nor was subtlety part of their journalistic repertoire. Many of the newspaper reports were frequently bombastic expressions of opinion with what would in today's terms be cause for slander and libel.

The territorial press' treatment of crime varied with community conditions just as the communities themselves differed in dealing with what they perceived to be crime and deviance. In the Southwest before 1870 newspapers generally had little interest in crime and violence chiefly because it was too commonplace. During the same period, however, newspapers became partisans in some of the most violent confrontations of the period between warring interest groups. In the decade following, when there was a new outbreak of violence the press supported vigilante action as a solution (Stratton, 1969). While sheer frequency of events may have contributed in some instances to a lack of press coverage, one must not overlook that these incidents were crimes that involved individuals (i.e., largely crimes against the person). These were not acts that threatened more established or elite interests. Once collective interests or struggles for economic and political power resulted in violence the territorial press' reportage increased, as did partisan editorials.

The remainder of this chapter will be a case study of how one northwestern frontier community newspaper reported crime in its pages. The subject of this study is the *Great Falls Tribune* in the territory of Montana during the year 1887–1888, the first year of the newspaper's existence and the latter part of the frontier period.

Prior to making some conceptual assertions and presenting a description and analysis of the data, some mention of the state of the territory and the social context in which the *Great Falls Tribune* operated is necessary.

Montana was organized as a separate territory in 1865 following the discovery of gold at Bannack, Alder Gulch, and Last Chance Gulch. The economy which developed after initial settlement and acted as an inducement to settlers was based on the territory's rich resources, not only in gold, soon to be mined out, but silver, copper, virgin timber, and grazing areas that sustained enormous herds of buffalo (Payne, 1960), to be replaced by cattle in the ensuing years.

When Lewis the explorer first saw the "great falls" the Indians had described to him, he is reputed to have stated: "[I] longed for the pen of an artist that [I] might be able to give to the enlightened world some just idea of this truly magnificent and sublimely grand object which has from the commencement of time been concealed from the view of civilized man" (Cheney, 1971).

Seventy-nine years after this discovery the first post office was opened in Great Falls, having been preceded by the first house by one year. The postmaster, a pragmatist, saw "possibilities in the vast resources of water power running to 'waste'" (Cheney, 1971), a prophetic statement of the subsequent history of the area.[2]

At the time the *Great Falls Tribune* opened its offices, Montana had already been a territory for over two decades and was vying for statehood. The town of Great Falls was a community in the process of establishing itself as a center of commerce by opening its gates to all who wished to exploit its rich resources and "wasted" water power for profit. The *Tribune* was to play its journalistic role in the promotion of this goal in a number of ways, not the least of which was in the managing of crime news.

It seems certain from the amount of column space and the tenor of the comments that the *Tribune* was concerned chiefly with building the local community and pressing for statehood. That these were the goals is clearly revealed in numerous stories concerning commerce and industrial development. The following items are representative:

> The lots of Great Falls have a frontage of fifty feet and depth of one hundred and fifty. There are also twenty-foot alleys in the center of all the blocks. These matters should be borne in mind when comparing values. The usual frontage of lots in Montana cities is only twenty-five feet, which is just one-half that of Great Falls. [May 19, 1887]

> Manufacturers are coming westward. . . . Great Falls will profit by this westward movement. The conditions are all favorable for the establishment of factories in this city and its vicinity. Waterpower, coal and iron are abundant. The Manitoba and Montana Central railroads will bring to our doors all the other raw materials that may be needed. . . . With such inducements persons who are about to establish factories will do well to settle in Great Falls where they will find public sentiment very strong in favor of all new industries. [May 20, 1887]

> The combination of mining, grazing, agricultural, and manufacturing interests which Montana affords will have strong inducements for the thousands who are now looking westward for homes. They will find Great Falls the best place to stay while preparing for any of these pursuits. They will be able to gather much practical information here, and will be in the heart of a mining, farming and grazing country. [May 25, 1887]

Any event considered to lend respectability to the community was applauded and given prominence in its pages.

Uppermost was development; an oft-repeated banner headline advertisement gave the following message to all who cared to read it:

> Great Falls is located at the falls of the Missouri, which furnish the greatest available water-power on the continent. It is within seven of the most extensive coal and iron districts in the West, immediately beyond which are rich gold, silver, and copper districts. It lays tributary to the best agricultural and grazing part of the Territory, and the pineries of the upper Missouri and its tributaries. It is especially adapted by its natural resources and geographical position to become the leading manu-facturing city between Minneapolis and the Pacific Ocean, and the principal railroad center of Montana. The trip to Great Falls will amply repay tourists by the beauty of the scenery on the way, and they will find here the most magnificent series of waterfalls in the world, while the surrounding country is rich in picturesque scenery.

That considerable attention was given to the building of an "establishment" may be seen in items hailing the creation of legal institutions; an editorial congratulating the chief justice on a job well done; and praising, as a great accomplishment, the opening of a district court. Repeatedly one finds columns lauding the attractiveness of the area for industrial and commercial ventures. Conflict between different commercial interests generally was reported in a spirit of amelioration in that there was "enough for everyone." This conciliatory stance, however, did not extend to real or perceived criticism of the community, which was promptly and sometimes sarcastically answered. Rivalries and animosities between neighboring communities were not uncommon as evidenced by argumentive columns duly presented in the pages of the paper.

In 1887, Great Falls became the county seat of newly created Cascade County. This in turn allowed for a strengthened push for manufacturers and population growth. An additional boon to further development was the extension of the Manitoba Railroad into Great Falls. This in brief is the context in which the *Great Falls Tribune* operated and in which its creation and management of crime news is examined.

Data and Method

Each issue of the *Great Falls Tribune* recorded on microfilm from May 16, 1887, to May 20, 1888, was examined (the newspaper circulated daily), and the number of crime news items were ascertained and counted. The time span used was the first year of the *Tribune's* publication, which coincided with the beginning of the town's life. A determination was made as to whether the item pertained to a local, territorial, elsewhere in the U.S., or foreign incident of crime. The type of incident was also noted. Each issue was then examined for news items relating to criminal justice matters—these included items related to the establishment of a new court, grand juries, judicial appointments, etc. Since newspapers did not sufficiently distinguish between news and editorials during this period, a distinction was made between news elaboration and editorial comment. If a news report included some slanting or opinion of the writer, it was termed a comment item; if the entire piece was a commentary on some crime event, it was termed an editorial. In either case the article was summarized. Thus tabulation was made of all crime news mentioned, and at least a summary statement of all editorial and news elaborations was recorded. It was assumed that these statements reflected gradations of persuasive intention by the newspaper under study. Stated differently, comments and editorials were considered to evidence strength of attitude of the editors toward crime.

There were a total of 168 crime news items reported during the period under study. Of these, 6 were foreign (i.e., events reported as having occurred in a foreign country); 107 were recorded as occurring elsewhere in the U.S.; 55 were within the territory, and of these 55, 18 events were reported as happening locally.

Discussion

It is clear that these figures do not indicate any overemphasis of crime reporting. In comparison with Southwestern territorial papers of the period (e.g., *The Tombstone*

Daily Nugget; Dodge City Times; Ford County Globe; Silver City Enterprise) the *Great Falls Tribune*'s crime coverage was minor. Crime certainly was not absent from the territory, for according to census reports by 1890 there were already 432 persons serving prison sentences. While this is by no means an accurate reflection of the state of crime, it is an indicator among the sparse crime data available for the period.[3] For purposes of this analysis crime rates are not crucial. What is of importance is the degree of seriousness ascribed by the local press to a variety of violating conduct based on its perception of the harm caused to the community by such conduct.[4] While crime news was generally de-emphasized, concern with crime was not. As we shall see, to the *Great Falls Tribune* crime was of two kinds—first, that which occurred outside the immediate confines of the community the newspaper represented, and second, that which was perpetrated by "outsiders" within the community.

An early issue of the paper gives the initial warning of the possible threat that some outsiders might pose and proposes a remedy:

> Action must be taken without delay to either enlarge the present one or build a new prison, for the accommodation of the "bad men" who will pour in upon us by the hundreds within a few weeks. The prison we now have is too small, and not only that, but it is filthy and wholly unfit to receive a prisoner, no matter what his condition may be or the magnitude of his crime. Situated as we are, a day's drive from the county jail, the incarceration of prisoners there for petty crimes would entail a heavy expense upon the county, and if they are let go, they will take it for granted that they can do as they please without fear of the law. Such a state of affairs is bound to exist here within the next sixty days unless effective measures are adopted at once.
>
> Another matter that must be looked after is the appointment of a sufficient number of officers to preserve the peace. If this is not done immediately the consequences may prove costly. Already a hard gang has begun to congregate, and their numbers will be rapidly augmented. Unless this element is given to understand that it is the intention to preserve the quietude and peace in the city, they will become a mob and will endeavor to

run things to suit themselves. The history of other western
towns has proved this to be only too true. . . . [May 25,
1887]

The intention to preserve order coupled with the threat the
influx of outsiders might bring was to be a frequent theme.
When the town experienced a few street fights, a not too
uncommon occurrence given the time, the *Tribune* was quick to
editorialize the harm that such behavior posed to the "good"
name of the town and more importantly to property. The need
for ordinances to protect these interests was considered essential.

> The "scrap" in the street today was no more heinous than
> the drunken fights which are a daily occurrence in the
> large cities. But this city has always been so orderly that it
> has naturally created surprise and indignation. The
> occurrence has brought home forcibly to the people the
> need of regular municipal government, which would
> establish ordinances and take measures for the
> preservation of the peace. . . . Until incorporation has been
> effected public vigilance should be exercised to suppress
> all disorders and keep the town clear of evildoers. Every
> property owner is interested in upholding the good name
> of the city . . . common interest should unite citizens in a
> solid phalanx against all persons who come here to have a
> "good" time when such means prizefighting and
> disorderly conduct. [June 8, 1887]

In other instances the outsider bringing evil is presented in
conjunction with statements of the community's desire to "put
down" crime and a chiding of those who wish to exaggerate the
number of crimes being committed.

> There is a strong determination in this city to put down
> lawlessness of all kinds, and render it too hot for those
> vultures who prey on industry and thrift of the hardy
> settler. More has been said on this subject than we care to
> report, for there are persons and newspapers always ready
> through malice or foolishness to exaggerate such matters,
> especially when a young Montana town is concerned.
> Enough has been done, however, to convince landjumpers
> and ranch-thieves that the people are a unit in resolving
> that such knavery must stop. . . . Fortunately the city has
> plenty of resolute men to enforce order, even when the

horde which follows the railroad builders arrive here. [June 16, 1887]

Along with the portrayal of crime as the work of outsiders the newspaper also tended to create the impression of an absolute difference, and generally adhered to the concept of a "criminal class."

> The advance guard of the bum element has arrived. He is a typical specimen of his class, and proffers his "will-you-give-a-poor-fellow-a-couple-of-bits" request in the quiet tones of one serene in virtuous purpose and confident of success. An occasional introduction to a wood-pile may have the effect of making his calls less frequent and ultimately rid the community of his presence. [February 25, 1888]

Suspicion also extended to those (perhaps not unwisely) deemed to be associated with criminals and "connivers." In this respect the newspaper probably reflected popular sentiment when it wrote:

> the legal fraternity are [sic] now well represented in our city. As a class they are genial citizens, but it is generally conceded that trouble always begins when they congregate in one place in any considerable number. [May 20, 1887]

Judges, however, were approved of as long as they were fair and a "terror to evil doers" [May 23, 1887]. In spite of protestations to the contrary, there were some who viewed the growing town not as virtuously as the *Tribune* wished to picture it, but criticism from the outside was not to be tolerated. When the newspaper of another Montana community wrote that Great Falls is full of "tramps and hoodlums" the *Tribune* replied forcefully that its town was an "orderly and law abiding community. . . . The court records show that there are few cases of crime and these are light" [August 15, 1887]. A similar response was given to a Wyoming newspaper that attempted to label Great Falls a "resort for criminals" [August 20, 1887].

The impression *Great Falls Tribune* readers were given was that crimes were events that happened elsewhere and tended to be viewed by the paper as acts committed by a class of people distinct from those living in Great Falls. The problem as the *Tribune* saw it, at least by implication, was to keep this "class" from entering, or if that proved impossible, to make an example of "them" for purposes of deterrence.

In keeping with this class distinction it should not be surprising that the *Great Falls Tribune*, like many other newspapers of the period, was racist in more than a few of its commentaries. Chinese, African Americans, and Native Americans were seen as "good" when they "kept their place," but to be watched because of their alleged criminal potential. For example, in one news article headed "Summary Justice," there was a detailed account of an African-American male who had been accused of shooting a white waitress; a lynch mob was formed but was foiled; the accused was placed in custody, but the lynchers burned down the jail, killing the suspect. According to the report: "The negro's body was *roasted* in the building" [September 16, 1887 (italics mine)].

While few local crime incidents were reported, several distinctions may be made. It is clear that the town paper saw local crime largely as an evil brought into the community by undesirables and not as a problem arising out of it, a point alluded to above. Second, the preservation of order was of paramount concern and tended to be stressed even though local crime coverage was restrained. This emphasis and reference to outsiders emerged in news elaboration and editorial comment.

Examples of underreporting are found in items such as a three-line report that a gunfight was avoided [June 4, 1887] or a three-line mention that some burglaries had been committed with the elaboration that the "tough element will bear close watching." On the other hand, when there was an assault on the main street which *visibly* threatened good order, the *Tribune* felt compelled to write ". . . when acts of violence such as this are committed upon the main thoroughfare and the thug escapes beyond hope of detection, it is time for law-abiding citizens to organize and rid the community of such as his ilk" [June 16, 1887]. Proper punishment was seen as a deterrent to the incoming evil doer as this editorial comment makes clear:

> Let it once be understood that when a crime is committed punishment will speedily follow, and there will be less of

it. With the large influx of population liable to come in the spring, crime will be rampant unless evil doers are stearnly [sic] dealt with. Let our magistrates stiffen their spinal columns and they will meet with the approval of law abiding citizens. [February 4, 1888]

Analysis

To understand the role of this territorial newspaper, particularly its management of crime news, it is important to recognize what was at stake. It must be remembered that a community was in the process of creating itself and in so doing was in a search for identity and stability. As an incentive to settlement and creation of permanence it could offer the rich potential of the vast resources of its environs. But the awareness of this potentiality needed to be communicated not only to draw settlers to the area, but also to those already resident in order to create purpose for a viable community. In Kai Erikson's terms, it was an emerging community that needed to define its boundaries; the newspaper acted as a catalyst in this process by representing the elite viewpoint of the emerging business-industrial sector. By continually placing before its readers the picture of an almost idyllic social and cultural space it aided in the coalescing of the people. Moreover, by picturing crime largely as an outside event or the result of those foreign or marginal to the community, it could readily solidify the people in pointing to the threat, and thereby create a definition of where the cultural boundaries should be. As Erikson (1966:13) explains: "Deviant forms of behavior, by marking the outer edges of group life, give the inner structure its special character and thus supply the framework within which the people of the group develop an orderly sense of their own cultural identity."

This process was to be aided through the press' major purpose: to attract industry and business to the area and to create more readership and advertising for its pages. It was, therefore, both in its interest and best for the elite it sought to represent to maintain a balanced posture of reporting.[5] While crime could have been given greater emphasis, and even the few local crimes reported could have been given more play, it was not advantageous for the *Tribune* to do so. Reporting too much crime or giving it too much emphasis might dissuade profitable settlement, and yet the threat needed to be stated; thus, a selective dwelling on order. Contrasting conditions existed for territorial news coverage in other areas such as the Southwest. Crime news was not lacking during the same period (see Stratton, 1969). The reasons for the difference may be discovered in the type of community the newspapers represented and in the stage of development of the community under consideration.

The frontier communities of the Southwest during their early phases, particularly those that depended on cattle trade, were towns that needed to rely on transient population for their economic well-being. In these communities certain forms of criminal activity were expected, especially from drovers, who spent months in isolation with cattle on the long drive to market. Personal disputes and assaults were frequent. Assaults that ended in shootings and sometimes death were not uncommon. Only when the level of crime went beyond a tolerance point, usually when local merchant interests were directly affected, was there a call for order. Indeed, some types of deviant and criminal activities such as prostitution and gambling were even encouraged, notwithstanding ordinances against them, simply because it was felt that these were essential to the town's hold on the cattle trade (Dykstra, 1968).

As long as these communities gained their economic well-being partially from the marginality of their transient population, there was no need for restraint in the reporting of crime news; those that were attracted to the community would not be dissuaded. The existence of a place where there was some "action" may have proved an attraction for some. Under these circumstances a newspaper's interest in crime was only in its newsworthiness and no significant effort or need to campaign for law and order was necessary. Although there were occasional calls for vigilante action when the order of the community seemed grossly disrupted, there was no sustained effort at reform until later.

The press took a reform stance when frontier communities gained a measure of stability through economic development and political and economic elites were establishing themselves. Hence the concern with order of the *Great Falls Tribune*. Newspapers became active in calling for reform only when there were power shifts in the economic or political structure that required an emphasis on law and order for these interests either to be established or to be able to carry out their affairs. When crime became disruptive of these interests, then the press seemed to have taken a more active role in its suppression.

For the *Great Falls Tribune* its area of influence had exploitive potential which depended on stable settlement and long-term investment and for which order was essential. News coverage of crime occurring elsewhere was safe and fulfilled the obligation to report newsworthy events. While local crime was not to be exaggerated, as the *Tribune* saw it, the community needed to protect itself against the marginals who made up the "criminal class," such as railroad workers and others needed for their labor, but who posed a potential threat to order and stability.

Given the infancy of the town, one may surmise that it was desirable to create and sustain an internal sense of community among the inhabitants of Great Falls. While this may not have been a conscious effort on the part of the newspaper, its emphasis on "outsiders" as criminals contributed to this end. This labeling (cf., Becker, 1963) was, however, selective and was reserved for those whose pariah status had already been established and whose "evil" was taken for granted. There was already a history of suppression of the indigenous population in the territory and an established myth to draw on to create this definition. As a consequence these outsiders-in-residence were given impermanent status, never to be considered a viable part of the community, but simply another resource to be exploited. Other "outsiders," chiefly businessmen and industrialists whose "good" was an assumed certainty, were encouraged to join the community as permanent members.

Summary and Conclusion

Two suggestions may be made with regard to the territorial newspaper's role in the establishment of early communities. The first relates to labeling of the outsider which has relevance for deviance theory. The second is related to the larger role newspapers played in community organization through their management of crime news.

The *Great Falls Tribune* practiced what might be termed labeling in reverse when it came to certain outsiders. While the general theoretical thrust of deviance theory in the interactionist tradition treats the outsider as an outcome of deviance definition (Becker, 1963; Schur, 1971), and views the outsider in essentially negative terms as a permanent outcast; the outsider may also be perceived positively as a desideratum to be attracted to form a more cohesive community.

The "outsider" in this sense is perceived as a potential ally of ruling elites' interests. Here the newspaper with its influence potential acted at least superficially as a power broker of these interests. Moreover, by attracting certain "outsiders" it assured its own future. This interpretation would support conflict theory assertions that the concern of power elites in maintaining their privileged position (in our case establishing it) is of greater import than boundary maintenance in community building (see Chambliss, 1976). What is divergent in this case study is at least the minimizing of deviance rather than its creation. What this suggests is that perhaps we are dealing with a continuum in the development of social control mechanisms, wherein definitions of deviance are interconnected with stages in the development of socioeconomic structures, rather than, as heretofore presented, as definitive processes of deviance creation. This leads to the second point.

As has been suggested, newspapers played active roles in community building and by their management of crime news were instrumental in the type of order and control resources that emerged primarily to protect economic interests. The manner in which crime was treated by the territorial press in large measure was related to the types of communities they were serving. Crime news coverage differed in the Northwest from that in the

Southwest chiefly because of the initial economics of the communities involved. Cattle town economics depended on trade and merchandising, service, and leisure-related enterprises, and there was no initial industrial development. The Northwest community herein described had an impulse toward industrialization from its beginning and the press championed this cause in its call for order and restrained crime reporting.

Given these conditions a tentative model (see Table 2.1) may be proposed that relates newspaper concern with crime to stage and type of community development. The model hypothesizes that in nonindustrially inclined frontier communities during their formative stages, newspapers report crime without restraint or great concern. At times there may be a call for order when local interests are threatened. In industrially disposed communities the reverse holds true. Newspapers tend to control their reporting of local crime and emphasize order to be achieved by proper procedure if possible, which is given secondary importance. During the latter stages of growth in nonindustrial towns there is a mixed newspaper management of crime events. There tends to be straight reporting with some reform movement development and more emphasis on order than on law. Finally, during the latter stages of the evolution of industrial towns, crime coverage becomes more objective with a reform emphasis as well as a call for legal constraints in the enforcement of community order.

It is recognized that these are not exclusive categories but it is suggested that they do represent tendencies which might profitably be investigated further in studies of community organization that include crime news management as a variable in their analysis, a subject heretofore largely ignored but one which holds promise toward a better understanding of how communities deal with crime, the function crime serves in their development, and the boundaries they create within their cultural space.

TABLE 2.1

Territorial Newspaper's Role in Crime News Reporting
and Stage and Type of Community Development

| | *Type of Community* | |
	Frontier nonindustrial	Frontier industrial
Stage of community development	Crime Coverage nonrestrained	Crime Coverage restrained
Early	Concern minor Order emphasis	Concern major Order and law emphasis
Late	Crime Coverage nonrestrained Some reform Order and law emphasis	Crime Coverage nonrestrained Reform movement Law and order emphasis

NOTES

* This article is a combined and slightly revised version of an article, *Crime News in the Old West—Social Control in a Northwestern Town, 1887–1888*, which appeared in *Urban Life* Vol. 8 No. 3 October 1979, 317–334; and a paper, *Crime News in the Old West—A Case Study of a Northwestern Town*, presented at the annual meeting of the Society for the Study of Social Problems, 1977, on which portions of the published article were based. Reprinted by permission of Sage Publications, Inc.

1. There is an extensive literature on the diverse nature of the U.S. frontier. An excellent bibliography may be found in Billington (1974).

2. For a more complete history of the area see: Howard, Joseph K. (1959) *Montana, High Wide and Handsome*, (rev. ed.). New Haven, CT: Yale University Press; Toole, Ross K. (1959) *Montana: An Uncommon Land*. Norman: University of Oklahoma Press; Burlingame, Merrill G. (1942) *The Montana Frontier*. Helena: State Publishing Co.; Burlingame,

Merrill G. & K. Ross Toole (eds.) (1957) *History of Montana*, 3 vols., New York: Lewis Historical Publishing Co.; Smurr, John W. & K. Ross Toole (eds.) (1957) *Historical Essays on Montana and the Northwest*. Helena: Western Press; Hamilton, James McClellan (1957) *From Wilderness to Statehood: A History of Montana 1805–1900*. Portland, OR: Binford and Mort Publishers.

3. While it is recognized that the data are not directly comparable, it is interesting to note in this connection that the rate of imprisonment for Montana by 1890 was 326.8 per 100,000 in the population; in 1973 the rate of imprisonment per 100,000 in the population was 42. See *Abstracts of Eleventh Census 1890*. Washington DC: Government Printing Office, 1896; and U.S. Department of Justice, *Census of Prisoners in State Correctional Facilities, 1973*. LEAA-NPS, 1976.

4. In a previous study of crime news coverage, Davis (1952) found that the amount of crime news in each of four Colorado newspapers varied independently of both the amount of crime in the state and the amount of crime news in other newspapers.

5. What may be seen here is an example of the constructed nature of news creating described by Molotch and Lester (1974; 1975). Public events, these researchers maintain, become news for the practical purposes these events serve, not because of any intrinsic objective importance they may harbor. Accordingly, "the sociological use of news is for its potential as a guide to the social purposes dominant in a society rather than as an indicator of what in some objective sense, actually happened [1975: 236]." More recent research has shown this to be equally true in the management of television news, see Fishman (1978).

REFERENCES

Becker, H. S. 1963. *Outsiders: Studies in the Sociology of Deviance*. New York: Free Press.

Bensman, J. 1971. "Social and institutional factors determining the level of violence and political assassinations in the operation of society: a theoretical discussion," 345–388 in W.J. Crotty (ed.) *Assassinations and the Political Order*. New York: Harper & Row.

Billington, P. A. 1974. *Westward Expansion: A History of the American Frontier*. New York: Macmillan.

Chambliss, W. J. 1976. "Functional and conflict theories of crime: the heritage of Emile Durkheim and Karl Marx," 1–28 in W. J. Chambliss and M. Mankoff (eds.), *Whose Law What Order? A Conflict Approach to Criminology.* New York: John Wiley.

Cheney, R. C. 1971. *Names on the Face of Montana: The Story of Montana's Place Names.* Missoula: University of Montana Publications in History.

Davis, J. F. 1952. "Crime news in Colorado newspapers." *American Journal of Sociology,* (January) 57: 325–330.

Dimsdale, T. J. 1866. *The Vigilantes of Montana.* Virginia City: Montana Post Press.

Dykstra, R. 1968. *The Cattletowns.* New York: Alfred A. Knopf.

Erikson, K. T. 1966. *Wayward Puritans: A Study in the Sociology of Deviance.* New York: John Wiley.

Fishman, M. 1978. "Crime waves as ideology," *Social Problems,* (June) 25: 531–543.

Gard, W. 1949. *Frontier Justice.* Norman: University of Oklahoma Press.

Great Falls Tribune. May 16, 1887, to May 20, 1888.

Miller, N. H. and J. W. Snell. 1963. *Why the West Was Wild: A Contemporary Look at the Antics of Some Highly Publicized Kansas Cowtown Personalities.* Topeka: Kansas State Historical Society.

Molotch, H. and M. Lester. 1975. "Accidental news: the great oil spill as local occurrence and national event," *American Journal of Sociology,* (September) 81: 235–260.

————. 1974. "News as purposive behavior: On the strategic use of routine events, accidents and scandals," *American Sociological Review,* (February) 39: 101–112.

Myers, J. M. 1967. *Print in a Wild Land.* Garden City, NY: Doubleday.

Payne, T. 1960. "Under the copper dome: politics in Montana," 181–205 in F. H. Jonas (ed.), *Western Politics.* Salt Lake City: University of Utah Press.

Schur, E. M. 1971. *Labeling Deviant Behavior: Its Sociological Implications.* New York: Harper & Row.

Shirley, G. 1957. *Law West of Fort Smith.* New York: Henry Holt.

Stratton, P. A. 1969. *The Territorial Press of New Mexico, 1834–1912.* Albuquerque: University of New Mexico Press.

Sundholm, C. A. 1978. "Social control on the American frontier: Comparative notes on early mining and cattle towns." Paper presented at the annual meeting of the American Sociological Association, San Francisco.

CHAPTER 3

Communal Violence and the Media: Lynchings and Their News Coverage by *The New York Times* between 1882 and 1930

Ira M. Wasserman
Steven Stack

In considering the general issue of news construction and crime, one should be aware that there are general problems related to the construction of news. News accounts of reality are always subject to distortions generated by a number of "structural" and "human" factors (see Breed, 1955, 1958; Tuchman, 1978; Gans, 1979; Bridges, 1989; Hardt, 1990). The structural factors have to do with such factors as the technological base (Levy, 1974) and the "invisible" hand of the market (Greenberg, Sacksman, Sandman and Salamone, 1989). The human factors have to do with the behavior or policies of interests or individuals who act to create a news agenda (see Stevens, 1990), or else censor this agenda (see Evans and Lundman, 1983). The construction of news involves a complicated interaction between the social producers of news and the objective external reality (Hartley, 1982; Manoff and Schudson, 1987).

In some sense there is a circularity in the construction of news, since the media tends to focus its attention on celebrities, who may be defined as "people who are known for being known" (Boorstin, 1962). Thus news stories tend to emphasize stories about people who have made the news. An example of this celebrity focus of news may be observed in the media presentation of suicide. In the United States in any one year there are over 20,000 suicides (Holinger, 1987), but the mass media only presents suicide information on celebrities (Bollen and Phillips, 1982; Wasserman, 1984; Stack, 1987), or else unusual public suicides. Almost all other suicide stories tend to be ignored by the national media.

The issue of how news is constructed is an especially important problem in the area of crime, since it involves behavior that may arouse strong public sentiments and impact on public policy. A number of studies (Antunes and Hurley, 1977; Dutton and Duffy, 1985; Pritchard, 1985) have found that the reporting on crime by the elite (e.g., *The New York Times, Harpers Magazine*) and the general mass media (e.g., local newspapers, mass circulation magazines, television news shows) is highly selective and biased. The news media is more likely to overreport violent crimes (e.g., homicide), and underreport other more routine crimes (e.g., larceny), or else ignore crimes where there is no clear victim (e.g., corporate crimes) (Evans and Lundman, 1983). Ethnic and racial factors may also influence crime reporting by the media (Martens and Cunningham-Niederer, 1985; Winkel, 1990), with an underreporting of crimes within ethnic and racial communities, and an overreporting of inter-ethnic and racial crimes.

An interest group, or unique individuals who may create a media interest in certain types of crime news, may be titled *moral entrepreneurs* (Becker, 1963; Molotch and Lester, 1974), i.e., groups or individuals who make the larger society socially aware of crime issues, and by so doing create news interest in these events. For example, by 1913 and thereafter, the national media in the United States publicized commercial prostitution, in part because of the activities of a commission chaired by John D. Rockefeller, Jr. (Kneeland, 1913). A recent example of this creation of news under the auspices of a moral crusade involves the "national war on drugs" (Reinariman and Levine, 1989). Prominent elites (e.g., Nancy Reagan) convinced the American public that a drug epidemic was occurring in the United States, and it was necessary to fight it. In general, struggles against many types of crime create crime ideologies (e.g., the view of a crime wave) which become publicized in the mass media (Fishman, 1981; Humphries, 1981; Gorelick, 1989). There may be no dramatic shift in criminal behavior, but moral entrepreneurs are able to convince the public that there is a serious social problem. The social concerns of elites may temper the crime news reporting on these events, as illustrated by the fact that in India crime waves, as reported in the Indian newspapers, involve public demonstrations—a major concern of Indian newspaper and political elites (Priyaharsini, 1984).

The presentation of crime news may also influence the general beliefs of a larger public, and the behavior of public officials. Presentation of large amounts of local crime news engenders increased fear among the larger public (Sheley and Ashkins, 1981; Brillon, 1987), while the presentation of large amounts of nonlocal crime news has the opposite effect of making a public feel safe by comparison with other areas (Liska and Baccaglini, 1990). The media presentation of crime news may also influence the behavior of public officials, causing them to construct certain agendas. For example, a study on the Milwaukee county prosecutors's office between 1982 and 1983 (Pritchard, 1986) found that the degree of news coverage of a crime influenced whether the District Attorney's office plea-bargained the case.

Almost all of the research on the interrelation between crime and media presentation of it has tended to focus on individual crimes, with little attention to communal or group crimes. The one exception to this rule involves the study of the media and riots in the 1960s. Examining riot news, Danzger (1975) discovered that whether the press recorded a city as having a riot or not was heavily influenced by whether there was an AP/UPI office in the city. However, Snyder and Kelly (1977) found that for more intense riots (e.g., the 1967 riots), the influence of media location was minimal. To further explore the factors that influence media presentation of communal violence, this chapter will investigate the structural factors which determined whether or not *The New York Times* would present stories on lynchings between 1882 and 1930.

Lynchings as a Form of Communal Violence

A form of communal violence that existed in the United States from the end of the Civil War until World War II was lynching. In a broad sense lynching can be defined as the illegal execution of an individual, or set of individuals, by another group of individuals, usually over fifty in number. Analytically it is necessary to differentiate two broad types of lynchings (Myrdal, 1944: 564): mob lynchings that were ritualistic communal illegal executions (Williamson, 1984: 185), and vigilante lynchings that were illegal executions where a restricted number of participants gave the victim a trial before execution (Brown, 1969). The latter form was caused by the lack of legal authority, and it ceased once legal authority was established. Another intermediate type was whitecapping (Holmes, 1969; Noble, 1973), which involved the illegal activities of lower-class members of secret societies to punish offenders who were not adequately dealt with by the law. Ross (1989), using historical data, has identified seven broad types of lynch mobs. Most lynchings in the previous time period were concentrated in the American South, an area with a plantation economy that employed cheap black labor (Mandle, 1978: 42). A vast majority of lynching incidents in the United States were interracial lynchings in which whites lynched blacks for a variety of real and imagined offenses.

The fact that lynchings were organized in different ways (Ross, 1989: 172–238) makes the precise definition of a lynching difficult and problematic. The activity may have reflected a nonoperative criminal justice system (e.g., vigilante mobs [Brown, 1969]), the presence of secret societies (e.g., whitecappers [Holmes, 1969]), or the illegal activity of law enforcement officials (e.g., rural southern posses [*The New York Times*, 1927]). At times local law enforcement officials dispensed "street-corner justice"[1] and these events were not classified as lynchings but as legal homicides. Also, in cases where a deputized posse killed someone they were pursuing, it was a judgment call as to whether they had lynched the person, or killed him/her in the line of duty.

There is also a problem with ascertaining the full extent of lynchings in the United States, since no officials records are available. The only available historic data sources are local and national newspaper accounts of this illegal behavior. Since these accounts are only indexed since 1882, this year is treated as the starting year of the study. After 1930 they became extremely rare, so 1930 is the last year that they are examined. A number of sources were utilized to locate national lynchings between 1882 and 1930. For eleven southern and border states[2] Beck, Tolnay and Massey (1991), through a National Science Foundation grant, verified newspaper lynching data. For the other states, which, except for Texas and Missouri, had relatively fewer lynchings, data collected by *The Chicago Tribune* (1883–1919) and the National Association for the Advancement of Colored People (1919) are employed to determine lynchings between 1882 and 1918. After 1918 a number of additional sources (Work, 1921; Guzman, 1948; Ginzburg, 1988; Wright, 1990) were employed to obtain further lynching data. Since this study is concerned with relating total lynchings to their national coverage in *The New York Times*, it examined all lynching accounts in *The Times* between 1882 and 1930, and if these individual accounts were not in the previous data set, they were included in it. The previous data represents the most comprehensive information on this illegal behavior.

The previous information was computer coded, and it was determined that 4,209 individuals were lynched between 1882 and 1930. However, many cases involved multiple lynching victims, with the number varying between one and eleven. Since this study is concerned with the national coverage of lynching incidents, it was necessary to convert the previous data into incident data. When the data was recoded in this manner, 3,403 incidents were specified. Figure 3.1 indicates the yearly distribution of lynching incidents in the United States between 1882 and 1930.

As can be seen from Figure 3.1, lynchings peaked until the 1890s, reached a maximum level in 1892, and then declined gradually, reaching a low level by the 1920s. In general, the period 1882 to 1900 was a period of high lynchings, the period

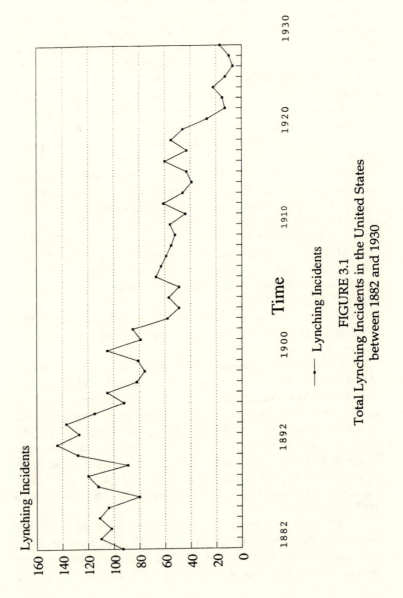

FIGURE 3.1
Total Lynching Incidents in the United States
between 1882 and 1930

1901 to 1920 was a period of moderate lynchings, and the period 1921 to 1930 was a period of low lynchings.

The purpose of this study is to determine the factors that were causally related to the national coverage of these events. In the period 1882 to 1930 a major national newspaper in the United States was *The New York Times*. *The New York Times* was founded in 1851 by Henry Raymond, and in 1896 it was purchased by Adolph Ochs, who continued its high journalism, while at the same time expanding its scope (Berger, 1970). It was a paper that opposed sensationalism, and followed a product concept that sells news by emphasizing high-quality content and printing (Thorn, 1987: 55–56). Gamson and Modigliani (1971: 152–168) examined *The New York Times* as a data source for examining the Cold War conflict between 1946 and 1962, and showed that it was a thorough and reliable source of information. Given the quality of this national information source, and the fact that it is the only national newspaper that possesses a yearly index between 1882 and 1930, which allows one to specify the yearly lynchings covered in this period, it will be utilized as the data source for determining the national coverage of lynchings in the United States between 1882 and 1930.

Causes of Variation in National Coverage of Lynchings

Let us now consider factors which might influence the national coverage of lynchings by *The New York Times* between 1882 and 1930. The first factor would be the year of coverage, with increased coverage more likely in later years compared with earlier years. Figure 3.2 displays the percentage (%) coverage of lynchings by *The Times* between 1882 and 1930.

It can be seen from the figures that as lynching incidents became rarer (see Figure 3.1), there was a greater tendency for *The Times* to cover these events (see Figure 3.2). Throughout the twentieth century the mass media has extended its scope and depth of coverage of national events (Matthews and Prothro,

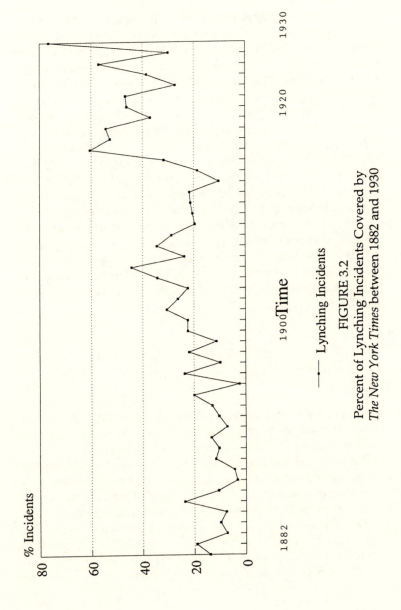

% Incidents

1882   1900Time   1920   1930

— Lynching Incidents

FIGURE 3.2
Percent of Lynching Incidents Covered by
The New York Times between 1882 and 1930

1966: 237–263), and one would expect these changes to be related to national newspaper coverage of lynchings, especially as they became more rare and unusual. The level of national coverage over time was also influenced by the fact that they were more likely to be publicly condemned by the mass public (see, for example, *The New York Times*, 1935), local elites, and media elites (Ames, 1938). For example, there were a number of lynchings in Tampa, Florida, between 1858 and 1935 (Ingalls, 1987), but it was after the 1920s that the local elites' came to strongly oppose them, whereas in earlier times they either condoned them or provided leadership for the local lynch mobs who attacked individuals who threatened the local establishment (rapists, strike organizers). In many communities prior to the 1930s, local elites supported this behavior for crimes that revolted communal mores (see, for example, *The New York Times*, 1903).

A second factor that might influence coverage was seasonal effects. As can be seen from Table 3.1, lynchings, and especially lynchings that were precipitated by sexual assaults, were more prevalent in the warmer months, and one might expect this seasonal pattern to influence national media coverage of them.

A third factor that might influence coverage would be geographic location. Lynchings were more commonplace in the South, which in the time period 1882 to 1930 was a more culturally isolated region (Woodward, 1951) that was less urbanized than the remainder of the nation (Weiher, 1977). Also, more lynchings in the South, with the exception of Louisiana, occurred in smaller, more rural political areas (Young, 1928). Other studies (e.g., Greenberg, Sacksman, Sandman and Salamone, 1989; Singer, Endreny and Glassman, 1991) of all types of natural disasters, including human and nonhuman ones, have found that unless the disasters are very intense (e.g., a major earthquake with significant loss of life), there is less coverage of them in more geographically isolated areas.

TABLE 3.1

Monthly Distribution of Lynching Incidents for all Lynchings, and Lynchings Triggered by Homicide and Nonsexual Assault and Sexual Assault

Month	All Lynchings	Homicide and Nonsexual Assault	Sexual Assault
	(%)	(%)	(%)
January	6.7	8.4	4.1
February	6.6	7.3	5.7
March	7.1	6.7	7.0
April	7.9	8.9	7.6
May	9.2	9.1	8.0
June	10.5	10.9	13.2
July	11.2	9.3	13.5
August	10.3	9.8	11.6
September	8.1	6.9	9.5
October	7.8	7.7	7.7
November	6.9	6.6	7.7
December	7.4	8.5	4.2
	(N = 3400)	(N = 1336)	(N = 931)
	$x^2 = 116.15$	$x^2 = 31.91$	$x^2 = 121.07$
	$p < .001$	$p < .005$	$p < .001$

A fourth factor that might influence national coverage would be the race and gender of the victim. Gender might be important because the lynching of women was rare, and one might expect that this would lead to greater coverage of these incidents. With regard to race, there might be lower coverage of black lynchings because of their greater prevalence. Lynchings generated a great fear in the black community which has continued to the present in more isolated areas. This fact is illustrated by a recent claim by family members of a black youth who was a victim of jail suicide. They alleged that he was lynched by local authorities, even though the evidence was very scant (Applebome, 1993). The fact that race might influence national coverage is illustrated by the coverage of two *altruistic lynchings* that occurred during World War I. In discussing homicide, Durkheim (1958: 110–120) defined altruistic homicide as murder that occurs when individual actors are seen as opponents of the collective order, and their homicide serves the current collective interests. During World War I two of these types of lynchings occurred. In August of 1917 a black preacher in South Carolina who opposed the draft law was lynched by an interracial mob [*The Augusta Chronicle*, 1917]. This unusual type of lynching was not covered by *The Times*. By contrast, the lynching of a white German-born Socialist who supposedly made disloyal remarks in Illinois in 1918 [*The New York Times*, 1918a] was given extensive coverage by *The Times*, and became an issue at the Berne, Switzerland, prisoners' conference in 1918 [*The New York Times*, 1918b].

A fifth factor that might influence coverage involved the nature of the precipitating event for the lynching. Lynchings that were brought about by murder and sexual assault were more likely to arouse strong community sentiments, have more individuals participate in the lynching, and increase the possible property damage from the lynching. These factors make it more likely that these types of lynchings would be covered by the national media.

A sixth possible causal factor could be the intensity of the lynching, as measured by the number of lynch victims. Lynchings where there were multiple victims tended to receive greater attention in a local area, aroused greater public emotions, and led to greater community disorders.

Methodology of the Study

As stated earlier in this chapter, the authors have collected a data set that determines the characteristics of 3,403 lynching incidents in the United States between 1882 and 1930, as well as whether each of these lynching incidents was covered by *The New York Times*, using the annual *New York Times Index* to make this determination. For each incident a dummy or indicator variable is created (Neter, Wasserman and Kutner, 1990: 349–

351) that takes a value of 0 if the incident is not covered by *The Times*. These indicators, or dummy variables are created throughout this study. For C classes of items (e.g., twelve months), C-1 indicator variables are created, one class being arbitrarily omitted. The relative strength of each of the C-1 variables is interpreted in relation to the arbitrarily omitted variable. For example, if one related homicide rates over time to eleven monthly indicator variables, arbitrarily omitting December, then the strength of the monthly indicator variables would be in relation to December, with significant estimated correlations and slope coefficients indicating that the homicide rate is significantly greater in a particular month than it is in December.

With regard to the historic time period, two indicator variables are created. The first indicator variable is one that relates 1882–1900, a period of high lynchings, to 1921–1930, a period of low lynchings; the second indicator variable is one that relates 1901–1920, a period of moderate lynchings, to 1921–1930. The results of Figure 3.2 would suggest that these two indicator variables should have a significant impact on *The Times* coverage of lynchings.

With regard to the measurement of seasonal effects, eleven monthly dummy variables are created, December being arbitrarily eliminated from the model. If *The Times* coverage is causally linked with the actual occurrence of lynchings, one would expect these monthly indicator variables to be most significant in the warmer summer months.

In order to measure geographical effects, the study differentiated deep southern states, upper southern states, border states,[3] and the remainder of the nation. The study arbitrarily eliminates states in the remainder of the nation from the model.

With regard to race and gender, white was defined as zero, and nonwhite as one, while male was defined as zero and female as one. With regard to the number of lynching victims, the actual number was used, except that four or more lynchings was defined as four, since the number of incidents in which there were more than four victims was very small. Thus the range of this variable was from one to four.

It was not possible to use ordinary-least-squares (OLS) to estimate the coefficients in the model because the dependent variable was an indicator variable. Rather, a logit estimation procedure was employed (Aldrich and Nelson, 1984; Walsh, 1987), and the SPSS statistical package (*SPSS*, 1990: 858–859) was utilized to compute the estimated coefficients in the model.

Findings

Table 3.2 specifies the estimated findings for the data set, displaying the correlation coefficient and the regression coefficient divided by the standard error. The correlation coefficient measures the individual strength of each variable. The regression coefficient/standard error, while "not strictly speaking a t-test can be interpreted as such" (Walsh, 1987: 180). The first estimator, i.e., the correlation coefficient, indicates the relative strength of the variable, while the second estimator, i.e, the regression coefficient/standard error, indicates whether the finding is significant at the .01 level, which means that the probability that the correlation coefficient is 0 is less than 1 percent. As might be expected from Figure 3.2, historic time periods have the greatest explanatory power, as indicated by the magnitude of the regression coefficient/standard error, and this effect diminishes over time, as illustrated by the magnitude of this coefficient for the period 1882 to 1900 in comparison to the time period 1901 to 1920. With regard to the seasonal effects, there is no warmer-month effect, but there is significantly lower coverage by *The Times* in January, February, and May. However, *The Times* did not increase its coverage of lynchings in the warmer months when lynchings were more common.

With regard to geography, there was less coverage by *The Times* of lynchings in deep and upper southern states in comparison to the remainder of the nation, but the level of coverage in the border states did not significantly differ from the remainder of the nation. The cultural isolation of the South between 1882 and 1930 (McKinney and Bourque, 1971) and its low level of urbanization (Weiher, 1977) probably account for these findings.

TABLE 3.2

Logit Coefficients Relating *The New York Times* Coverage
of Lynchings to a Set of Independent Variables

Variables	Correlation R	Regression Coefficient Standard Error
Constant	——	21.929*
(a) *Historic Period Effects*		
Period 1882–1900	–.256	–14.254*
Period 1901–1920	–.131	–7.416*
(b) *Seasonal Effects*		
January	–.035	–2.534*
February	–.038	–2.534*
March	.000	–1.301
April	.000	.636
May	–.035	–2.379*
June	.000	–.674
July	.000	–1.128
August	.000	–.700
September	.000	–.766
October	.000	–1.185
November	.000	–1.794
(c) *Geographic Effects*		
Deep Southern States	–.061	–3.658*
Upper Southern States	–.053	–3.267*
Border States	.000	–.778
(d) *Race and Gender*		
Race	–.063	–3.750*
Gender	.000	–0.020
(e) *Type of Precipitating Event*		
Rape or Sexual Assault	.054	3.323*
Murder or Serious ssault	.072	4.218*
(f) *Intensity of Lynching*		
Number of Lynching Victims	.130	7.326*

*Significant at .01 level

Gender had no significant impact on national coverage, probably because almost every woman lynched between 1882 and 1930 was black, and this fact caused the effect of gender to be subsumed under race. Race did have a significant impact on national coverage, with a significantly lower coverage of black lynchings.

With regard to the precipitating events, those lynchings precipitated by rape or sexual assault, and murder or serious assault, had a higher probability of coverage by *The Times*.

Similarly, the number of victims had a strong impact on national coverage, with greater probability of coverage when there were multiple victims. As an illustration of how these three effects influenced national coverage, consider two lynching incidents in Georgia in 1904 and 1910. In 1904 a black male was lynched by a small party of unknown men for being impudent to a white woman [*The Atlanta Constitution*, 1904], and this incident was not covered by *The Times*. By contrast, in 1910 two blacks were lynched for the murder of a law enforcement official who attempted to arrest them in a gambling raid [*The Atlanta Constitution*, 1910], and this latter incident was covered by *The Times*. There were more participants in the latter incident, and it received wider local coverage in Georgia, increasing the probability that it would be covered by *The New York Times*.

Discussion

The previous findings on the newspaper reporting of communal violence are in many ways consistent with the findings that relate individual crimes and the media reporting of these crimes. Geographical location influenced the findings, with lynchings in the more culturally isolated South being less likely to be reported in the national media.

The fact that the reporting of lynchings in the border states was not significantly different from the remainder of the nation would suggest that these states were less culturally isolated than the South. There was no significant linkage between the temporal patterning of lynchings and their reporting in *The Times*, as evidenced by the fact that the seasonal pattern for *The Times* coverage was not similar to the actual seasonal patterns of lynchings (see Table 3.1). Gender did not significantly influence the coverage because most of the women lynched were southern black women. Race influenced the level of coverage, with the more common black lynchings having a lower probability of national coverage. Finally, lynchings triggered by more violent incidents (i.e., sexual assault and murder) and those in which there were multiple victims had a greater probability of national coverage.

The relatively low level of lynching reporting by *The Times* prior to 1900 was probably caused by the structural weakness of the media system in the nation. While *The New York Times* was a national newspaper throughout its history (Berger, 1970; Thorn, 1987), it expanded its national coverage significantly after 1896 when it was purchased by Adolph Ochs, with field representatives being sent to many major cities in the nation. The low level of urbanization in the South prior to 1897 (Weiher, 1977), and its social and cultural isolation, limited national coverage of southern lynchings. In this time period the South was a relatively isolated subregion. After 1900 a number of events and social transformations increased the coverage of lynchings in the South. The lynching of Leo Frank outside Atlanta in 1915 (Dinnerstein, 1968) shocked the nation, and aroused Jewish and ethnic antagonisms against the South. The fact that an organized mob could remove a person from a state prison, lynch him, publicize the event in the local media [*The Atlanta Constitution*, 1915], and not be apprehended or punished, suggested a high level of social and legal chaos in this subregion ("the rotten borough"). The increased migration of blacks from the South, in part because of lynching fears (Fligstein, 1981), increased racial tensions in other areas of the nation, since it caused lynchings and race riots outside the South [*The New York Times*, 1923], causing the national media to pay greater attention to this violent behavior in the subregion. On the other hand, this increased black migration because of lynchings caused many southern plantation owners to pressure local law enforcement officials to prevent it, since these lynchings might cause their cheap black labor to migrate from the region (Tolnay and Beck, 1962).

While rare and violent events have greater probability of being covered by the national media, it is still surprising that lynchings were so extensively covered by *The Times* after 1920. One reason for this increased coverage may have been the role of *moral entrepreneurs* in publicizing the evils of this communal behavior.

Prior to World War I many local civil groups in the South denounced lynching as a moral evil [*The New York Times*, 1904; *The Atlanta Constitution*, 1916], although they did reluctantly approve of it for one "unspeakable crime" (i.e., rape and sexual assault). However, in this same historic period within the South there were racist politicians and groups that saw its use as necessary to control an unruly black population [*The New York Times*, 1901, 1905].

In 1892 the black activist Ida B. Wells began a crusade against lynching in Memphis, Tennessee (Aptheker, 1977), but she was run out of town by local racist elements. In 1894 a visiting British representative of the Anti-Lynching Committee, a British moralist society, spoke out against lynching as a question of law and order, but he was denounced by southern political leaders [*The New York Times*, 1894]. After 1900 a number of civic, religious and social organizations came to oppose it (Southern Commission on the Study of Lynching, 1931; Miller, 1957; Reed, 1968; Grant, 1975), and after it was formed in 1909, the National Association for the Advancement of Colored People (NAACP) made its elimination the main focus of their political activities (Zangrando, 1980). By the 1920s a federal bill to control this communal violence, which was becoming rarer at this time, was introduced into Congress (Dyer and Dyer, 1928). The bill was opposed by southern legislators because they feared that its enactment would lead to further federal control that might weaken the southern racist state (James, 1988). In all types of political behavior, moral entrepreneurs, whether they were organizations (e.g., KKK [Lipset and Raab, 1978]) or individual actors (e.g., Senator Joseph McCarthy and the anticommunist crusade [Rogin, 1967]), have influenced public opinion and altered the public perception of a social problem. In the case of lynchings it is likely that moral entrepreneurs sensitized the public to the moral evils of this communal behavior and increased national coverage of it.

Conclusions

Over time the national press, as exemplified by *The New York Times*, gave greater publicity to lynchings, in part because they were seen as a potential threat to social stability, and in part because of the activities of moral entrepreneurs. One may raise the question as to how effective this increased national coverage of lynchings after 1920 was in controlling this behavior. In his Milwaukee study, Pritchard (1986) suggested that media coverage of crime influenced plea bargaining procedures. The identification of communities where it occurred did act to stigmatize these communities (Wolf, Thomason, and LaRocque, 1987), although this stigmatization was probably less effective as a means of social control than it was after 1950 when the nation was more integrated economically and politically (e.g., the fact that after the 1957 school disturbance in Little Rock, Arkansas few new industries located in the community). Reed (1969) suggested that increased national media coverage operated to force local sheriffs to prevent lynchings, but he offered no convincing proof of this hypothesis.

In the period after 1920, lynchings declined less because of national pressure and more because of greater state control (Wager, 1940), linked with the increased political integration of the counties in the region (Pratt, 1910), and because of increased local elite opposition to mob rule (Ingalls, 1987). The limited ability of the national press to influence behavior and public policy in this time period is illustrated by the failure of Congress to enact federal anti-lynching legislation between 1920 and 1948. The national press supported such legislation as a means of controlling this communal violence but southern legislators, fearful of increased federal control, strongly opposed it, and utilized their political power in Congress to block such legislation, usually through the use of the filibuster in the Senate. In this time period southern legislators were quite powerful in Congress because of the seniority and committee systems. This political clout is illustrated by their ability to shape the Social Security Act of 1935 to exclude black rural tenants from coverage (Quadagno, 1988). Many national political elites were appalled by this communal violence, but they also wished to maintain political ties with this powerful southern elite. For example, in 1938 Walter Lippmann, the prominent American political philosopher and journalist, justified the southern filibuster that opposed anti-lynching legislation on the grounds that in a democracy the rights of a political minority (i.e., southern whites) must be protected.[4] Opponents of lynching overestimated the power of the national media to control this communal behavior [*The New York Times*, 1930], which was rooted in irrational communal fears.

While the national press in this time period did not significantly alter the southern political system by changing social conditions that might prevent such atrocities, it did sensitize the American public and political elites to the social pathology of the southern political system and its use of extra-legal means to maintain racial control. When the more dramatic social and political changes occurred in the southern political system in the 1950s and 1960s, the national political elites were more sensitized to the social pathologies of this subregion of the nation.

NOTES

1. At times the political authorities allowed and encouraged this behavior. For example, in 1917 Governor Cole Blease of South Carolina offered a $500 reward for the corpse of a black fugitive [*The Atlanta Constitution*, 1917].

2. This study checked newspaper accounts of lynching behavior for the eleven southern and border states of Alabama, Arkansas, Florida, Georgia, Kentucky, Louisiana, Mississippi, North Carolina, South Carolina, Tennessee and Virginia.

3. Using Matthews and Prothro (1966: 169–170), the deep South was identified as Alabama, Georgia, Louisiana, Mississippi and South Carolina; the upper South was identified as Arkansas, Florida, North Carolina, Tennessee, Texas and Virginia; the border South was identified as the states of Kentucky, Maryland, Missouri, Oklahoma and West Virginia.

4. "He [Lippmann] . . . supported a southern filibuster against a federal anti-lynching law in 1938. 'If the spirit of democracy is to be maintained,' he wrote, 'a minority must never be coerced unless the reasons for coercing it are decisive and overwhelming.' Lynching was apparently not an overwhelming reason" (Steel, 1980: 552).

REFERENCES

Aldrich, J. H. and F. D. Nelson. 1984. *Linear probability, logit and probit models.* Beverly Hills: Sage Publications.

Ames, J. D. 1938. "Editorial treatment of lynching." *Public Opinion Quarterly*, 2, 77–84.

Antunes, G. E. and P. A. Hurley. 1977. "The representation of criminal events in Houston's two daily newspapers." *Journalism Quarterly*, 54: 756–760.

Applebome, P. 1993. "Death in a jailhouse: The ruling, a suicide; The fear, a lynching." *The New York Times*, (February 21), p. 12.

Aptheker, B. 1977. "The suppression of free speech: Ida B. Wells and the Memphis lynching, 1892." *San Jose Studies*, 3: 34–40.

The Atlanta Constitution. 1904. "Negro is shot for impudence." (May 3), p. 1.

———. 1910. "Another black pays penalty." (November 9), p. 7.

———. 1915. "Mob's own story in detail." (August 18), pp. 1, 2.

———. 1916. "18 southern colleges will fight lynch law." (April 7), p. 3.

———. 1917. "Blease offers $500 for corpse of Negro." (May 7), p. 16.

The Augusta Chronicle. 1917. "Negro preacher dead from injuries." (August 24), p. 3.

Beck, E. M., S. E. Tolnay and J. L. Massey. 1991. *Lynchings in the American South. 1882–1930.* Athens: Department of Sociology, University of Georgia.

Becker, H. 1963. *The Outsiders.* New York: The Free Press.

Berger, M. 1970. *The Story of the New York Times: The First 100 Years 1851–1951.* New York: Arno Press.

Bollen, K. and D. P. Phillips. 1982. "Imitative suicides: A national study of the effect of television news stories." *American Sociological Review,* 47: 302–309.

Boorstin, D. J. 1962. *The Image or What Happened to the American Dream.* New York: Atheneum.

Breed, W. 1955. "Social control in the newsroom: A functional analysis." *Social Forces,* 33: 326–335.

———. 1958. "The mass media and socio-cultural integration." *Social Forces,* 37: 109–116.

Bridges, J. A. 1989. "News use on the front pages of the American daily." *Journalism Quarterly,* 66: 332–337.

Brillon. Y. 1987. *Victimization and Fear of Crime among the Elderly.* Translated by D. R. Crittensten. Toronto: Butterworths.

Brown, R. M. 1969. "The American vigilante tradition." pp.154–225 in H.D. Graham and R. Gurr (eds.) *Violence in America: Historical and Comparative Perspective.* New York: Bantam Books.

The Chicago Tribune. 1883–1919. *Annual Listing of Lynchings in the United States the Previous Year.* Chicago: The Chicago Tribune Corporation.

Danzger, M. H. 1975. "Validating conflict data." *American Sociological Review,* 46: 570–584.

Dinnerstein, L. 1968. *The Leo Frank Case.* New York: Columbia University Press.

Durkheim, E. 1958. *Professional Ethics and Civic Morals.* Translated by C. Brookfield. Glencoe, Illinois: The Free Press.

Dutton, J. and J. Duffy. 1985. "Bias in the newspaper reporting of crime news." *British Journal of Criminology,* 23: 159–165.

Dyer, L. C. and G. C. Dyer. 1928. "The constitutionality of a federal anti-lynching bill." *St. Louis Law Review,* 13: 186–199.

Evans, S. S. and R. J. Lundman. 1983. "Newspaper coverage of corporate price-fixing." *Criminology,* 21: 529–541.

Fishman, M. 1981. "Crime waves as ideology." pp. 98–117 in S. Cohen and J. Young (eds.) *The Manufacture of News*. Beverly Hills: Sage Publications.

Fligstein, N. 1981. Going North: *Migration of Blacks and Whites from the South 1900–1950*. New York: Academic Press.

Gamson, W. A. and A. Modigliani. 1971. *Untangling the Cold War: A Strategy for Testing Rival Theories*. Boston: Little, Brown and Company.

Gans, H. J. 1979. *Deciding What's News: A Study of CBS Evening News, NBC Nightly News, Newsweek and Time*. New York: Pantheon Books.

Ginzburg, R. 1988. *100 Years of Lynchings*. Baltimore: Black Classic Press.

Gorelick, S. M. 1989. "Join our war: the construction of ideology in a newspaper crimefighting campaign." *Crime & Delinquency*, 35: 421–436.

Grant, D. L. 1975. *The Anti-Lynching Movement: 1883–1932*. San Francisco: R and E Research Associates.

Greenberg, M. R., D. B. Sacksman, P. L. Sandman and K. L. Salamone. 1989. "Risk, drama and geography in coverage of environmental risk by network TV." *Journalism Quarterly*, 66: 267–276.

Guzman, J. P. (ed.) 1948. *The Negro Yearbook 1941–1946*. Tuscaloosa, Alabama: Tuscaloosa Press.

Hardt, H. 1990. "Newsworkers, technology and journalism history." *Critical Studies in Mass Communication*, 7: 346–365.

Hartley, J. 1982. *Understanding News*. London: Methuen.

Holinger, P. C. 1987, *Violent Deaths in the United States*. New York: The Guilford Press.

Holmes, W. F. 1969. "Whitecapping: Agrarian violence in Mississippi." *Journal of Southern History*, 35, 165–185.

Humphries, D. 1981. "Serious crime, news coverage and ideology: A content analysis of crime coverage in a metropolitan paper." *Crime & Delinquency*, 27: 191–205.

Ingalls, R. P. 1987. "Lynching and establishment violence in Tampa, 1858–1935." *The Journal of Southern History*, 53: 613–644.

James, D. R. 1988. "The transformation of the southern racial state: Class and race determinants of local state structures." *American Sociological Review*, 53: 191–208.

Kneeland, G. J. 1913. *Commercialized Prostitution in New York City.* Introduction by J. D. Rockefeller, Jr. New York: The Century Company.

Levy, S. G. 1974. "Distance of politically violent events from newspaper sources over 150 years." *Journalism Quarterly*, 51: 28–32.

Lipset, S. M. and E. Raab. 1978. *The Politics of Unreason: Right-Wing Extremism in America 1790–1977.* Second Edition. Chicago: The University of Chicago Press.

Liska, A. E. and W. Baccaglini. 1990. "Feeling safe by comparison: Crime in the newspapers." *Social Problems*, 37: 360–374.

McKinney, J. C. and L. B. Bourque. 1971. "The changing South: National incorporation of a region." *American Sociological Review*, 36: 399–412.

Mandle, J. R. 1978. *The Roots of Black Poverty: The Southern Plantation Economy after the Civil War.* Durham, North Carolina: Duke University Press.

Manoff, R. and M. Schudson. 1987. *Reading the News.* New York: Pantheon Books.

Martens, F. T. and M. Cunningham-Niederer. 1985. *Federal Probation*, 49: 60–68.

Matthews, D. R. and J. W. Prothro, 1966. *Negroes and the New Southern Politics.* New York: Harcourt, Brace & World.

Miller, R. M. 1957. "The Protestant church and lynching 1919–1939." *The Journal of Negro History*, 62: 118–131.

Molotch, H. and M. Lester. 1974. "News as purposive behavior." *American Sociological Review*, 39: 101–112.

Myrdal, G. 1944. *An American Dilemma.* New York: Harper & Row.

National Association for the Advancement of Colored People. 1919. *Thirty Years of Lynching in the United States. 1889–1918.* New York: The National Association for the Advancement of Colored People.

Neter, J., W. Wasserman and M. H. Kutner. 1990. *Applied Linear Statistical Models.* Homewood, Illinois: Irwin.

The New York Times. 1894. "Sir John Gorst's report." (September 10), p. 8.

———. 1901. "Tillman favors lynching." (August 5), p. 1.

———. 1903. "Preacher praises lynching." (June 29), p. 2.

———. 1904. "Start anti-lynching crusade." (March 21), p. 6

———. 1905. "Wants lynching legalized." (October 7), p. 1.

————. 1918a. "German is lynched by an Illinois mob." (April 5), p. 4.

————. 1918b. "Germans magnify lynching here." (September 9), p. 11.

————. 1923. "Mob fights milita; 1 killed, three hurt." (June 20), p. 1.

————. 1927. "Posse kills Negro." (June 18), p. 14.

————. 1930. "Sees end of lynching in the next ten years." (January 12), p. 29.

————. 1935. "Service of indignation planned in Tampa today." (December 15), III, p. 2.

Noble, M. M. 1973. "The White Caps of Harrison and Crawford County Indiana: A Study in the Violent Enforcement of Morality." Unpublished Ph.D. Diss., University of Michigan.

Pratt, J. H. 1910. "Good road movement in the South." *The Annals of the American Academy of Political and Social Science*, 35: 105–113.

Pritchard, D. 1985. "Race, homicide and newspapers." *Journalism Quarterly*, 62: 500–507.

————. 1986. "Homicide and bargained justice: The agenda-setting effect of crime news on prosecutors." *Public Opinion Quarterly*, 50: 143–159.

Priyaharsini, S. 1984. "Crime news in newspapers: A case study in Tamil Nadu, India." *Deviant Behavior*, 5: 313–326.

Quadagno, J. S. 1988. *The Transformation of Old Age Security: Class and Politics in the American Welfare State*. Chicago: University of Chicago Press.

Reed, J. S. 1968. "An evaluation of an anti-lynching organization." *Social Problems*, 16: 172–182.

————. 1969. "A note on the control of lynching." *Public Opinion Quarterly*, 33, 268–271.

Reinariman, C. and H. Levine. 1989. "The crack attack: Politics and media in America's latest drug scare." pp. 115–137 in J. Best (ed.) *Images of Issues*. New York: Aldine de Groyter.

Rogin, M. P. 1967. *The Intellectuals and McCarthy: The Radical Specter*. Cambridge: The M.I.T. Press.

Ross, J. R. 1989. "At the Bar of Judge Lynch: Lynching and Lynch Mobs in America." Unpublished Ph.D. Diss. Texas Tech University.

Sheley, J. F. and A. D. Ashkins. 1981. "Crime, crime news and crime views." *Public Opinion Quarterly*, 45: 492–506.

Singer, E., P. Endreny and M. B. Glassman. 1991. "Media coverage of disasters: Effects of geographic location." *Journalism Quarterly*, 68: 48–58.

Snyder, D. and W. R. Kelly. 1977. "Conflict intensity, media sensitivity and the validity of newspaper data." *American Sociological Review*, 42: 105–123.

Southern Commission on the Study of Lynching. 1931. *Lynchings and What They Mean*. Atlanta: The Southern Commission on the Study of Lynching.

SPSS. 1990. *SPSS Reference Guide*. Chicago: SPSS Inc.

Stack, S. 1987. "Celebrities and suicide: A taxonomy and analysis, 1948–1983." *American Sociological Review*, 52: 401–412.

Steel, R. 1980. *Walter Lippman and the American Century*. Boston: Little Brown and Company.

Stevens, J. 1990. *Sensationalism in the News*. New York: Columbia University Press.

Thorn, W. J. (with M. P. Pfeil). 1987. *Newspaper Circulation: Marketing the News*. New York: Longman.

Tolnay, S. and E. M. Beck. 1962. "Migration in the American South, 1910 to 1930." *American Sociological Review*, 57, 103–116.

Tuchman, G. 1978. *Making News: A Study in the Construction of Reality*. New York: The Free Press.

Wager, P. W. 1940. "State centralization in the South." *The Annals of the American Academy of Political Science*, 207: 144–150.

Walsh, A. 1987. "Teaching understanding and interpretation of logit regression." *Teaching Sociology*, 15: 178–183.

Wasserman, I. M. 1984. "A re-examination of the Werther effect." *American Sociological Review*, 49: 427–436.

Weiher, K. 1977. "The cotton industry and southern urbanization." *Explorations in Economic History*, 14: 120–140.

Williamson, J. 1984. *The Crucible of Race: Black-White Relations in the American South since Emancipation*. New York: Oxford University Press.

Winkel, F. W. 1990. "Crime reporting in newspapers: An exploratory study of the effects of ethnic reference in crime news." *Social Behavior*, 5: 87–101.

Wolf, R., T. Thomason and P. LaRocque. 1987. "The right to know vs. the right of privacy: Newspaper identification of crime victims." *Journalism Quarterly*, 64: 503–507.

Woodward, C. V. 1951. *Origins of the New South 1877–1913*. Baton Rouge: Louisiana State University Press.

Work, M. M. 1921. *The Negro Year Book: Eleventh Annual Report for the Year 1920*. New York: National Association for the Advancement of Colored People.

Wright, G. C. 1990. *Racial Violence in Kentucky 1865–1940*. Baton Rouge: Louisiana State University Press.

Young, E. F. 1928. "The relation of lynching to the size of political areas: A note on the sociology of popular justice." *Sociology and Social Research* 12: 348–353.

Zangrando, R. L. 1980. *The NAACP Crusade Against Lynching 1909–1950*. Philadelphia: Temple University Press.

CHAPTER 4

Crime in the News Media: A Refined Understanding of How Crimes Become News*

Steven Chermak

Introduction

Crime is an important news topic, *every day*. One might think that its importance has increased corresponding to public concern over a growing crime problem. However, crime news has long been an information priority. Court reporting can be traced as far back as 1830, and early newspapers sensationalized crime to increase circulation. For example, in the late 1880s when Joseph Pulitzer changed the news focus of the *New York World* from political news to crime and tragedy, circulation jumped from 15,000 to 250,000. William Randolph Hearst used the same prescription to increase circulation of the *New York Journal* at the beginning of the 1900s (Lotz, 1991: 10–11). According to Marsh (1988: 11–12), early crime news literature (1893–1929) emphasized the salience of crime in the news.

People become informed about crime in a variety of ways. Some people commit crime and others are victimized. Some people learn about crime from friends, relatives, or neighbors who have been involved in the criminal justice system as workers or as clients. Most people, however, do not have direct or indirect exposure to crime as either defendants or victims. These people, the vast majority, rely on the mass news media for their information about crime and victimization (President's Task Force, 1967; Meyer, 1975; Sherizen, 1978; Skogan and Maxfield, 1981). In this way, the news media act as a surrogate for members of the public who have limited exposure to crime and violence and as a supplement to those with more direct exposure (Surette, 1992). Accordingly, the news media can be influential in shaping opinions and attitudes about crime. Studying the media and their role in understanding crime and justice is an important topic to examine.

The media provide information about events that are significant to us, and in one sense paint a portrait of society. However, it is a limited picture of crime and victims alike because of selection decisions that are made based on organizational constraints. Because of this limited image, the public at large and politicians in particular not only come to form distorted views about crime and victims, but they also support policies that may or may not make sense when compared to what some may argue are the more informed pictures shared by criminologists and victimologists. By studying crime news production, students of crime and crime control can develop an important understanding of the news media's role in shaping society's attitudes and policies towards crime and victims (Ericson, Baranek, and Chan, 1987, 1991; Surette, 1992).

This chapter presents data on the prevalence of crime in the news. More specifically, it examines the newsmaking process used to generate the large number of stories that help shape the general public's view of criminals and victims. Finally, a typology on different types of crime stories is developed that helps to refine our understanding of the crime news production process.

The Production of Crime News

A number of studies have examined how news media produce crime news (Roscho, 1975; Chibnall, 1977; Sherizen, 1978; Fishman, 1980; Hall, Critcher, Jefferson, Clarke and Roberts, 1978; Cohen and Young, 1981; Voumvakis and Ericson,

1984; Ericson et al., 1987; 1989; Grabosky and Wilson, 1989). These studies have relied on some of the theoretical models generated in the larger communication's literature to explain crime news production (White, 1950; Breed, 1955; Tuchman, 1973, 1978; Sigal, 1973; Epstein, 1973; Gans, 1979). One of the most popular models used to explain the production of crime news is one that examines how news organizations affect and are affected by the influences of source organizations (Chibnall, 1977; Cohen and Young, 1981; Voumvakis and Ericson, 1984; Ericson et al., 1987, 1989). A brief review of the research that examines how this relationship affects the production of crime news will be helpful in highlighting important variables in the production of news.

Crime news is among the most popular topics for both the media and the public. It is popular for media organizations because it is convenient to discover and it helps sell newspapers (Sherizen, 1978; Chibnall, 1977; Grabosky and Wilson, 1989). The public uses the media to learn about the amount and type of crime in society (Skogan and Maxfield, 1981) which reaffirms and evokes threats to the consensual morals of society (Hall et al., 1978: 66). However, what the news media present and what the public learns about crime are specialized images that are distorted by the newsmaking process.

This process involves condensing a significant amount of crime into a limited amount of news space. The news media have a large number of stories to choose from because crime is consistently available and abundant (Tunstall, 1971). In order to make the production of crime news more manageable, the media routinize their task by putting themselves in a position to get easy access to crime news (Tuchman, 1973; Gans, 1979; Voumvakis and Ericson, 1984; Ericson et al., 1987; 1989). Thus the production of crime news becomes a routine with a standardized news format in which the reporter simply changes the details of what was involved, who was involved, and what the authorities are planning to do about it. This is why crime news reads much like a police blotter and the image that is produced has "little to do with the realities or complexities of crime" (Sherizen, 1978: 206).

The media do not distort reality in a random fashion; in fact, it is done systematically (Ericson et al., 1987). The structure, division of labor, and decisions made within news organizations determine what stories eventually get selected (Breed, 1955; Sigal, 1973; Epstein, 1973; Gans, 1979). Reporters and editors gather crime news from a limited number of sources, and the type of information presented is influenced by the inter-relationships between the news organization, journalist, and criminal justice agency (Sherizen, 1978; Voumvakis and Ericson, 1984; Ericson et al., 1987; 1989; Grabosky and Wilson, 1989).

News organizations are dependent on sources to produce crime news. However, source organizations are equally dependent on the media. A symbiotic relationship between the media and news source develops because of their dependency on each other. The media cite sources in order to underscore their own authority and maintain objectivity (Chibnall, 1977; Hall et al., 1978; Tuchman, 1973; Ericson et al., 1989). Thus the media enhance their own legitimacy by expanding and relying on their surrounding environment. Reciprocally, because sources are cited as the authoritative voice in regard to crime news, source organizations appear more credible (Gans, 1979). The evolving interrelationship between these two forces determines what is presented and what is not.

Source organizations have their own organizationally determined set of criteria that influence the presentation of crime. Sources decide what information should be revealed and in what form, what details should be highlighted or discarded, and when stories should be released (Ericson et al., 1989: 6). When producing crime news, the police are the primary source used by the media, and the information they provide is partial to their own interests and particular to their own version of crime (Sherizen, 1978; Fishman, 1980; Chibnall, 1977; Hall et al., 1978; Ericson et al., 1989; Grabosky and Wilson, 1989). An analysis of source organizations in Canada illustrates that the police have become more open to the media so that they can control their environment, protect their organization's vulnerability, and legitimize their work (Ericson et al., 1989: 11).

News organizations selectively choose the source organization's version of the "truth" to produce a story. The media have their own set of independent criteria for determining what news captures the most consumers. These criteria affect editors' story selection, production, and assignment decisions. They affect reporters' decisions regarding what angle to use, source selection and how much follow-up should be used when producing a story. Then these criteria affect the lengthy editing process which every story undergoes. The media may choose not to present a story if it does not fall within one of their organizationally driven criteria. Studies of the general news process in America (Galtung and Ruge, 1981; Johnston, 1979; Fishman, 1980), in Australia (Grabosky and Wilson, 1989), in Canada (Ericson et al., 1987) and in England (Chibnall, 1977; Hartley, 1982; Hall et al., 1978; Roshier, 1981) have illustrated the criteria that determine newsworthiness and influence the production of crime news.

Stories that are more likely to be selected for presentation as crime news are those crimes which are novel and dramatic (Chibnall, 1977; Roshier, 1981; Hartley, 1982; Ericson et al., 1987; 1991; Grabosky and Wilson, 1989). Ordinary crime is not news. The news media presents exceptional, unusual, and violent crimes because these stories sell newspapers. Crime news must be simple and unambiguous so that the story can be placed quickly within an already established framework that can be easily followed by the audience (Chibnall, 1977; Hartley, 1982; Ericson et al., 1987). If a celebrity is involved, then the story is more likely to be presented (Chibnall, 1977; Roshier, 1981; Hartley, 1982; Ericson et al., 1987). When a particular story does meet one or more of these criteria, the story then competes against other selected stories because of time and space limitations (Chibnall, 1977; Hartley, 1982; Hall et al., 1978; Grabosky and Wilson, 1989). The more selection criteria that a story satisfies, the more likely that story will be presented and the more likely the selection criteria will be emphasized in presentation.

Research Methodology

Most research examining crime in the news media has utilized one of two research methodologies. First, content analysis has been used frequently. When examining the content of crime stories, researchers scrutinize the product that gets *presented* to the public for consumption. The second method typically employed is ethnography. Research using ethnography considers the news *process* that occurs to produce crime stories. Examination of crime news using both methods has produced two separate bodies of research: a presentation and a process component. Research has generally failed to consider the linkage between the two methods even though the news production process can clearly affect what gets presented as crime news (Ericson et al., 1987, 1989).

The data on crime, victim, and defendant characteristics presented here are from a larger project that collected information from both newspapers and television, and which combined these two classic research methodologies. Data for the newspaper content analysis were collected from six newspapers: *The Albany Times-Union, The Buffalo News, The Cleveland Plain Dealer, The San Francisco Chronicle, The Dallas Times Herald,* and *The Detroit News.* Television data were collected from stations in Albany, Cleveland and Dallas. In total, more than 2,700 different news stories were examined. In addition, ethnographic analysis of the selection, production, and editing decisions of both a newspaper and television station were observed in a large midwestern city. Throughout this chapter, the newspaper that was observed will be referred to as the *Midwest Tribune,* and the television station as the *Midwest Nightly.*[1]

Importance of Crime News

Crime news can be found throughout an entire newspaper or at any time during a broadcast. The majority of crime stories appear in the first two sections of a paper as both routine crime stories and feature stories. Stories about specific crime incidents proliferate in these sections. Crime is frequently commented on by editors and citizens in the opinion sections of a paper. Topics such as the death penalty, legalization of drugs, and gun control are analyzed, rebutted, and reanalyzed ad nauseam. Crime stories, however, are not presented only in these sections. For example, crimes committed by Mike Tyson, Pete Rose, and Darryl Strawberry can appear in the sports page. Illegal activities by actors and entertainers such as Pee Wee Herman and James Brown can be found in the entertainment section. Crimes committed by Michael Milken, Ivan Boesky, and a variety of other financiers are often relegated to the business section. Thus, unlike most other major news topics, crime spans all sections of a newspaper.

The amount of daily crime news that is "newsworthy," when compared to other topics, is large. Table 4.1 presents the number and percentage of all news stories by combining results from the television and newspaper analysis. Approximately 11 percent of all news stories were crime stories, which was the fourth largest category behind sports, business and general interest stories. This is similar to other research that found crime news as the third largest category in newspapers (Sherizen, 1978: 208).

Sports and business stories are among the most popular topics for readers. Each of these have designated newspaper sections because of their popularity and a large number of stories must be written to fill these sections. A wealth of international, national, state, and local sports events are used to fill the sports section. Oftentimes, in order to satisfy the space requirements, newspapers will simply provide a laundry listing of stories regarding particular events. For example, at the height of summer there are between ten and thirteen professional baseball games each evening and newspapers report the highlights of each game. This skews the results because other topics, such as crime, are not afforded similar space to air their laundry.[2] When the sports and business sections are excluded from the calculations, the prevalence of crime stories, compared to other stories without designated sections, is large. Approximately 16 percent of the total number of stories were crime stories. Table 4.2 presents these results.

TABLE 4.1

Total and Percent of Story
By type of news story

	Total	Percent
Sports	5,627	20.8%
General interest[a]	3,691	13.6
Business technology	3,616	13.4
Crime	2,879	**10.6**
General stories[b]	2,749	10.2
Domestic affairs	1,990	7.3
Foreign affairs	1,966	7.2
Science[c]	1,175	4.3
Schools	889	3.3
International affairs	724	2.7
Death[d]	613	2.3
Celebrations[e]	418	1.5
Environment	310	1.1
Automobile accidents	163	0.6
Fires	138	0.5
Presidency[f]	133	0.5

n = 27,081

[a] Includes stories about arts, entertainment, people, gardening, etc.

[b] Stories about specific incidents such as chemical leaks, gas leaks, power outages, missing persons.

[c] Includes medical and health issues.

[d] Includes accidents, suicides, plane crashes, and death by natural disaster.

[e] Includes ceremonies and parades.

[f] These are not political stories, but those stories about activities by the president, such as playing golf.

TABLE 4.2

Total and Percent of Story
By type of story without sections

	Total	Percent
General interest[a]	3,691	20.7%
Crime	2,879	**16.1**
General stories[b]	2,749	**15.4**
Domestic affairs	1,990	11.2
Foreign affairs	1,966	11.0
Science[c]	1,175	6.6
Schools	889	5.0
International affairs	724	4.1
Death[d]	613	3.4
Celebrations[e]	418	2.3
Environment	310	1.7
Automobile accidents	163	0.9
Fires	138	0.7
Presidency[f]	133	0.7

n = 17,838

[a] Includes stories about arts, entertainment, people, gardening, etc.

[b] Stories about specific incidents such as chemical leaks, gas leaks, power outages, missing persons.

[c] Includes medical and health issues.

[d] Includes accidents, suicides, plane crashes, and death by natural disaster.

[e] Includes ceremonies and parades.

[f] These are not political stories, but those stories about activities by the president, such as playing golf.

Is there too much space devoted to crime news coverage? This topic has generated a considerable amount of debate. Some argue that news simply mirrors society, and that the large amount of crime in the news reflects its occurrence in society. Some critics believe that the amount of crime in the news is excessive and that news organizations sensationalize crime, distort it, and unjustifiably promote fear and contribute to public misconception of crime (see Gottfredson and Hirschi, 1990: 35). Others disagree, arguing that the current presentation of crime raises the public's consciousness and makes them take the necessary steps to avoid victimization (Heath, 1984). Regardless of which position is more correct, the more important question remains as to why news organizations seem to rely so heavily on crime news. We now turn to five traditional explanations for the prevalence of crime news in the production of television and print journalism.

Crime News as Information. One justification for the large amount of crime news is that it provides the public with protection and knowledge. News informs the public regarding scandal and corruption, and provides information that allows citizens the opportunity to protect themselves against crime. When asked why crime news is so important, B. D., a general assignment reporter who covered news for over thirty years for the *Midwest Tribune*, said "I think the police and newspapers have a responsibility to let the public know what's going on. . . . An informed citizenry is an armed citizenry and it can protect itself a hell of a lot better if it knows when it is in danger" (Chermak interview notes, 6/4/91). Petty crimes are typically not newsworthy. They can be, however, if a reporter notices some peculiar repetition or pattern, such as a number of burglaries occurring in a particular neighborhood, or a number of purse snatches that occur on a certain street. These stories are news because the media are attempting to inform the public about the potential danger.

Oftentimes, the media justify overzealous tactics, arguing that the public has a right to know. Rape and child sexual abuse pose particular difficulties within news organizations when trying to balance the need to keep the public informed about certain dangers while not infringing upon an individual's right to privacy. G. M., a police beat reporter for less than a year, struggled to find this balance when covering rapes. On the one hand, the police will not give up information on rape victims because of evidentiary concerns. Reporters do not like contacting victims, and when they do, victims typically do not want to talk to the reporter. However, G. M. notes that rapes are a huge problem, one of the most underreported crimes and something the public should know about. Another reporter from the *Tribune*, K. E., echoed these thoughts. He acknowledged that ordinary common rapes are not news, but they become news when reporters discern interesting patterns or trends: "If reporting rapes in a certain neighborhood helps people to become aware of the problem so they can be looking over their shoulder, then we need to let the public know" (Chermak field notes, 5/14/91: A38).

Crime News as Deterrent. Another justification for presenting crime in the news is for its deterrent effect. Assuming that potential criminals pay attention to the news, the presentation of crime, of criminals getting caught, and being sentenced to years in prison might deter them from committing crime. One objective of criminal justice source organizations is to deter law violators from committing certain types of crime. Source organizations use the news media to assist them with this objective. For example, police departments publicize the utilization of weekend sobriety checkpoints and holiday speed traps to deter individuals from driving drunk or speeding. News follow-ups on the productiveness of these police tools are presented in the hope of deterring future law violators. Some research has indicated that publicizing executions in the media has a deterrent effect on homicide rates. For example, Stack (1987: 536) found that thirty fewer homicides occurred in those months where executions were publicized compared to those months where no executions were publicized.[3]

Reporters from the *Tribune* and *Nightly* thought coverage of crime might deter individuals from committing crime. Y. B., a television reporter, thought that covering crime might have deterrent effects:

> If people see a massive police effort, we got cameras rolling and we do a story on, say a major drug bust, it might make some kid think twice when they see the police with their helmets and their goggles, and they go busting in their doors, it might scare them, and maybe it will scare them to a point where they say I am not going to get involved in this because I don't want it to happen to me. (Chermak interview notes, 7/18/91)

Crime News as Entertainment. Crime delivered through any medium capitalizes on the public's fascination with gore and pathos (Gans, 1979). Crime stories provide real-life drama and entertainment that can stir a host of emotions, making such stories more appealing to the public. Crime stories can make you laugh (the burglar who terrorized a suburban neighborhood by breaking into homes in the evening and stealing the owners' underwear while asleep); cry (the minister who spent his entire life advocating for the poor, and was doing so when bludgeoned to death); reflect (one teenage driver killed by another when both were drinking); and they can make you rejoice (story about the donations a family received for their child who was in the hospital after he was thrown from his bike, which was stolen with the flowers he bought for his mother on Mother's Day. The family was unable to pay his hospital bills because the father had two broken legs and was unemployed, and his mother had recently had a stroke). Whether a person laughs, cries, reflects, rejoices, or reads with disinterest depends on the reader's own "symbolically created reality" (Altheide, 1984; Surette, 1992).

Crime News Reflecting the Nature of Criminal Justice. The prevalence of crime stories in the news can partially be explained by the nature of the criminal justice system. If a crime is discovered and reported, its discovery is only the initiation of the criminal justice process. Each crime goes through a number of stages in order to be fully processed by the system. This may take months or years. Because of this, crime stories are ongoing, and the same story might be covered at each stage of the process. For example, a crime story might be written when a homicide victim is discovered. A few days later, another story might update the public on the continuing investigation. If a suspect is arrested, an arrest story might be done and another on the suspect's arraignment. One might be done on a pretrial motion raised by the defense. If the suspect pleads, a story is presented. If tried, stories on opening remarks, salient witnesses, closing remarks and the verdict might be done across a number of days or weeks. The media could also be there at sentencing, at incarceration, at a number of parole hearings, and on release.

Since the criminal justice process is arduous, media organizations have a steady supply of newsworthy crime stories across this process. Table 4.3 presents the percentage of crime stories by each stage of the process for crime incident stories. Crime stories are more newsworthy at the beginning stages of the criminal justice system than at later stages, resembling an inverted criminal justice funnel. Official discovery of a crime incident was the most frequent stage cited in crime stories. Clearly, certain stages (discovery, arrest, arraignment, and sentence) are more newsworthy than other stages because they are definitive. For example, arraignment begins the court process and the sentence ends it. Most stories report on either police (38 percent) or court stages (44 percent).

Coverage of the trial stage is frequently presented (9.2 percent of crime incident stories) because trials typically span a number of days or weeks. Also a trial affords the news organization a wealth of information with minimal effort on the news organization's behalf. When a crime is newsworthy, a trial gives the media organization the opportunity to continually update the public on the progress of the trial. Reporters can attend the trial at their convenience and write stories based on whichever witness testifies when they arrive. For example, a man who at one time was a Hell's Angel was on trial for the rape and murder of his stepdaughter. The *Midwest Nightly* had a reporter at the courthouse to cover his trial. A story was done on the opening arguments, key prosecution witnesses, expert testimony, defense rebuttal witnesses, and concluding remarks. These stories were in the news every weekday for over two weeks. However, the *Nightly* did not have a reporter at the trial everyday. If the organization was unable to send a reporter to cover a certain aspect of the trial, a crime story was still aired by having a reporter call both the prosecution and the defense in regard to what had occurred on that particular day, and film was used from previous days to finish the story. Similarly, if court reporters from the *Midwest Tribune* missed testimony from certain witnesses, or even a verdict, they could still write a story for the paper by talking briefly with the attorneys because they were already familiar with the case.

Steven Chermak

TABLE 4.3

Crime Stories
By stage of criminal justice process[a]

Stage of Process	Percent
Discovery of crime	18.7%
Investigation	4.2
Arrest	15.4
Charged	13.3
Pretrial	3.0
Plea	2.7
Trial	9.1
Jury deliberation	0.4
Verdict	3.9
Sentence	7.3
Extradition	0.7
Appeal	2.3
Supreme Court decision	0.8
Probation	0.1
Commitment to prison	0.4
Parole behavior	1.8
Pardon request	0.3
Release from prison	1.1
Execution	0.5
Follow-ups[b]	12.7
Other[c]	1.4

n = 1,979

[a] This analysis includes only specific incident stories.

[b] These are either victim, defendant or crime follow-ups. For example, a story on the impact that a crime has had on a victim's family.

[c] Includes other court settlements.

The Newsmaking Process Used to Fill this Gap. A large news hole exists for crime stories that must be filled everyday because of their popularity. Graber (1980: 49–50) notes that 95 percent of the respondents in her study cited the mass media as their primary source of information about crime and criminal justice. The content analysis performed for this study revealed that, on average, the six newspapers covered nine crime stories a day, and the three television stations covered four. The media establish convenient access to source organizations from which a pool of potential newsworthy crimes are available for story selection to fill the gap. Thus criminal justice sources are critical to the production of crime stories. The rest of this chapter discusses how crime is selected and produced into crime stories.

Crime News Selection

The news organization routinizes the crime newsmaking process in order to satisfy its organizational needs by developing mutually convenient relationships with criminal justice sources in order to process crime news and keep it entertaining (Tuchman, 1973; Gans, 1979; Voumvakis and Ericson, 1984; Ericson et al., 1987, 1989). This routinization insures that the organization is able to transform the large amount of crime that occurs into crime stories, and process them in a simple, cost-effective manner (Sherizen, 1978; Roshier, 1981). The number of crimes available is larger than is necessary to fill the crime news gap because the media's access to criminal justice organizations is largely uninhibited.

Police reporters from the *Midwest Tribune* had an office located at police headquarters, and court reporters had an office in the county courthouse. This gave the reporters the opportunity to interact with key crime sources on a daily basis. Police beat reporters started each day on the telephone with sources. Reporters made daily police calls to all city police districts, all divisions (e.g., homicide division), suburban departments, emergency medical personnel, hospitals, the coroner's office, fire departments, the coast guard, and airport security. These calls are made throughout the day to ensure that late-breaking stories are not missed. Each of the sources contacted is willing to give the information, if they have any, without question. Police reporters had easy access to arrest sheets, police booking reports, and the primary police source, affectionately referred to by reporters as the "mouthpiece," who had an office located next to the chief's, and said he spent at "least 40 percent of [his time] dealing with the media" (Chermak field notes, 5/16/91: A46).

Court beat reporters typically began their day by checking the court calendar to see whether they recognized any cases that were newsworthy. Court reporters had convenient access to indictments, motions that were filed, returned search warrants and appellate decisions. Reporters were never once questioned when walking behind desks to peruse these materials and did not have to pay anything when they decided to copy something that interested them using county copy machines. Court reporters would mingle with clerks and district and defense attorneys in judges' chambers. When a popular area doctor was on trial for prescription drug sale and all seats in the courtroom were filled, the judge announced at the beginning of the session that "any media could sit in the jury box." Television reporters are provided the same access, but do not use it because the number of stories needed is less and they can fill their space by contacting sources from the station by telephone.

In order for a crime to become news, there first must be an official acknowledgment of it by a criminal justice source. The media-source routine, and its resulting access, ensure that individuals working for police and court organizations are the primary sources cited within crime stories. This reliance on criminal justice sources is convenient for the media because they are culturally accepted as being legitimate and credible crime sources. Thus reliable sources are cited while the media maintain a cloak of objectivity (Chibnall, 1977; Ericson et al., 1987; 1989; Surette, 1992). Table 4.4 provides data from the current analysis regarding the sources used for incident information in crime stories.[4] The media's heavy reliance on criminal justice sources is illustrated by the fact that, of the 6,300 sources that provided information within crime stories, nearly half were either a police or court source. Moreover, this large amount actually underestimates the media's dependence on criminal justice sources. Close to 7 percent of the sources cited in this analysis were not specific. These are those instances where reporters attribute the information to "sources say," "authorities say," or "officials say." These are typically criminal justice sources that refused to be identified by name.

TABLE 4.4

Crime Incident Sources
By type of source

Type of Source[a]	Percent
Police	29.4%
Court	25.3
Defendant	8.9
Not specific[b]	6.9
Victim acquaintance	3.7
Documents[c]	3.7
Victim	3.6
Witness/juror	3.6
Politician	3.0
Citizen	2.6
Media	2.1
Other[d]	1.9
School/church	1.4
Defendant acquaintance	1.3
Hospital[e]	0.9
Expert	0.9
Corrections	0.8

[a]Presented by rank order.
[b]Source cited as "sources say," "officials say," "authorities say."
[c]Police or court documents.
[d]Highway spokesman, community groups, weather service, etc.
[e]Includes doctors cited, emergency medical service, and coroner.

Source organizations benefit equally from the media's reliance on them because they determine the pool of crimes available for crime news selection (Ericson et al., 1989). Sources control which crimes are presented, as well as what is provided about them. The police and courtroom actors pass along crimes which reflect their own perspective where seriousness and the dangerousness of the street are emphasized. Source organizations benefit because this helps them accomplish their objectives. For example, arguably one of the primary objectives of the criminal justice system is to punish. A court reporter at the *Tribune* assisted a district attorney in accomplishing this objective. While eating lunch one day with a *Tribune* reporter, this district attorney thanked one of the reporters for attending a shock parole hearing of a woman who murdered her abuser and was sentenced to five to twenty-five years. Before the hearing, the D.A. asked numerous media to attend. The woman's sentence was not commuted. The prosecutor suggested that the presence of the media deterred the judge from reducing the defendant's sentence because the elected judge did not want to be publicly identified as soft on crime.

The news media rarely cover award ceremonies (see Tables 4.1 and 4.2). This is the case despite the fact that they receive a tremendous number of news releases announcing such awards. For example, while at the *Nightly*, over thirty press releases on awards, dedications, and ceremonies were received for a one-month period of time. Most of these did not even make a list of potentially newsworthy stories that are discussed during their afternoon editorial meeting, and few were covered. D. K., who was the managing editor of the *Nightly* and was responsible for generating the list of stories, explained that, although they were important for the people directly involved, these stories were of little significance to the general public (Chermak field notes, 8/8/92: C68). However, when individual police officers are awarded, and the police mouthpiece notes the significance of the awards to the officers involved, both print and electronic organizations covered the ceremonies, promoting a positive image of the police.

Selections are based on a number of discretionary decisions made by both individuals and organizations determining what crimes become news. The source organization develops policies on their relationships with the media; they decide on the level of access that is achieved by the media organization; and they attempt to garner public support by promoting particular programs within the media. Individual sources interpret their organizational policies regarding the media. Their interpretation influences whether stories are released, what about each story is released, and when the information is released. Some information is withheld regardless of the organization's policy. For example, each day the beat reporters choose between five and seven blotter reports that might be newsworthy. These blotter reports provide little more than basic demographic information. In order to be able to decide whether a story should be done on any of these reports, the reporters have to ask the police mouthpiece to provide the full report. Typically, he will reject one or two of their requests each day. The reporters do not question his withholding of information because he does it consistently, and provides them with other reports that satisfy daily story requirements.

Sometimes specific individuals within the same organization interpret the organization's policy quite differently. An ongoing problem between the police beat reporters and one particular source, D. L., illustrates this. D. L., who was in charge of the sex crimes division of the police department, refused to provide the police reporters with any information regarding rapes or child sexual abuse cases that occurred. The reporters, however, thought these crimes should be covered on occasion, because they were a significant problem that needed to be addressed. One morning, when the police mouthpiece stopped down to the reporter's office to drop off a memorandum about an award ceremony occurring on that day, the reporters noted the problem and thought that it was significant enough that the mouthpiece should set up a meeting with the police chief. "D. L. needs to be aware of what we do for you," G. M. pointed out (Chermak field notes, 5/15/91: A61). When trying to explain why D. L. would not provide any information, the mouthpiece hypothesized that D. L. felt she was acting according to the police organization's policy. Conversely, the mouthpiece had no problem providing them with the information. "I don't mind providing a victim's name, or even a rape victim's name to you guys. It is up to you to decide what you do with the name. All I ask is that you are balanced and provide both sides of the issue" (Chermak field notes, 5/15/91: A60).

The media organization and the individuals working within the organization have an equally large range of possible discretionary decisions that are made when selecting stories or interacting with the source. The organization decides what news is covered, how it is covered, and policies regarding its coverage (Ericson et al., 1987, 1989). For example, the *Tribune* had recently "commissioned a major study to measure readership of every element of the newspaper" and opened suburban news bureaus to assist them in making these decisions (Organizational document No. 1: 1). Individual reporters can also make a variety of discretionary decisions. Police reporters, after perusing a two-inch stack of blotter reports, decide which to pull and peruse. Court reporters decide which indictments/appellate decisions and other court documents examined are followed up on, which court sessions to attend, and how long they attend. Each individual reporter, while in constant contact with editors, decides how a story is covered, the angle and source(s) used, its lead, as well as its length.

Selection decisions are influenced by mutual cost/benefit calculations made by both the media and source organization. Each reporter must weigh the costs of pushing a particular issue when evaluating source performance. Sometimes, when a reporter is "insistent and persistent and aggressive in his asking of questions" to the President at an orchestrated White House Press Conference, the reporter loses his job [*New York Times*, 3/1/92: A21]. Most of the time, costs are not this extreme. However, reporters do stand to lose information access if they negatively reflect on source performance. For example, one of the police reporters at the *Midwest Tribune*, M. D., was faced with weighing a number of costs. M. D., who puts a story together much like a seasoned police detective puts together a case, received a call from a homeowner who had complained, on a number of occasions, about cars illegally parked on his front lawn whenever an auction, which was held once a week, took place nearby. Even after the homeowner posted warning signs, an unmarked police car parked on his lawn. When the man threatened to tow the car, the officer identified himself and went off to the auction. The man towed the car anyway, but then was arrested for motor vehicle theft and destruction of property. M. D. met with the police mouthpiece about the story. The mouthpiece asked an officer who was involved in the confrontation to attend the meeting. This was the first and only time during my observational tenure at the *Tribune* that the mouthpiece asked an officer who was involved in a specific incident to attend. M. D. left after listening to the police side of the story, and mentioned that he thought the police were lying. The story was never printed for a couple of reasons. First, the benefits were unknown. M. D. thought that both the police and the homeowner were not telling the whole truth. Second, the costs would have been great. M. D. was fairly new to the *Midwest Tribune*, and was still developing a relationship with the primary police source. He was afraid that access to police information might have been limited or totally cut off. Not covering the story did not leave an unfilled news gap on that particular day. There was still more than enough crime stories that were covered.

The media are less likely to critically evaluate criminal justice performance because of these heavy costs. Rarely do stories examine the causes of crime, the motive for a particular crime, or the effectiveness of the criminal justice system (Graber, 1980). The current analysis of six newspapers and three television stations revealed that causes of crime were mentioned in approximately 2 percent of all crime stories; motives for specific crime incidents were presented in about 20 percent of specific incident stories; police effectiveness was evaluated in less than 4 percent of the total number of stories, and courts were evaluated in less than three percent. Table 4.5 presents the number of cases where the police or courts were evaluated (either positively or negatively) by the media. Table 4.5 indicates that when the police or courts are evaluated in crime stories the media evaluate them by their performance in a specific instance. This indicates that even when their effectiveness is evaluated, whether it is a positive or negative evaluation, the problem is assumed to be isolated, not ongoing or systematic.

TABLE 4.5

Crime Stories Where Police or Courts Are Evaluated
By type of evaluation

Type of Evaluation	Police	Court
Overall positive evaluation	12.3%	1.6%
Overall negative evaluation[a]	10.3	21.3
Overall mixed evaluation	5.1	NA
Evaluation in specific instance	69.1	77.1
Other	3.2	0.0

n = 97   n = 61

NA = Not Applicable

[a] This category includes those instances where police or courts are criticized for performance in a specific situation. For example, a victim might be angered at an investigation, or a prosecutor might have been criticized for selectively prosecuting a particular individual.

Sources use a similar cost/benefit framework when deciding whether to release a story. Sources release some stories because they simply do not care. That is, they do not care whether a particular crime gets presented, as well as what gets presented about it. Other stories are released because they are beneficial and help accomplish an objective. For example, the district attorney who asked the print and electronic media to attend the shock parole hearing. Others are withheld because of their sensitive nature. A court reporter from the *Tribune* became extremely upset when that same district attorney forgot to tell her about a hearing that was being held that day regarding a prosecutorial misconduct allegation against him.

The Production of Crime Stories

The media select a limited number of stories from the large pool of crimes that are available. Some are excluded because a reporter decides that they are not news; some might be news, but the organization does not have the resources needed to do the follow-up necessary to determine whether they are news; other crimes are news, but are not covered because of their relationship with the source. Some crimes become important news stories, some are interesting, and others are written simply to satisfy organizational space needs.

Reporters and the media organization consider each crime as potentially filling four different levels of news space. These levels are determined by the newsworthiness of the story, and are produced differently depending on its determined level of newsworthiness. Examining these different levels, and why certain stories are chosen to fill each of these different levels, is a unique and more comprehensive way to understand the crime news production process. The four levels are "tertiary," "secondary," "primary," and "super primary." Table 4.6 provides a summary that compares the characteristics of these different levels and how the production of these stories varies.

Tertiary Crime Stories. Tertiary level stories are space fillers which appear in the news everyday. These are easy to put together and can be done quickly by contacting sources over the telephone. These are brief stories usually not more than five story inches in length. These stories are written to ensure that at least some crime gets into the paper without taking much news space, and can be easily disposed of if a more newsworthy crime occurs. Very few sources are contacted for these stories, and reporters typically do not get bylines for them. Compared to the other levels, tertiary crime stories are not interesting and only basic demographics are provided about the victim and defendant.

Coverage of these stories cannot be justified by the fact that they are informative or entertaining, but are included daily as news stories because they satisfy organizational needs. The organizational purpose for requiring tertiary input from their reporters is to fill the sections of a newspaper designated for "local briefs" and they are used to fill unexpected news holes that are left when all stories are in. Reporters write these stories because it's required by the organization, and because they have an unknown potential to develop into a higher level news story. Additionally, tertiary stories are sometimes covered because of

TABLE 4.6

Levels of Crime Stories

By characteristics of these stories

Characteristic	Tertiary	Secondary	Primary	Super Primary
Frequency	Everyday	Everyday	Infrequently/frequently	Rarely/infrequently
Length/coverage	3–7 story inches	7–14 story inches	14+ inches; covered across a number of days and criminal justice stages.	14+ inches covered across a number of days/weeks and criminal justice stages; numerous stories appear on same date; anniversary dates provide opportunity to do another story.
Level of difficulty	Simple; done by one reporter.	Burdensome; done by one reporter.	Burdensome; done by one reporter.	Burdensome; numerous reporters work on various aspects.
Number of sources contacted	1 or 2	Exhaustive –	Exhaustive	Exhaustive +

Type of sources contacted	Only criminal justice lower level (e.g., patrol officer, police said.)	Criminal justice; exhaust other sources; hit dead ends; time constraints.	Criminal justice; source able to provide newsworthy information; contact individuals directly and indirectly involved.	Criminal justice sources; individuals involved; other experts; community members; sources are higher level sources (e.g., police chief says).
Byline	No	Yes	Yes	Yes; some reporters noted as contributors.
Disposable	Yes	Yes	No	No
Justification	Organizational; nature of the criminal justice system.	Organizational; nature of the criminal justice system.	Organizational; nature of the criminal justice system; can be informative and/or entertaining.	Organizational; nature of the criminal justice system; can be informative and/or entertaining.

the nature of the criminal justice system. For example, if the discovery of a tertiary homicide is printed in the briefs section on a particular day, another tertiary story will be done if a defendant is arraigned.

Reporters from both the police and court beats are expected to contribute between two and three tertiary level crime stories each day. Typically, tertiary stories taken from the police beat are taken directly from a police report and are supplemented with one or two source contacts serving as the authority on the story. When making morning police calls, for example, a police beat reporter finds out about a shooting that occurred. The reporter then asks the mouthpiece to provide him with the full report, and then he contacts the investigating homicide detective to have a source for which to attribute crime incident information, and contacts the coroner to be able to attribute information about the victim. Similarly, tertiary court stories are easily put together by sitting in briefly on a court session, or calling either a bailiff or any of the attorneys involved.

Secondary Crime Stories. The second level of crime story going upward are secondary crime stories. Secondary level crime stories have the potential to be important news. Thus the reporter goes to great lengths to generate these stories by exhausting the number of sources that might be able to provide information about the crime. Unfortunately for the reporter, often the sources cannot provide the information necessary to increase the salience of the story so it ends up being nothing more than a tertiary story with one or two additional elements or quotes in them. Secondary stories take up a fair amount of news space (between six and twelve inches), and consume a fair amount of resources on the particular day that they are put together. Reporters will get a byline for these stories, but they are really nothing more than back page news.

These stories occur almost every day because they fill organizational needs; however, they are more burdensome than tertiary stories. The reporter contacts a number of sources, but these sources are unable to provide enough information. This occurs because sometimes sources cannot be contacted, or they refuse to provide information about a crime for fear of jeopardizing an investigation. These stories are also burdensome to the organization because they are not disposable by any means, but there is not really anything entertaining about them.

For example, while at the *Tribune*, M. D. and I went to the east side of the city to cover a gang-related drug shooting that left one deceased victim and another in critical condition. M. D. thought that the story had the potential to be more newsworthy because another shooting occurred in the same area the night before, and he thought that they might be linked together. The reporter went out on the streets to put this together with the hope of finding an important crime story.

He was disappointed. The shooting had occurred at about two in the morning outside of a bar. The crime scene was cold in the sense that the only things physically left there that could be included in the story were blood stains on the cement and bullet holes in a nearby restaurant. M. D. had to dig. First we went inside the bar, but none of the patrons nor the waitress saw anything. Fortunately the night manager, who was there when the shooting occurred, was still there and took us over to the crime scene and explained what he had heard happened. The manager had some good information, but did not want to be identified, so the reporter had to continue to dig. M. D. then proceeded to talk to people on the streets and in a number of nearby restaurants and gas stations, but nobody saw anything. When we went back to the crime scene, M. D. saw a woman in an overlooking window and he called up to her. She really did not see much, but gave him a lead because she knew both of the victims and where one of their girlfriends lived. We went to the girlfriend's apartment complex, skirted security, and were lucky enough to bump into one of the girlfriend's friends who was with the two victims immediately before the shooting occurred. She was able to give some details about the crime, but did not want to be identified.

The reporter was stuck. He did not have time to go to the hospital to interview the victim's family, and it was late in the day. In order to write the story, he ended up calling the homicide division to be able to attribute quotes regarding the crime, called the hospital for quotes on the surviving victim, and contacted the coroner for quotes on the deceased victim. The information for the story that was written was collected in about fifteen minutes, but it was a story that the reporter worked on all day. The *Tribune* placed this story at the bottom of page 4 of the metro section with a four-inch headline. It ran about seven inches long, which is close to being a tertiary-level story.

Primary Level Crime Stories. The third level consists of primary stories. These are stories that take up primary space, but editors are glad to give these stories space and reporters enjoy working on them. If the story discussed above had panned out and the reporter had been able to link the two separate shootings together, it *could* have been a primary-level story. These stories take the best sections of the paper, either the front page or the front page of the metro section, and editors are more liberal with the amount of space given these stories. With tertiary and secondary stories, reporters are told the amount of space to which they have to limit the story even before they start to write. Reporters will work on these stories all day, and an exhaustive list of sources that might have information about the crime is used.

There are a number of newsworthy elements to these stories. A reporter sometimes is able to tie the story into some larger community concern and typically the story is supplemented with a good picture or film. These stories do occur fairly infrequently, however, but when they do occur they are covered across a number of stages of the criminal justice system. These stories can be informative and entertaining, and news organizations provide them larger amounts of space because of their ability to attract consumers.

The best example of a primary-level story occurred while working at the *Tribune* with M. D. The crime involved a six-month pregnant woman who was hit in the stomach with a brick by another woman, a friend of the family, who was arguing with another family member over the length of a woman's skirt. The woman's baby was born prematurely, lived for a couple of hours, and then died. It was eventually ruled a homicide. There were a number of newsworthy elements within this story. First, the crime was serious; seriousness is a key factor in determining whether any crime becomes newsworthy. An ordinary, everyday homicide can be a tertiary story, but an ordinary, everyday purse-snatching cannot be. A second newsworthy element to this story was the status of the victim. Old people and children are seen as being special victims who are deserving of special protection. A third newsworthy element to this crime was the stupidity of the crime. M. D. wanted to lead with the fact that the baby was murdered over an argument about the length of a woman's skirt. Another element was that it happened near Mother's Day, and the reporter emphasized the mother whose child was taken from her so close to that day. Finally, this story was tied to the larger community concern of abortion. The story led with the abortion tie because the editors wanted that to be the lead.

It took all day to assemble this story. M. D. found out about the story from the police mouthpiece who provided him with the report. He then contacted a sergeant in the district where it occurred, called the captain in charge of the district, and called the homicide detectives who were investigating the case. He called the coroner for information about the deceased victim, and contacted the hospital regarding the status of the mother. He called an attorney regarding whether the person could be charged with murder, and called the district attorney to find out whether the woman who threw the brick would be charged with murder. He also contacted a national abortion organization. Finally, he was able to talk with the mother and get permission to send a photographer out to her house to get a picture. This story ended up on the front page of the metro section (where the mother's picture appeared), and was the lead story on all of the area television stations.

Super Primary Stories. Super primary stories are sensational crime stories. When a mayor such as Marion Barry gets arrested for smoking crack, or a sports celebrity such as Mike Tyson gets convicted of rape, these are examples of super primary stories. They are stories with national and international appeal in terms of their newsworthiness. Not only is a lead story written that describes the incident, but three or four follows-up to that story occur on the same day. For example, there might be a community impact story, a victim impact follow, an analysis of the causes of crime, procedural issues that might come up at trial, or even an editorial written on the same day. A number of personnel resources from the organization are diverted to cover all aspects of these stories. A number of reporters exhaust the sources that can provide information about the incident and each reporter who assisted is noted as contributing to the story. Other sources are contacted to generate the follow-up stories.

These are large stories that fill vast amounts of news space, are typically covered for a number of days after the incident occurred, and continue to be at least a primary story as the case moves through the system. These stories are infrequent; however, when they do occur organizational resources are set aside to continually follow up and develop different aspects of the story. Although rare, these are the most intriguing and entertaining crime stories.

A super primary story occurred while observing the *Nightly*. At the beginning of my tenure there, the Milwaukee police discovered serial murderer Jeffrey Dahmer. Dahmer's story was important for a number of reasons. There were a large number of victims (seventeen); he used unusual methods to dispose of his victims (boiled their skulls to preserve them and destroyed the dismembered parts by sticking them into a vat of acid); the crime scene (bones, body parts, and smells); as well as how Dahmer was initially captured (one of his victims escaped and flagged down police). Dahmer's story was aired across the country that evening, and appeared on the front page of newspapers the morning after. In New York, Missouri, and California, the lead story on the eleven o'clock news was Dahmer. In addition, what increased the newsworthiness of this particular story was the fact that Dahmer grew up near the city where I was doing my research, thus giving reporters the local angle. They now could contact his family, friends, teachers, past employers, and neighbors, which made it an even a bigger story. Thus, not only was Dahmer the lead and second story on the news for that particular day, but also the third and fourth.

Later, when it was found out that his "first victim" was murdered in this hometown when he was a youth, it made the story even larger, to such an extent that approximately twenty-five satellite trucks and seventy-five news organizations showed up to cover the dig for his first victim, and this little midwestern town, for at least four or five days, was known as the city where

Jeffrey Dahmer began his career as a serial murderer. A great many stories were produced from this small city across a number of days. These stories ranged from the actual dig and the number of bones it produced to psychological evaluation of Dahmer's behavior in his youth; the community's economic benefits from having such a large influx of reporters eat at its restaurants and stay at its hotels; and even a story on the two little girls who made about $25 profit by selling lemonade to reporters and interested bystanders. Observing the coverage of this story gave insight into the news production of a sensational story.

Conclusion

Crime is an important source of news for media organizations. Thus the news organization routinizes a process that efficiently operates to produce crime news. Regardless of how the amount of crime in the news is justified, the public is exposed to a lot of it. Violent, property, white collar, victimless, and political crimes can be newsworthy. A traffic offense, disorderly conduct, or even jaywalking might be a story under the right set of circumstances. Some crimes are ordinary and not spectacular. Others, such as the woman who was held hostage as a sex slave, are bizarre primary news stories which are deemed deserving of more news space. Some crime stories are secondary because they are ludicrous (the Kuwaiti who was sentenced to fifteen years in prison for wearing a Saddam Hussein T-shirt). *Any* crime has the potential to be a news story, and its level of newsworthiness determines the process that will be used to produce the story.

Examining how the newsmaking process varies across these four levels of newsworthiness is a better way to understand crime news. It helps highlight the factors that influence whether or not a crime becomes news. Some crimes, for example, become increasingly newsworthy as the public and politicians define them as being more important. Story-specific factors including the type of crime, the victim, and the defendant involved can raise the importance of a story. Ordinary, everyday homicides can be news because of their seriousness. Ordinary, everyday burglaries or motor vehicle thefts are not news. They can be, however, when additional factors exist, such as when auto thieves demonstrate an increasing tendency to steal cars at gunpoint with the passengers still in them. There has to be a plug, a twist, or a lead that makes these crimes newsworthy. Future research needs to consider how the presentation of crime varies across these different levels, as well as why these additional elements raise the newsworthiness of crime.

NOTES

*An earlier version of this chapter was presented at the 1992 annual meeting of the Academy of Criminal Justice Sciences in Pittsburgh.

1. The names of the organizations and individuals involved in the study are fictitious to preserve anonymity.

2. Some newspapers, on occasion, will do this where they have a "crime page" which will present all crimes that appeared in the police blotter over a period of time. This is atypical.

3. There has been a considerable amount of research that has looked at this topic producing inconsistent results. Stack (1987) and Phillips (1980) find deterrent effects. However, Bailey and Peterson (1989) and Bailey (1990) find none.

4. Up to nine sources were coded for each crime story. Three who provided information about the actual incident (results provided above); three who provided information about the victim; and three who provided information about the defendant. If more than three sources existed that provided information on either the crime, victim, or defendant, the first, third, and fifth source were chosen.

REFERENCES

Altheide, David L. 1984. "TV news and the social construction of justice: Research issues and policy." In Ray Surette (ed.), *Justice and the Media*. Springfield, IL: Charles C. Thomas, pp. 292–304.

———. 1976. *Creating Reality: How TV News Distorts Events*. Beverly Hills: Sage.

Bailey, William C. 1990. "Murder, capital punishment, and television: Execution publicity and homicide rates." *American Sociological Review*. 55: 628–633.

Bailey, William C. and Ruth D. Peterson. 1989. "Murder and capital punishment: A monthly time-series analysis of execution publicity." *American Sociological Review*. 54: 722–743.

Breed, Warren. 1955. "Social control in the newsroom." *Social Forces*, 33: 326–335.

Chibnall, Steve. 1977. *Law and Order News*. London: Tavistock.

Cohen, Shari. 1975. "A comparison of crime coverage in Detroit and Atlanta newspapers." *Journalism Quarterly*, 52, 4: 726–730.

Cohen, Stanley. 1972. *Folk Devils and Moral Panics*. London: MacGibbon and Kee.

Cohen, Stanley and Jock Young. 1981. *The Manufacture of News: Deviance, Social Problems and The Mass Media*. London: Constable.

Epstein, Edward J. 1973. *News From Nowhere*. New York: Vintage.

Ericson, Richard V. 1991. "Mass media, crime, law and justice: An institutional approach." *The British Journal of Criminology*, 31, 3: 219–249.

Ericson, Richard V., Patricia M. Baranek, and Janet B. Chan. 1991. *Representing Order: Crime, Law, and Justice in the News Media*. Toronto: University of Toronto Press.

———. 1989. *Negotiating Control: A Study of News Sources*. Toronto: University of Toronto Press.

———. 1987. *Visualizing Deviance: A Study of News Organization*. Toronto: University of Toronto Press.

Fishman, Mark. 1980. *Manufacturing the News*. Austin: University of Texas Press.

———. 1978. "Crime waves as ideology." *Social Problems*, 25: 531–543.

Galtung, Johan and Mari Ruge. 1981. "Structuring and selecting news." In Stanley Cohen and Jock Young, (eds.), *The Manufacture of News: Deviance, Social Problems and The Mass Media*. London: Constable, pp. 52–63.

Gans, Herbert J. 1979. *Deciding What's News: A Study of CBS Evening News, Newsweek and Time*. New York: Pantheon Books.

Gordon, M. and Linda Heath. 1981. "The news business, crime and fear." In D. Lewis (ed.), *Reactions to Crime*. Beverly Hills: Sage.

Gottfredson, Michael R. and Linda Hirschi. 1990. *A General Theory of Crime*. Stanford, CA: Stanford University Press.

Graber, Doris. 1980. *Crime News and the Public*. New York: Praeger Publishers.

Grabosky, Peter and Paul Wilson. 1989. *Journalism and Justice: How Crime is Reported*. Leichhardt, AUS: Pluto Press.

Hall, Stuart, Chas Critcher, Tony Jefferson, John Clarke, and Brian Roberts. 1978. *Policing the Crisis*. London: Macmillan.

Hartley, John. 1982. *Understanding News*. London: Methuen.

Heath, Linda. 1984. "Impact of newspaper crime reports on fear of crime." *Journal of Personality and Social Psychology*, (August) 47: 263–276.

Johnston, Donald H. 1979. *Journalism and the Media*. New York: Barnes and Noble.

Lotz, Roy E. 1991. *Crime and the American Press*. New York: Praeger.

Marsh, Harry L. 1988. *Crime and the Press: Does Newspaper Crime Coverage Support Myths about Crime and Law Enforcement?* (Ph.D. Dissertation: Sam Houston State University). Ann Arbor, MI: University Microfilms International.

Meyer, John C., Jr. 1975. "Newspaper reporting of crime and justice: Analysis of an assumed difference." *Journalism Quarterly*, 52, 4: 731–734.

Phillips, David P. 1980. "The deterrent effect of capital punishment: New evidence on an old controversy." *American Journal of Sociology*, 86: 139–48.

President's Commission on Law Enforcement and Administration of Justice. 1967. *Task Force Report: Crime and Its Impact*. Washington, D.C.: U.S. Government Printing Office.

Rock, Paul. 1973. "News as eternal recurrence." In Stanley Cohen and Jock Young (eds.), *The Manufacture of News*. London: Constable: 73–80.

Roscho, Bernard. 1975. *Newsmaking.* Chicago: University of Chicago Press.

Roshier, Bob. 1981. "The selection of crime news by the press." In Stanley Cohen and Jock Young (eds.), *The Manufacture of News: Social Problems, Deviance and the Mass Media.* Beverly Hills: Sage Publications, pp. 40–51.

Sherizen, Sanford. 1978. "Social creation of crime news: All the news fitted to print." In C. Winick (ed.), *Deviance and Mass Media.* Beverly Hills: Sage, pp. 203–224.

Sigal, Leon. 1973. *Reporters and Officials.* Lexington, Mass: D.C. Heath.

Skogan, Wesley G. and Michael G. Maxfield. 1981. *Coping With Crime: Individual and Neighborhood Reactions.* Beverly Hills: Sage.

Stack, Steven. 1987. "Publicized executions and homicide, 1950–1980." *American Sociological Review.* 52: 532–540.

Surette, Ray. 1992. *Media, Crime, and Criminal Justice: Images and Realities.* Pacific Grove, California: Brooks/Cole Publishing Company.

Tuchman, Gaye. 1978. *Making News: A Study in the Construction of Reality.* New York: The Free Press.

———. 1973. "Making News by doing work: Routinizing the unexpected." *American Journal of Sociology,* 79, 1: 110–131.

Tunstall, Jeremy. 1971. *Journalists at Work.* London: Constable.

Voumvakis, Sophia E., and Richard V. Ericson. 1984. *News Accounts of Attacks on Women: A Comparison of Three Toronto Newspapers.* Toronto: Centre of Criminology, University of Toronto.

White, David M. 1950. "The 'gate keeper': A case study in the selection of news." *Journalism Quarterly,* 27, 4: 383–390.

CHAPTER 5

Predator Criminals as Media Icons

Ray Surette

> In the ranks of these ogres are assassins and those who
> lynch them; stranglers of women and torturers of children;
> practitioners of patricide and killers of offspring; and
> among them we find the quiet veteran who converts his
> home town into a target range. Such men strike terror for
> several reasons: for one, they cast doubt on the sanctity of
> life, because they assault victims who have done them no
> harm and who are frequently unknown to them; they raise
> questions about the meaningfulness and predictability of
> human motives, because their lives typically do not
> foreshadow their tragic fate. Frequently these are the
> mildest, gentlest souls, immune to anger and unconcerned
> with their surroundings. Frequently they are shy,
> brooding, and shadowy, unnoticed until the moment
> when they explode into horrible prominence. (Toch, 1969:
> 214)

Predator Criminals and the Social Construction of Criminality

The crimes that dominate the public consciousness and
policy debates are not common crimes but the rarest ones.
Whether in entertainment or news, the crimes that define
criminality are the acts of predator criminals. Our desire to
understand and control these seemingly incomprehensible and
uncontrollable criminals is long-standing and is reflected in

much of our classic literature.[1] However, the modern mass media have raised the specter of the predator criminal from a minor character to a common, ever-present image. Predator criminals are modern icons of the mass media. As with other icons, they represent a largely unquestioned set of beliefs about the world, a constructed reality that, as the aphorism "perception is reality" suggests, has the ability to shape the actual world to fit the media image. In the world of crime and justice, the icon of predator crime pushes life to imitate art.

How does the media's portrait of predator crime construct social reality? To understand this process it is useful to conceptualize social reality as a changing, socially created phenomenon, not as fixed or universal but as evolving and subjective. In dealing with society, people use world models to group and understand factual information and to simplify and direct their decisions and social behavior.[2] These models are constructed over time from information gained through social interactions and personal experiences. An individual's direct experiences make up what has been termed "objective reality."[3] Because knowledge of it is first hand, this objective reality has the strongest influence on the social reality each individual constructs and subsequently on his or her behavior, attitudes and perceptions. For most creatures, knowledge of the world is gained only through their objective reality or direct experiences.[4] Humans, however, have access to another source of knowledge about the world. This second source is termed "symbolic reality" and is obtained from our extensive capability to manipulate abstract symbols as representations of objects and concepts. Examples of symbolic systems include written and spoken language, art, music, and mathematics. Symbolic reality provides a vast amount of communicated knowledge of the world and allows individuals to employ knowledge of experiences that they have not directly undergone, and to incorporate that knowledge into their world models. For modern people, most of our worldly knowledge is gained not from objective reality but from symbolic reality.

In the final world-model construction step, the objective and symbolic realities are combined by each individual to create a "subjective" reality model.[5] In sum, in the social construction-of-reality process each individual constructs a social reality based upon interaction with an objective reality (the physical world) and information received from a culture's symbolic reality (language, art, the media) to create a subjective reality that directs his or her social behavior.[6] In advanced, urbanized societies such as the United States, the mass media play a crucial role in the social construction of reality because knowledge of many social phenomena is obtained solely through the media rather than through direct experience (Meyrowitz, 1985), and social institutions must rely on the mass media to distribute their reality-molding information (Altheide and Snow, 1991). Furthermore, when other sources of knowledge are not available the media play a greater role in the construction and dissemination of social reality. The mass media has evolved in present-day America to become the dominant player in the symbolic reality realm and, by default, in the subjective reality construction process.

The social construction-of-reality process and the media's role in it has been regarded as particularly important in the area of crime and justice. Relatively few people have direct experience with crime, and so the entertainment and news media are major sources of crime-related information and have been forwarded as important elements in the construction of crime and justice reality.[7] In the crime and justice area, one result of the media's central role is the construction of mass media-supported crime myths (Kappeler et al., 1993).[8] Although individual crime myths fade and are cyclic in nature, their effect on our conception of crime and justice linger because they provide knowledge that becomes permanently incorporated into our socially constructed world models. This process is enhanced as new events are constructed within the framework of previously constructed myths. The most prevalent, longest-running crime myth promulgated by the media is that of predator crime: a media icon that has been unchallenged for a century.

The Genesis of the Predator Icon

The history of the predator icon reveals that this image has long dominated the news and entertainment media. By 1850 the dominant image of the criminal in the popular print media had shifted from earlier romantic, heroic portraits to more conservative, negative images. The two most popular media genres of the period, detective and crime thrillers (found in magazines, serials, and dime novel books) describe crime as originating in individual personality or moral weakness (Papke, 1987). In this regard, the crime and justice portrayals produced during the late 1800s are surprisingly similar to today's efforts. Both present images that reinforce the status quo, state that competent, often heroic individuals are pursuing and capturing criminals, and encourage the belief that criminals can be readily recognized and crime ultimately solved through direct law enforcement efforts (Papke, 1987). Detective and crime thrillers mark the beginning of a more violent entertainment crime media that is less critical of social conditions. They laid the groundwork for the construction of a social reality of crime which is predatory and rooted in individual failures rather than social ills (Papke, 1987).

Following the print media's lead, the first film criminals are descendants of violent western outlaws, but unlike the western bandits, the early twentieth-century film criminal was usually portrayed as an urban predator (Rosow, 1978). The most frequent portraits of these urbanized criminals depicted a common use of ruthless and corrupt business techniques and pursuit of wealth, and this businessman/criminal portrait has remained a prevalent part of the media crime image to this day (Rosow, 1978). In the 1930s and 1940s, the portraits of violence became more graphic as gangsters and undercover policemen and detectives appeared (McArthur, 1972; Rosow, 1978). The predator image was quickly adopted by television in the 1950s and television's portrait of crime greatly overemphasizes individual acts of violence.[9] Murder and robbery dominate, with murder comprising nearly one-fourth of all crimes.[10] In a representative content study by Lichter and Lichter (1983), murder, robbery, kidnapping, and aggravated assault made up 87 percent of all television crimes.[11]

The repeated message in the entertainment media is that crime is perpetrated by predatory individuals who are basically different from the rest of us and that criminality stems from individual problems. In the media, crime is behavior criminals choose freely, and media criminals are not bound or restrained in any way by normal social rules and values.[12] Over the course of this century an evolution in the portrayal can be observed. Media criminals have become more animalistic, irrational and predatory (a process paralleled by media crime fighters), and their crimes more violent, senseless and sensational, while their victims have become more random, helpless, and innocent. The public is led to see violence and predation between strangers as a way of life (Scheingold, 1984).

The news media have mirrored the entertainment media in the pursuit of predator criminality. Emphasis on predator criminality in the contemporary news media can be traced to the 1890s with the introduction of a new mass entertainment-focused news journalism, known as "yellow journalism" (Papke, 1987: 35). Represented by the Hearst and Pulitzer newspapers in New York, this new style of journalism devoted space and importance to disasters, scandals, gossip, and crime. In particular, personal violent crime was emphasized. Eventually dominating justice news, today crime news is composed largely of violent personal street crimes such as murder, rape and assault while more common offenses such as burglary, theft, and fraud are notably underplayed.[13] The vast majority of crime coverage pertains to violent or sensational crime. With similar orientations, it is not surprising that the image of the criminal that crime news propagates is similar to the image of the criminal found in the entertainment media. And when crimes are reported without perpetrator descriptions, since most crime news is of violent interpersonal crime, it follows that the blank image is filled by the public with a faceless predator criminal (Graber, 1980; Sheley and Ashkins, 1981).

Lastly, with the recent merging of the entertainment and news in high visibility, dramatic court trials and info-tainment, tabloid-style crime shows represent the culmination of the icon-construction process.[14] Such shows and trials represent the final step in a long process of merging the news and entertainment components of the mass media—often resulting in multi-media products and exploitations.[15] Crime in these productions symbolize the uncertainties of modern life, that criminals are evil, abnormal people, and that victims are vulnerable (Cavender and Bond-Maupin, forthcoming). Media crime is nearly universally due to individual characteristics rather than social conditions and the causes of crime are rooted in individual failings rather than social ills.[16] Since crime is viewed as an individual choice, other social, economic or structural explanations are irrelevant and can be ignored. Although other crimes and criminals are sometimes shown, the predatory stranger who preys upon unsuspecting victims dominates the news and the public's image of criminality.[17] In the final analysis, the media projects the horrendous crime as the norm (Elias, 1986).

Sometimes a constructed subjective reality is found to be significantly different from the objective reality that empirical data suggest actually exists. Such is the case with predator criminality. Although predator criminality dominates our image of crime and predator criminals direct our criminal justice policies, predatory criminal events are rare. If that is true, the potential seriousness of the misleading effects of the predator icon can be garnered from looking at the empirical reality of predator crime.

The Empirical Reality of Predator Crime

Gottfredson and Hirschi (1990) argue that media emphasis on the atypical but highly publicized crime is a serious source of misinformation and false perceptions of the true nature of crime. A simple direct measure of predator crime is not available but some proxy measures are. The first is the victimization rate for violent crimes by strangers calculated by the United States Bureau of Justice Statistics. The Bureau bases its calculations on annual National Crime Victimization Surveys. The most recent estimated rate (per 1,000 persons age 12 and older) of violent victimization by strangers is shown in Table 5.1.

TABLE 5.1

Crimes of Violence by Strangers*
(Rape, Robbery, and Assault)
1990

Crime	Rate Per 1,000
All Crimes of Violence	18.0
Rape	0.3
completed	0.1
attempted	0.2
Robbery	4.6
completed	3.2
attempted	1.5
Assault	13.2
Aggravated	5.1
completed	0.1
attempted	0.2
Simple	8.1
completed	0.1
attempted	0.2

*Source: *Criminal Victimization in the United States, 1990* (1992) Bureau of Justice Statistics, Table 37, Page 55 "Number of Victimizations and Victimization Rates for Persons Age 12 and Over, by Type of Crime and Victim-Offender Relationship."

Table 5.1 reveals that the probability was slightly less than two out of one hundred (.018) of being victimized by a stranger in 1990.[18] Note that this value includes both completed and attempted victimizations and is largely comprised of simple assaults. Without simple assaults the probability drops to about one in a hundred (.0099). If only completed crimes are included the probability drops to about one-third of one percent or 1 in 300 (.0034). There are also indications that the rate of victimization has been slowly declining over the past fifteen years. The rate per 1,000 for crimes of violence (stranger and nonstranger combined) has dropped from a peak of 35.3/1,000 in 1981 to 29.6/1,000 in 1990 and has been under 30/1,000 for the past five years.[19]

But of course, being the victim of a predator crime is normally a more harmful, serious event than other crime victimizations, so yearly probabilities do not fully account for the threat. In 1987, the Bureau of Justice statistics published an estimate by Herbert Koppel of lifetime likelihood of victimization. Koppel estimated that based on 1975–1984 victimization rates, eighty-three out of every one hundred people will be victims of violent crime (rape, robbery, and assault, either completed or attempted) at least once during their lives.[20] Stranger versus nonstranger victimization is not separated in the Bureau's lifetime likelihood estimate, but assuming that the ratio of stranger to nonstranger crime remains similar to that found in 1990 (a ratio of .611 or about three out of five violent crimes committed by strangers), of the eighty-three out of one hundred persons the Bureau estimates to be victimized during their lifetimes, about fifty-one will be victimized by strangers. At first blush, over a lifetime the likelihood of being a victim of at least a simple assault by a stranger appears significant. However, the likelihood of victimization declines significantly with age and the number of people in any group who are victimized more than once is substantially greater than if victimization were equally probable for all members of a group. In reality, persons inordinately susceptible to being victimized are likely to continue in their high susceptibility (Koppel, 1987). Thus, if it were true that we all equally share the likelihood of victimization, violent crime would be a common lifetime experience. But some carry more risk than others. Although violent victimization is a devastating act and cannot be trivialized, the reality is that a relatively small "at-risk" core of citizens carry a significant portion of the victimization risk. Hence, about one-third of U.S. residents report ever having been punched or beaten by another person in their entire lives.[21] In any one year risk of violent crime by a stranger is small, over a lifetime it can be significant, but with a substantial portion of the risk concentrated in high-risk groups, particularly young, urban, and minority males.

In terms of the most serious predatory crime, murder, the reality of predation also differs from media appearances. Again the estimation of victimization rates is derived from the Bureau of Justice Statistics data.[22] The number of murders has been increasing over the last thirty years from a low of 7,990 in 1964 to 20,045 in 1990.[23] Even with steady annual increases, murder remains a minute piece of all violent crime, comparing in 1990 for example to over 100,000 rapes, 600,000 robberies, and 1,000,000 aggravated assaults,[24] or about one-fourth of one percent of all violent crime. The 1990 figures also categorize 14.4 percent of murders known to the police as committed by strangers.[25] It is likely, however, that a proportion of the 6,956 uncategorized murders are also committed by strangers. Assuming that the proportion of stranger murders in the unidentified group is similar to the identified group, 1,537 of the unidentified relationship murders would be by strangers and of the total 20,045 murders in 1990, a total of 4,424 or 22.1 percent would be stranger-committed. Murder in general thus comprises a small proportion of all violent crime and predatory murders by strangers comprise about one-fourth of all murders.

Regarding the epitome of the predator criminal, the serial killer, in discussing the media generation of a serial killer panic in the 1980s, Philip Jenkins (1988) reports that although evidence of a true increase in the number of active serial killers since the 1970s exists, in total, serial killers account for no more than 300 to 400 victims a year, or 2 to 3 percent of all American homicides. They are not the dominant homicide problem in the United States, as their media image suggests. Furthermore, the "roaming serial killer" media stereotype is even rarer. Serial killing is a regional, not a national problem, concentrated primarily in the states of California, Texas, and Florida. Kappeler and his colleagues (1993) argue that recent media coverage provides the reinforcement and linkage necessary for a unified image of violent predatory crime to be established with the roaming serial killer stereotype as the lead element. The multimedia coverage of serial murderers such as Jeffrey Dahmer and Ted Bundy and the movie *Silence of the Lambs* link real and fictional cases together allowing the coverage of actual predator crimes to blend with popular fiction.

All told, the available statistics suggest that the empirical reality of predator crime is a serious but not representative component of the crime picture. Most victimizations are simply not that serious, assaultive, injurious, or life-threatening (Skogan and Maxfield, 1981). The media's attraction to predator crime cannot be understood by its pervasiveness and can be only partly understood by its popularity. To a degree, some interest can be attributed simply to its rarity. However, reasons for the public's devotion and the media's myopic exclusion of competing images are not readily apparent.[26]

Devotion to the Predator Icon. The public's devotion to the predator icon and an understanding of the media's role in its proselytization can be better understood from looking at the United States' cultural tradition. Noted as a dominant cultural trait first by Alexis de Tocqueville in the 1830s, a key feature in American culture is the central role that individualism plays.[27] Individualism in America demonstrates itself in two ways. First, at the personal level, it is related to an American focus on close individual relationships and an avoidance of contact with large groups and organizations. Second, regarding the conduct of other individuals, they are nearly universally held directly responsible for any problems and difficulties they may experience and for fashioning any solutions; collective responses are seldom conceived or pursued. This firm belief in individual responsibility is reflected in our vigilante tradition (Scheingold, 1984) and it is apparent in our popular crime and justice literature, which relies on the rugged individualist as problem-solver (Gans, 1988). In practice, Americans traditionally focus on small personal "micro" communities and avoid contact with the "macro" community and large organizations. In private life, individualism forwards the pursuit of life-style enclaves, artificially created private havens of safety and privacy. These enclaves share external features of life (built around a golf course or a marina for example) but are less than a community. They have no history, no social interdependence, and no external political involvement (Bellah et al., 1985).

In practical effect, individualism leads to micro-social solutions to crime—security devices, guns, private protection agencies. And when enclaves feel threatened by crime, the ones that can afford it become garrison communities. The culture of individualism also affects our perceptions of the causes of crime, forwarding personal and interpersonal moral explanations. Predating the mass media, the traditional causes of crime have been seen as individual flaws or flawed relationships between individuals; social or organizational relationships traditionally have not been given much weight (Gans, 1988). And although the media do not argue any clear set of policies, they reflect the cultural focus on the micro-community of family, close friends, and individuals in their content regarding social problems and their solutions. In our media and in our culture, social problems are generated and solved at the individual level. Because of this, Americans lack the cultural resources to deal with relationships between culturally, socially or economically different citizens (Bellah et al., 1985). Large organizations, government, and business corporations are shown as distant, distrustful and frequently dishonest, things to be avoided wherever possible (Bellah et al., 1985).

For criminal justice, another effect of individualism is its orientation toward deviants as inherently different. The culture desires to isolate troublemakers and to perceive them as distinct (Schur, 1969). In the crime and justice arena, the myopic focus on predator crimes is thus heightened by the perception of criminals as a separate breed, encouraging the perception of social and economic factors as irrelevant (Scheingold, 1984). The mainstream American response to crime is drawn from a commonsense perspective which focuses on morally deficient criminals and on preventing them from committing crime. However, this focus tends to ignore the social generation of morally deficient criminals. In sum, when crime is solely blamed on individual failure, even nonpunitive anti-crime policies will emphasize intensive individual rehabilitative or educational efforts rather than policies that deal with social contributors (Gans, 1988). This emphasis on individual explanations and solutions in turn hurts people at the bottom of the social hierarchy who need a package of policies that incorporates both social solutions as well as individual responsibility.[28]

A second cultural feature of more recent vintage is the general acceptance of a largely invisible and incomprehensible social complexity as a basic American reality of modern economic, organizational and political life. The acceptance of an incomprehensible, complex society developed early in this century along with modernization; the emergence of the United States as a world power; the growth of professional "careers" as the defining feature of work; and a reliance on individual-based therapy (Bellah et al., 1985; Gans, 1988). All of these developments occurred simultaneously with the development of the mass media in the United States. An immediate effect of the perception of an invisible, incomprehensible complexity was to heighten the avoidance mechanism Americans already held toward large organizations and differing social groups. Acceptance but avoidance of complexity also means that Americans do not strive to be greatly informed about many aspects of society. A conscious decision to remain uninformed is strong and we intermittently "keep up" through the news media (Gans, 1988). Thus, as with other areas of public life, we avoid the criminal justice system unless immediately involved and turn over responsibility for crime to its specialized experts and bureaucratic managers as the only sensible course.[29] The "administrative despotism" de Tocqueville feared 160 years ago has been realized. This deferment to expertise and bureaucracy is palatable because it allows individuals to follow our natural cultural tendency to concentrate on micro-society relationships and enclave living while avoiding the macro society.

Hence, the cultural reflex is to turn over complex, seemingly incomprehensible problems such as crime to large organizations staffed with the technical expertise and bureaucratic experts to deal with them. And because social problems tend to be scanned from a distance and policy development and administration ignored, involvement increases only as threat to personal private life increases. As most crime falls on the poor and disadvantaged it is easy for most to avoid it as a public policy issue that requires close attention. Individual acts of crime are significant to individuals or small groups of people but specific crime policy is left the responsibility of government and, in practice, the monopoly of the professionals and experts of the criminal justice system (Heinz, 1985). As long as it is founded on individualism, crime and justice policy is mostly a government concern. Deemed the place where you find crime experts, by extension the criminal justice system's enhancement is seen as the natural solution to the crime problem. In addition, the short-term immediate effect of alternative solutions to crime not based on individualism or punitiveness would mobilize middle America (Gans, 1988). Therefore, although the status quo may be ineffective or even counter-effective in the long run, it is more acceptable in a repeating cycle of short-term politically defined periods demarcated by elections.

This reluctance to change is also found within the criminal justice system. It is best understood by conceiving of the criminal justice system as a collection of manufacturing firms sharing a marketplace. They influence one another's activities but they do not have direct authority over one another. In such a market there are few actions big firms can take easily and inexpensively and one of the easier ways of responding to criticism is symbolically (Gans, 1988: 85). Thus, change in the criminal justice system's policy would require many parts of the system to change simultaneously and the costs of not changing must be high before any change will occur. It is not surprising then that real policy change, except to increase punitiveness, is rare and that the criticism leveled at most criminal justice system innovations is that they are more symbolic than real. And it is in the realm of symbols, of course, that the mass media has its greatest influence.

Within the media construction of social reality, two myths symbolizing society are focused upon (Knight and Dean, 1982). The first myth is of simpler times when prompt solutions could be achieved through direct, disciplined action. The second myth is that of optimism for technology to create a better future through exotic, technological solutions. The first myth is an outgrowth of the cultural tenet of individualism, the second an outgrowth of the tenets of expertise and complexity. Both help in bolstering the cultural support structure for the predator icon and both are supported in turn by a high level of fear of crime in society. Media content, dominated by the predator icon, has been credited as the single greatest source of fear of crime.[30]

This is because perceived vulnerability is more important than actual victimization, and, further supporting predator-based policies, those who see themselves as vulnerable are more punitive in their attitudes (Langworthy and Whitehead, 1986). Thus the media portrayals and politicians' manipulations of the media result in increased support for punitive policies above the levels that victimization would alone establish. The effect is summarized by Bazelon:

> The true source of the public's anxiety is not, I believe, the problem of crime as such. People are afraid instead about their personal safety. It is not white collar crime that causes us to lock our doors so firmly at night. It is not organized crime, which corrupts our politics and business life, that causes us to lock them, either. Locking our doors against crimes of passions is, of course, like locking the fox 'inside' the chicken coop. What makes us fear for our safety are the random muggings and burglaries, the assaults on our sense of security and repose committed by people we don't know, for reasons we cannot fathom, let alone understand. (1978: 13)

This effect is not a conspiracy but the convergence of the goals of politicians seeking an issue, punitive predispositions of the public (due to our heritage of individualism), the content focus of the news and entertainment media, and the professional proclivities of the crime control establishment, especially the police (Scheingold, 1984). The media are encouraged by our cultural history to project the predator icon, risk little social criticism by emphasizing it, and are rewarded by continuing popularity. The icon is a safe and expected image for crime and justice. That both the news and entertainment components of the media project the predator icon ad nauseam has, however, led to some concern over its effects on society and criminal justice policy. Audience fear, mystification of the criminal justice system, artificially generated support for punitive criminal justice policies, and increased tolerance for illegal law enforcement practices are all concerns.[31]

   Icon Effects. The social effects of the icon are multiple. First, the mass media have been forwarded as a crucial factor in the development of general public policy and have been cited as especially important for criminal justice policy developments.[32] The most notable relationship between the icon and policy is the simultaneous shift toward individual focused retributive policies in the United States during the 1970s and 1980s and the growth of the resurgence of predator criminals in the media. A causal relationship is not asserted but both developments point to the underlying cultural forces discussed earlier. Exemplifying this process is the rise of the predator icon of the serial killer which ascended to cultural prominence in the 1970s. The serial killer presents a recent extreme image of a more conservative predator stereotype. Representing an explanation of crime in terms of objective, external evil, the resulting quest for evil denotes the culmination of the historic effort to differentiate dangerous offenders from the law-abiding (Rennie, 1978). As other causative theories of crime were discounted, public policy and criminological research shifted. By the late 1970s, criminology tended to emphasize the offender as a rational, responsible, deterrable creature. As a generalized group, criminals were less the victims of society and more the ruthless predators upon it. Stereotyped as serial killers, sexual abusers of children, and devil-worshipers, criminals were portrayed not only as predators but creatures of extreme, pathological evil (Jenkins, 1988). In the process, crime was transformed into a war being fought by semi-human monsters versus society.

The new, refined serial-murderer predator icon is important because it solidified and confirmed the traditional notion of an overwhelming social threat from lethal criminal predators. The media-induced serial killer panic of the early 1980s was readily embraced not only because of the media sensationalism that accompanied the campaign but also from the manipulation of the media by government agencies and the public's embracing of a quest for evil as an all-encompassing crime explanation and solution. Our cultural traditions set the tone and prepared a receptive social setting for the 1980s interaction between the mass media, public officials, and the public (Jenkins, 1988). In the end, public resources and law enforcement efforts have been heavily diverted to address serial killers; a policy directed at a perception of the crime problem rather than at the reality of crime (Jenkins, 1988).

Besides influencing resources, the icon also affects police practices. This is not surprising in that the early steps of the justice process, law enforcement, investigation, and arrests, are emphasized in entertainment programming to the near-exclusion of other subsequent steps (Carlson, 1985; Garofalo, 1981). Law enforcement not only dominates, but dominates as a glamorous, action-filled detective process which often legitimizes the use of violence (Culver and Knight, 1979). The media crime fighters are the dramatic embodiment of the dominant American ideology of individualism and action and the media's criminal justice system usually ends with the arrest or killing of the offender (Bortner, 1984; Dominick, 1978). Info-tainment news-style shows cement the image that police work is dangerous and pitted against an established class of predator criminals, images that match the self-promotions of law enforcement "wars" against crime and on drugs (Kappeler et al., 1993: 124). Thus a parallel icon of a dangerous, exciting world of crime-fighting ties into the image of the predator criminal icon, the two reinforcing each other. Indeed, the police image of stressful, dangerous, crime-fighting work needs the predator criminal image to maintain its credibility (Kappeler et al., 1993).

There is also evidence that the media predator image influences police recruits in their expectations of police work. In a pre- and post-academy training survey of police recruits by Surette (1993) it was noted that police recruit expectations of police work show a significant relationship with their media usage, a relationship that persists following police academy training. Even after the effects of other independent variables are taken into account, the greater a recruit's preference for television crime shows and belief in the reality of programming, the more likely that recruits will expect that police work will involve greater amounts of crime-fighting, that officers will more often fire their weapons, and that more arrests will be violent encounters. When the media's crime and justice message is subscribed to by police recruits, the predator icon results not surprisingly in predator-hunting, predator-focused police.

The predator criminal icon has also helped to make the United states one of the most punitive countries on the planet, while ironically simultaneously forwarding the myth that we are overly lenient.[33] Our reality is that we are both more violent than most Western societies and more punitive. We incarcerate at nearly four times the rate of our nearest competitor, the United Kingdom (388 versus 97.4 per 100,000 in 1988) and we have been increasing our death row, prison, parole and probation populations annually and significantly since the early 1980s. However, punitiveness has not brought security. For example, in 1990, 56 percent of Americans feared violent victimization,[34] 44 percent were afraid in their neighborhoods to walk alone at night,[35] 38 percent were more uneasy on the streets than they were the previous year,[36] 30 percent were more than a little fearful of being attacked or robbed at home, and 48 percent while traveling.[37] Fear and concern outrun risk, while increasing criminal justice expenditures do not seriously reduce the crime problem (Tauchen et al., 1992).

A single, unified, and very popular conception of crime in America emerges from the predator criminal icon. Predator crime is a metaphor for a world gone berserk, for life out of control. Forging a partnership between the police, the media, and the audience, these images of dangerous fugitives in a violent and uncertain world encourage broad social controls and justify increased social surveillance.[38] In an ultimate irony, myth creates reality. The pursuit of the icon in the real world fosters aggressive law enforcement policies and ignores social conditions that make the icon both more credible and threatening. Alternatives challenging the icon tend to be expelled from normal reality as dangerous, bizarre, and comical (Knight and Dean, 1982).

Conclusion

The most basic effects of the predator icon are to generate fear, degrade social networks, increase reliance on the media, and foster social isolation and polarization. We abandon society and its real problems to the media (Kappeler et al., 1993). When all external causes of crime are rejected, individual punishment emerges as the only logical social response to crime while criminology is demoted from a quest for understanding to the pragmatic task of crime detection. Offenders are stereotyped as monolithic, pathological, and violent; crime is analyzed from a simplistic prey-predator paradigm; and crime policy is fixated in a punitive defensive posture (Kappeler et al., 1993). The continued exposure to media violence, especially among those in which violence is likely to be perceived as a way of life, offers little hope that the media are orienting our society in a less violent direction. Instead it suggests that the media play an important role in reinforcing the norm of justified violence (Israel et al., 1972).

The result is that the media-attending public evaluates the criminal justice system poorly while paradoxically supporting more crime control-oriented law enforcement and punitive-based policies (Graber, 1980). Victor Kappeler and his colleagues (1993: 236, 247–248) conclude:

> Through our growing panic, we have enhanced law enforcement resources, developed task forces, implemented national programs, and created vast bureaucracies to deal with crime myths. Once created these machines are seldom dismantled and they consume an ever expanding amount of resources as they widen their sphere of influence. . . . Police will be limited to vigorously tracking stereotyped criminals, social service aspects of policing will be reduced to rhetoric, the courts will be pushed to the assembly line model of crime control, and we will fill the new prisons with those deemed different while continuing to search for new technologies to widen the system's net of social control.

The empirical reality of crime will be molded and offered as supportive evidence for the mythical icon of crime. A closed, tautological system will have been created that, despite the criminal justice system being presented and perceived as waging a losing war, its enhancement, at least as a law enforcement and punitive system, will be offered as the best hope against a sea of violent crimes and predator criminals. The continuing disparity between the media-constructed reality of crime and justice and the nonmedia reality of crime and justice results in the public receiving an unnecessarily distorted image that supports only one anti-crime policy approach, an expanded and enhanced punitive criminal justice system—an approach lacking evidence of success.[39]

NOTES

1. A prime attempt is Dostoevski's psychological study of a murderous burglar in *Crime and Punishment*.

2. These world models can be considered analogous to the world-views of George Gerbner and his colleagues (1976, 1978, 1979, and 1980).

3. See Adoni and Mane, 1984; Cohen et al., 1990; Schneider, 1985.

4. With some supplemental behaviors provided by instinctive patterns.

5. Thus the constructed reality is subjective in that each individual's world model will differ slightly from every other individual's model. This is because the knowledge mix will differ slightly from individual to individual. However, people exposed to similar experiences (objective reality) and similar communicated knowledge (subjective reality) will naturally construct subjective realities that are also similar. One can conceive of "culture" and "cultural heritage" as a set of similar products created from long-term social reality construction under similar objective and symbolic realities.

6. See Altheide, 1984; Altheide and Snow, 1991; Cohen and Young, 1981; Knight and Dean, 1982; Lichter, 1988; Quinney, 1970; and Tuchman, 1978.

7. See Barber, 1987; Best, 1989; Cohen et al., 1990; Dominick, 1978; Graber, 1979; Greenberg, 1969; Hawkins and Pingree, 1982; Knight and Dean, 1982; Quinney, 1970; Stroman and Seltzer, 1985; and Surette, 1992.

8. Kappeler and his colleagues (1993) describe the process of rapid electronic-based communication systems enabling myths to spread in unprecedented numbers and with frightening speed. Quoting Sutherland (1950: 143), they state: "Fear is produced more readily in the modern community than it was earlier in our history because of increased publicity." What was once restricted to small groups is now instantly projected to millions of people internationally by the mass media. (Kappeler et al., 1993: 4). In addition, myth-makers do not simply uncover crime and transmit information: they serve to structure

reality by selecting and characterizing events—thereby cultivating images of crime (Kappeler et al., 1993: 14 citing Lang and Lang, 1969; Gerbner, 1972; Schoenfeld, Meier and Griffin, 1979).

9. See Bortner, 1984; Jones, 1976; Antunes and Hurley, 1977; Pandiani, 1978; Sherizen, 1978; Graber, 1980.

10. See Estep and MacDonald, 1984: 5; Lichter and Lichter, 1983: 10.

11. The single most common portrait of a television criminal is an upper-middle-class person gone berserk with greed. See Estep and MacDonald, 1984: 7–8; Pandiani, 1978. Regarding corrections, they are often referenced via indirect negative allusions to an alumni group of ex-con offenders. In that habitual criminals outnumber first offenders by more than four to one, any rehabilitative ability of corrections is shown as marginal in the entertainment media (Lichter and Lichter, 1983: 29). Instead, corrections are suggested as being simple way stations for predatory criminals, frequently returning worse criminals to society than they receive. While corrections have not been ignored by the film industry, unfortunately its image in film is just as negative (Zaner, 1989).

12. An associated feature in these media portrayals involves the use of violence. The evolution of twentieth-century media crime violence has been to portray the crime fighter and criminal as more and more violent and aggressive and to show this violence more graphically (Rosow, 1978: 326–327; Shadoian, 1977: 212). The distinction between the crime fighter and criminal has become insignificant. Regarding weapons, they have become more technical and sophisticated but less realistic over the years. The portrayal of their effectiveness, especially of handguns, is often either ridiculously benign, so that misses are common and wounds minor and painless (usually when the hero is shot at), or ridiculously deadly (usually when the hero is shooting) so that shots from handguns accurately hit moving, distant people, killing them quickly and without extensive suffering (Stark, 1987; Bortner, 1984).

13. In one study by Sheley and Ashkins (1981: 499–500), murder and robbery account for approximately 45 percent of newspaper crime news and 80 percent of television crime news. Similarly, Graber (1980: 39–40) reports that murder constituted 0.2 percent of the crime known to the police, whereas it was 26.2 percent of crime news, and while nonviolent crime equaled 47 percent of crimes known, it comprises only 4 percent of crime news stories. Two examples of molding news coverage to fit the predator icon are offered by Best and Horiuchi's study of Halloween poison candy stories that were broadcast as anonymous predator criminal attacks but were in actuality family

member poisonings. They state (1985: 490): "... neither case fit the image of a maniacal killer randomly attacking children. Five-year-old Kevin Toston died after eating heroin supposedly hidden in his Halloween candy. ... Newspapers gave less coverage to the fact that Kevin had found the heroin in his uncle's home. ... Eight-year-old Timothy O'Bryan died after eating candy contaminated with cyanide. Investigators concluded that his father had contaminated the treat." See also Bortner, 1984: 3; Dominick, 1978: 108; Marsh, 1991; and Roshier, 1973: 32.

14. See Surette, 1989, 1992.

15. See Surette, 1992 and Cavender and Bond-Maupin, forthcoming, for reviews.

16. Nearly 66 percent of the cases reported in Graber's study were due to personal quarrels, greed, and the like, and the public perceives the cause of crime as clearly residing in offender deficiencies (Graber, 1980: 70–71).

17. Cavender and Bond-Maupin, forthcoming, citing Katz (1987) and Best (1989).

18. Note these values do not include murders. The rate for all violent crime (stranger and nonstranger) victimization in 1990 is 29.5 per 1000.

19. *Sourcebook of Criminal Justice Statistics 1991* (1992), Table 3.2, "Number and Rate (per 1000 units of each respective category) of Personal and Household Victimizations," p. 257.

20. Due to the assumptions underlying the estimates of victimization likelihood, estimates tend to show a slightly larger number of people being victimized at least once than is actually the case. This positive bias is counterbalanced somewhat by an underestimation bias regarding series victimizations. See Koppel, 1987, p. 5.

21. *Sourcebook of Criminal Justice Statistics 1991* (1992), Table 3.3, "Respondents Reporting Whether They Have Been Hit by Another Person," pp. 288–289. Since 1986 the rate has held fairly steady between 36 percent and 34 percent of respondents responding yes to the question: "Have you ever been punched or beaten by another person?" The percentage peaked in 1983 when 46 percent answered yes.

22. In their statistics they combine murders and non-negligent manslaughters together.

23. *Sourcebook of Criminal Justice Statistics 1991* (1992), Table 3.128 "Percent Distribution of Murders and Non-Negligent Manslaughters Known to Police," p. 398. The peak year was 1981 with 21,860 murders.

24. *Sourcebook of Criminal Justice Statistics 1991* (1992), Table 3.127 "Estimated Number and Rate (per 100,000 inhabitants) of Offenses Known to Police," p. 372.

25. *Sourcebook of Criminal Justice Statistics 1991* (1992), Table 3.140 "Percent Distribution of Murders and Non-Negligent Man-slaughters Known to Police," p. 399.

26. For a discussion of the demographics and general exposure of viewers to media violence, see Israel, Simmons and Associates, and Robinson (1972).

27. See de Tocqueville, 1981; Bellah et al., 1985; Gans, 1988.

28. While it unduly benefits those at the top who get personal credit for the successes of the organizations or corporations they head (Gans, 1988: 96).

29. For example, Anne Heinz (1985) notes that professions dominate the criminal justice process, especially prosecution-oriented groups that tend to criminalize behavior and increase punitiveness.

30. Langworthy and Whitehead (1986 citing Sheley, 1985) list three sources of fear of crime; victimization experiences, political campaigns, and general media content. They see the media playing a role in all three sources.

31. See Barrile, 1984; Cavender and Bond-Maupin, forthcoming; Hennigan et al., 1982; Reiner, 1985; Surette, 1985.

32. For an overview, see Doppelt and Manikas, 1990; Surette, 1992.

33. It has been noted that during periods of increased stress from multiple, simultaneous social problems, the American cultural traditions of individualism and avoidance result in increased support for punitiveness and law and order (Scheingold, 1984: 75).

34. *Sourcebook of Criminal Justice Statistics 1991* (1992), Table 2.24 "Fear of Violent Victimization," p. 191.

35. *Sourcebook of Criminal Justice Statistics 1991* (1992), Table 2.27 "Attitudes toward Walking Alone at Night and Safety at Home" p. 195.

36. *Sourcebook of Criminal Justice Statistics 1991* (1992), Table 2.26 "Attitudes toward Crime Rate in Own Area and Uneasiness on the Streets," p. 195.

37. *Sourcebook of Criminal Justice Statistics 1991* (1992), Table 2.29 "Reported Fear of being Attacked or Robbed," p. 198.

38. Cavender and Bond-Maupin (forthcoming, citing Gitlin, 1979 and Schattenberg, 1981) discuss similar ideas in terms of reality crime programming.

39. Eliot Currie (1985), David Duffee (1980), Diana Gordon (1990), and Stuart Scheingold (1984) all discuss the lack of evidence regarding the criminal justice system's effects.

REFERENCES

Adoni, H. and S. Mane. 1984. "Media and the social construction of reality." *Communication Research*, 11, 3: 323–340.

Altheide D. 1984. "TV news and the social construction of justice: Research issues and policy." in *Justice and The Media*. R. Surette (ed.). Springfield, IL: Charles C. Thomas Pub.

Altheide, D. and R. Snow. 1991. *Media Worlds in the Postjournalism Era*. New York: Aldine de Gruyter.

Antunes, G. and P. Hurley. 1977. "The representation of criminal events in Houston's two daily newspapers." *Journalism Quarterly*, 54: 756–760.

Barber, S. 1987. *News Cameras in the Courtroom*. Norwood, NJ: Ablex Pub.

Barrile, L. 1984. "Television and attitudes about crime: Do heavy viewers distort criminality and support retributive justice?." in *Justice and the Media*. R. Surette (ed.). Springfield, IL: Charles C. Thomas Pub.

Bazelon, D. 1978. "The hidden politics of American criminology." In John Conrad, *The Evolution of Criminal Justice*, pp. 12–27. Newbury Park, CA: Sage.

Bellah, R., R. Madsen, W. Sullivan, A. Swidler, and S. Tipton. 1985. *Habits of the Heart*. Berkeley: University of California Press.

Best, J. (ed.). 1989. *Images of Issues: Typifying Contemporary Social Problems*. New York: Aldine de Gruyter.

Best, J. and G. Horiuchi. 1985. "The razor and the apple: The social construction of urban legends." *Social Problems*, 32: 488–499.

Bortner, M. A. 1984. "Media images and public attitudes toward crime and justice." In *Justice and The Media*, R. Surette, (ed.). Springfield, IL: Charles C. Thomas Pub.

Carlson, J. 1985. *Prime Time Law Enforcement*. New York: Praeger.

Cavender, G. and L. Bond-Maupin. forthcoming. "Fear and loathing on reality television: An analysis of 'America's Most Wanted' and 'Unsolved Mysteries.'" *Sociological Inquiry*.

Cohen, A., T. Adoni, and C. Bantz. 1990. *Social Conflict and Television News*. Newbury Park, CA: Sage.

Cohen, S. and J. Young. 1981. *The Manufacture of News*. Newbury Park, CA: Sage.

Criminal Victimization in the United States, 1990. 1992. Bureau of Justice Statistics U.S. Department of Justice, Washington, D.C.: U.S. Govt. Printing Office.

Culver, J. and K. Knight. 1979. "Evaluating TV impressions of law-enforcement roles." In *Evaluating Alternative Law Enforcement Policies*. R. Baker and F. Mayer, (eds.). Lexington, MA: Lexington Books.

Currie, E. 1985. *Confronting Crime*. New York: Pantheon Books.

Dominick, J. 1978. "Crime and law enforcement in the mass media." In *Deviance and Mass Media*. Newbury Park, CA: Sage, pp. 105–128.

Doppelt, J. and P. Manikas. 1990. "Mass media and criminal justice decision making." In *The Media and Criminal Justice Policy*. R. Surette (ed.). Springfield, IL: Charles C. Thomas Pub.

Duffee, D. 1980. *Explaining Criminal Justice*. Cambridge, MA: Oelgeschlager, Gunn and Hain.

Elias, R. 1986. *The Politics of Victimization*. New York: Oxford University Press.

Estep, R. and P. MacDonald. 1984. "How prime-time crime evolved on TV, 1976 to 1983." In *Justice and the Media*. R. Surette (ed.). Springfield, IL: Charles C. Thomas Pub.

Gans, H. 1988. *Middle American Individualism*. New York: The Free Press.

Garofalo, J. 1981. "Crime and the mass media: A selective review of research." *Journal of Research in Crime and Delinquency*, 18: 319–350.

Gerbner, G. 1972. "Communication and social environment." *Scientific American*, 227: 153–160.

Gerbner, G. and L. Gross. 1980. "The violent face of television and its lessons." In *Children and the Faces of Television*. E. Palmer and A. Dorr. (eds.). New York: Academic Press.

———. 1976. "Living with television: The violence profile." *Journal of Communication*, 26: 173–199.

Gerbner, G., L. Gross, M. Jackson-Beech, S. Jeffries-Fox, and N. Signorielli. 1978. "Cultural indicators: Violence profile no. 9." *Journal of Communication*, 29: 176–207.

Gerbner, G., L. Gross, M. Morgan, and N. Signorielli. 1980. "The mainstreaming of America: Violence profile no. 11." *Journal of Communication*, 30: 10–29.

Gerbner, G., L. Gross, N. Signorielli, M. Morgan, and M. Jackson-Beech. 1979. "The demonstration of power: Violence profile no. 10." *Journal of Communication*, 29: 177–196.

Gitlin, T. 1979. "Prime time ideology: The hegemonic process in television entertainment." *Social Problems*, 26: 251–266.

Gordon, D. 1990. *The Justice Juggernaut*. New Brunswick, NJ: Rutgers University Press.

Gottfredson, M. and T. Hirschi. 1990. *A General Theory of Crime*. Stanford, CA: Stanford University Press.

Graber, D. 1980. *Crime News and the Public*. New York: Praeger.

———. 1979. "Evaluating crime-fighting policies." In *Evaluating Alternative Law Enforcement Policies*. R. Baker and F. Meyer (eds.). Lexington, MA: Lexington Books.

Greenberg, B. 1969. "The content and context of violence in the media." In Baker, R. and Ball, S. (eds.). *Violence and The Media*. Washington, D.C.: U.S. Govt. Printing Office, pp. 423–449.

Hawkins, R. and S. Pingree. 1982. "Television's influence on social reality." *Television and Behavior: Ten Years of Scientific Progress and Implications for the Eighties*. Vol. 2: Technical Reviews David Pearl, Lorraine Bouthilet, Joyce Lazar, (eds.). Washington, D.C.: U.S. Govt. Printing Office.

Heinz, A. 1985. "The political context for the changing content of criminal law." In E. Fairchild and V. Webb, *The Politics of Crime and Criminal Justice*. Newbury Park, CA: Sage.

Hennigan, K., L. Heath, J. Wharton, M. Del Rosario, T. Cook, and B. Calder. 1982. "Impact of the introduction of television on crime in the United States." *Journal of Personality and Social Psychology*, 42: 461–477.

Israel, H., W. Simmons and Associates, and J. Robinson. 1972. "Demographic characteristics of viewers of television violence and news programs." In E. Rubinstein, G. Comstock, J. Murray (eds.). *Television and Social Behavior, Reports and papers*, Vol. IV, *Television in Day-to-day Life Patterns of Use*. Washington, D.C.: U.S. Govt. Printing Office.

Jenkins, P. 1988. "Myth and Murder: The Serial Killer Panic of 1983–85." *Criminal Justice Research Bulletin*, 3, 11.

Jones, E. T. 1976. "The press as metropolitan monitor." *Public Opinion Quarterly*, 40: 239–244.

Kappeler, V., M. Blumberg, and G. Potter. 1993. *The Mythology of Crime and Criminal Justice*. Prospect Heights, IL: Waveland Press.

Katz, J. 1987. "What makes crime news?" *Media, Culture and Society*, 9: 47–75.

Knight G. and T. Dean. 1982. "Myth and the structure of news." *Journal of Communication*, (Spring) 32, 2: 144–161.

Koppel, H. 1987. "Lifetime likelihood of victimization." *Bureau of Justice Statistics Technical Report*, U.S. Department of Justice. Washington, D.C.: U.S. Govt. Printing Office.

Lang, K. and G. Lang. 1969. *Television and Politics*. Chicago: Quadrangle Books.

Langworthy R. and J. Whitehead. 1986. "Liberalism and fear as explanations of punitiveness." *Criminology*, 24, 3: 575–591.

Lichter, S. 1988. "Media power: The influence of media on politics and business." *Florida Policy Review*, 4: 35–41.

Lichter, L. and S. Lichter. 1983. *Prime Time Crime*. Washington, D.C.: The Media Institute.

McArthur, C. 1972. *Underworld*. New York: Viking Press.

Marsh, H. 1991. "A comparative analysis of crime coverage in newspapers in the United States and other countries from 1960–1989: A review of the literature." *Journal of Criminal Justice*, 194: 67–79.

Meyrowitz, J. 1985. *No Sense of Place*. New York: Oxford University Press.

Pandiani, J. 1978. "Crime time TV: If all we knew is what we saw. . . ." *Contemporary Crises*, 2: 437–458.

Papke, D. 1987. *Framing the Criminal*. Hamden, CT: Archon Books.

Quinney, R. 1970. *The Social Reality of Crime*. Boston: Little, Brown and Co.

Reiner, R. 1985. *The Politics of the Police*. New York: St. Martin's Press.

Rennie, Y. 1978. *The Search for Criminal Man*. Lexington, MA: Lexington Books.

Roshier, B. 1973. "The selection of crime news in the press." In S. Cohen and J. Young (eds.). *The Manufacture of News*. Newbury Park, CA: Sage, pp. 28–39.

Rosow, E. 1978. *Born to Lose*. New York: Oxford University Press.

Schattenberg, G. 1981. "Social control functions of mass media depictions of crime." *Sociological Inquiry*, 51: 71–77.

Scheingold, S. 1984. *The Politics of Law and Order: Street Crime and Public Policy*. New York: Longman.

Schneider, J. 1985. "Social problems theory: The constructionist view." *Annual Review of Sociology*, 11: 209–229.

Schoenfeld, A., R. Meier, and R. Griffin. 1979. "Constructing a social problem: The press and the environment." *Social Problems*, 27: 38–61.

Schur, E. 1969. *Our Criminal Society*. 4th ed. Englewood Cliffs, NJ: Prentice Hall.

Shadoian, J. 1977. *Dreams and Dead Ends*. Cambridge: MIT Press.

Sheley, J. 1985. *America's Crime Problem: An Introduction to Criminology*. Belmont, CA: Wadsworth.

Sheley, J. and C. Ashkins. 1981. "Crime, crime news, and crime views" *Public Opinion Quarterly*, 45: 492–506.

Sherizen, S. 1978. "Social creation of crime news." In C. Winick (ed.). *Deviance and Mass Media*. Newbury Park, CA: Sage.

Skogan, W. and M. Maxfield. 1981. *Coping with Crime: Individual and Neighborhood Reactions*. Newbury Park, CA: Sage.

Sourcebook of Criminal Justice Statistics 1991. 1992. Bureau of Justice Statistics, T. Flanagan and K. Maguire (eds.). The Hindelang Criminal Justice Research Center. Washington, D.C.: U.S. Govt. Printing Office.

Stark, S. 1987. "Perry Mason meets Sonny Crockett: The history of lawyers and the police as television heroes." *University of Miami Law Review*, 42: 229–283.

Stroman, C. and R. Seltzer. 1985. " Media use and perceptions of crime." *Journalism Quarterly*, 62: 340–345.

Surette, R. 1985. "Television viewing and support of punitive criminal justice policy." *Journalism Quarterly*, 62: 373–377,450.

————. 1989. "Media trials." *The Journal of Criminal Justice,* 17: 293–308.

————. 1992. *Media Crime and Criminal Justice: Images and Realities.* Pacific Grove, CA: Brooks/Cole.

————. 1993. "Police Recruits and The Media." Unpublished manuscript.

Sutherland, E. 1950. "The diffusion of sexual psychopath laws." *American Journal of Sociology,* 56: 142–48.

Tauchen, H., A. Witte, and H. Griesinger. 1992. "Criminal deterrence: Revisiting the issue with a birth cohort." BNDD Working Paper.

Toch, Hans. 1969. *Violent Men: An Inquiry into the Psychology of Violence.* Chicago: Aldine.

Tocqueville, Alexis de. 1981. *Democracy in America* (abridged). Thomas Bender, trans. New York: Random House.

Tuchman, G. 1978. *Making News: A Study in the Construction of Reality.* Glencoe, IL: Free Press.

Zaner, L. 1989. "The screen test: Has Hollywood hurt corrections' image?" *Corrections Today,* 51: 64–66, 94, 95, 98.

CHAPTER 6

University Professor or Sadistic Killer? A Content Analysis of the Newspaper Coverage of a Murder Case

Harry L. Marsh

In December 1982, the body of a young man was discovered in a field in rural Vermillion County, Indiana. The young man, later identified as Steve Agan of Terre Haute, Indiana, had been brutally beaten and stabbed many times:

> On a cold December night in 1982 a young man agreed to accompany two other men to an abandoned farm in rural Indiana. The young man had agreed to participate in a "bondage scene." At the farm, the three men entered a barn together, only two were to leave alive. Upon entering the barn one of the two men bound the young man's wrists and ankles and suspended him from one of the barn's wooden suspension beams. The other man began to masturbate and to take photographs of the young man who was being bound and suspended from the beam above him. The young man's eyes were covered with an elastic bandage and his mouth was covered with four layers of duct tape, so as to muffle his voice. After the young man was bound and gagged, his pants were pulled down, and then the man with the camera directed his accomplice to "kill the motherf-----." The second man then stabbed the bound man in the chest. The man with the camera then grabbed the knife and began to stab the victim while continuing to masturbate. After the victim was dead one of the men beat the lifeless body with a

piece of wood. Then the two men released the body from the beam and dragged it outside. There the man with the camera ordered the second man to finish the victim off, and as he continued to take photographs, the second man sliced open the victim's chest cavity with a knife. The two men then got into their vehicle and returned to their residence, where they prepared for their Christmas vacations.[1]

On October 21, 1990, an article in *The Tribune-Star* linked Agan's death to convicted murderer Larry Eyler, who was awaiting execution in Illinois for an unrelated murder (Kaufman, 1990). During a courtroom confession in December 1990, Larry Eyler accused Dr. Robert David Little, a professor at Indiana State University, Terre Haute, Indiana, of directing and actively participating in the murder of Steve Agan in December 1982 [Baker, December 13, 1990; Pastore, December 14, 1990]. From October 21, 1990, to July 18, 1991, two newspapers, *The Tribune-Star (TTS)* and *The Daily Clintonian (TDC)*, would publish a combined total of 124 news items pertaining to this case. Much of this coverage contained statements and information that could be construed as being prejudicial or biased toward Professor Little.

Literature reviews have disclosed that newspaper coverage of crime has been a source of criticism for more than a hundred years and alleged bias in newspaper crime coverage has been a research topic since the 1960s. The research in the area of newspaper bias has generally focused on one or more of the following issues: racism, the portrayal of victims and offenders in criminal cases, or agencies of the criminal justice system (Marsh, 1989; 1991).

Research findings regarding alleged racism have been mixed. Four studies reported the existence of racial bias (Abbott and Calonico, 1974; Karmen, 1978; Einstadter, 1979; Humphries, 1981), while three studies reported finding no racial bias (Dulaney, 1969; Fedler and Jordan, 1982; Galliher and Tyree, 1985). One study found that only the prosecutor's point of view was normally reported in criminal cases (Drechsel et al., 1980: 78). This is important to the current study as, generally, the prosecutor's view would be contrary to that of the alleged offender. Karmen found that victims are generally viewed in a favorable light, while personal data regarding suspects is usually not favorable (1978: 187). Karmen's findings are of paramount concern herein, as this study is concerned with the possible deleterious effects newspaper coverage might have on the defendant in a murder trial.

Research Concerns and Questions

Portrayal of the Defendant/Victim

Several research issues had to be considered prior to embarking on this content analysis of newspaper crime coverage. First, there has been little research regarding the portrayal of offenders and alleged offenders in the newspapers (Cromer, 1978: 226). A notable exception is Wilkie's (1981) study of the press coverage of Bruno Richard Hauptmann's trial for the kidnap/murder of Charles Lindbergh's baby. However, the Hauptmann trial can hardly be equated with the average murder trial. For example, Wilkie states that the Lindbergh kidnapping could be characterized "as a crime of national importance" as Charles Lindbergh was a "recognized symbol of American ideals" (1981: 103). The defendant and victim in the current study were relatively unknown outside a small circle of friends, family, and co-workers. Thus the coverage of the trial should more closely approach the average murder trial than did that of the Hauptmann trial.

Guilt Attribution

A second concern is the possible effect of newspaper coverage on the reader's perception of the defendant's guilt or innocence. Surette has stated that there is "some evidence that the media's impact on courtroom participants may be declining . . ." (1984: 326). This may be true as today's citizens are exposed to a variety of news sources including television, radio and various news magazines.

However, the researcher must be cognizant of other areas in which the defendant's life may be affected. For example, Shaffer reported that "most of the literature finds that pretrial publicity increases the probability of guilt attribution, even after jury deliberation" (1986: 156). This suggests that even though the defendant has been acquitted by a jury, a segment of the population may continue to believe that he or she is guilty.

There are two possible causes of this attribution of guilt. One possibility is that kind of "news which, however legitimate, may not be relevant by judicial standards . . ." (Friendly and Goldfarb, 1967: 87). For example, the newspaper may report that the defendant refused to take a polygraph examination. This may imply guilt to the reader, but it has little relevance in the courtroom. Another possibility occurs when the press prints statements of unqualified people it often invests "with a 'halo effect' and the material with authenticity" (Shelton, 1965: 120). This could result, for example, from a statement by a witness at the trial that the prosecutor or defense attorney did not "ask the right questions." This might imply that if the witness had been asked the "right" question, the outcome of the trial would have been different.

Prejudicial Factors

The final concern is the determination of which newspaper coverage is, or is not, prejudicial to the defendant. In a qualitative study it is important that the prejudicial factors selected be acceptable to other researchers. Friendly and Goldfarb suggest that prejudicial factors may be "specific items of news that either do not make their way into evidence at the trial or that come to the attention of jurors before the trial, unconfronted and unexamined . . ." (1967: 86). Wilkie suggests a number of factors that could be prejudicial to include: "identity, testimony, or credibility of witness . . . possibility of guilty plea . . . opinions as to guilt or innocence of the accused . . . characterization of the crime itself" (1981: 101). The foregoing suggests that the factors that could be prejudicial to an accused individual are many and they are varied in nature.

Three Core Questions

This study is concerned with trying to obtain the answers to three core questions: How was the accused portrayed in the newspaper coverage of this murder case? Did the coverage attribute guilt to the accused after the jury had reached its verdict of innocence? What, if any, prejudicial factors against the accused were incorporated into the newspaper coverage of this crime? The answers to these questions should provide some insight on the issue of newspaper bias in crime and criminal justice coverage.

Data and Methodology

The data for this study was obtained from two newspapers. One newspaper, *The Tribune-Star*, is located in Vigo County and Terre Haute, Indiana, where the accused lives and works and where the victim lived prior to his death. The other newspaper, *The Daily Clintonian*, is located in Vermillion County, Indiana, where the murder occurred and the trial was conducted. *The Tribune-Star* is a regional newspaper that serves a number of western Indiana and eastern Illinois counties and communities. The newspaper is published seven days a week. *The Daily Clintonian* is a local newspaper with a circulation primarily confined to Vermillion County and the city of Clinton, Indiana. The newspaper is published Monday through Friday. There are no Saturday or Sunday editions.

Coverage of the case by *The Tribune-Star* and *The Daily Clintonian* was divided into three stages found in the criminal justice process (see Tables 6.1 and 6.2). The stages are: pre-arrest/arrest, pretrial/trial, and post-trial. The newspapers' coverage of the murder case included articles by reporters, editorials, and letters to the editor.

TABLE 6.1

Coverage by *The Tribune-Star* (n=94)

CJ stage	Articles by Reporters	Editorials	Letters to the Editor
Pre-arrest/ Arrest	10	0	0
Pre-trial/ Trial	61	4	5
Post-trial	12	1	1
Totals	83	5	6

TABLE 6.2

Coverage by *The Daily Clintonian* (n=30)

CJ stage	Articles by Reporters	Editorials	Letters to the Editor
Pre-arrest/ Arrest	7	0	0
Pre-trial/ Trial	19	0	0
Post-trial	1	0	3
Totals	27	0	3

These stages of the criminal justice process were used in an attempt to determine the potential impact of the coverage at the pretrial, trial and post-trial stages. The pretrial and trial stages are important in assessing how the defendant is portrayed in the newspaper coverage and the post-trial stage is important in ascertaining the possible impact on the attribution of guilt question.

The types of coverage are important for two distinct reasons. First, those articles attributed to the reporters and newspaper editors tend to reflect the views of the agencies (e.g., law enforcement and prosecution) and individuals (e.g., police and witnesses) involved in the case. The editorials tend to reflect the views of either the newspaper or editors. The letters to the editors reflect the views of the readers and they help to ascertain the impact of the coverage on these individuals. However, whether the letters reflect the general view of the population at large is beyond the scope of this study.

In order to facilitate the reading of this study, and to give credit where it is due, the names of the contributing reporters will be used when possible. *The Daily Clintonian's* coverage of this murder case (twenty-seven articles) was accomplished by one reporter, Gene Baker, II. *The Tribune-Star's* primary coverage was the work of one reporter, Patricia Pastore. She wrote seventy-two of the eighty-three articles that appeared in her newspaper. Of the remaining eleven articles, three were written by one reporter, two by another reporter, two other reporters wrote one article each, and the four remaining articles were not credited to a specific reporter.

Content analysis research is necessarily concerned with what is written or said about a particular person or topic. For this study it was necessary to select a number of "prejudicial factors" that could be interpreted as being biased against the accused. The works of Friendly and Goldfarb (1967) and Wilkie (1981) were most helpful in determining what prejudicial factors to look for. The following is a list of six prejudicial factors selected for this study:

1. Characterization of the crime.
2. Characterization of the accused.
3. Statements or information that were not submitted or allowed in court.
4. Statements or testimony given untested or unsupported authenticity.
5. Individuals given untested or unsupported credibility.
6. Opinions about the guilt of the accused.

Findings

Each of the news articles pertaining to this case was scrutinized for statements or information that could be interpreted as being prejudicial in content. A number of statements were found to be potentially prejudicial toward the defendant in this case. However, fourteen of these statements have been singled out due to the repetitiveness of their appearance in the newspapers' coverage of Professor Little's case (see Table 6.3 and Table 6.4). It should be noted that the total (159) number of times the fourteen statements were repeated (Tables 6.3 and 6.4) exceeds the number (124) of articles published (Tables 6.1 and 6.2) because some of the articles contained more than one prejudicial statement. The combined number of times the prejudicial statements were repeated in the two newspapers through the pre-arrest and trial stages varied from a high of twenty-nine (Table 6.3, Statement 3) to a low of five (Table 6.3, Statements 6, 7, and 10). Two prejudicial statements were repeated twice in each newspaper during the post-trial stage (Table 6.4, Statements 1 and 2). Furthermore, the majority of the statements (151) were published during the pre-arrest through trial stages, rather than the post-trial stage (8).

Pre-Arrest/Arrest Stage

On October 21, 1990, Kaufman's article linked Eyler's name to Steve Agan and a series of unsolved murders of male homosexuals that occurred during the early 1980s. Kaufman indicated that Steve Agan was not known to be gay or to hustle for sex; however, she quoted one unnamed reporter as saying of the murders of gay men: "'So a queer is killing queers—who cares? Good way to get rid of 'em'" [Kaufman, 1990: C,3].

On December 14, 1990, Pastore [*TTS*: A,6] wrote an article titled "Larry Eyler tells court about night of wild sex acts that led to murder" which in itself could be deemed as prejudicial in nature. This article also contained several statements that could be considered prejudicial towards Little. The statements were made by Eyler during his appearance in court to plead guilty to Agan's murder. Eyler and his attorney had arranged a plea bargain wherein Eyler was to receive a sixty-year sentence if he confessed to Agan's murder and testified against anyone else involved in the killing.

During his court appearance Eyler implicated his housemate Little in Agan's murder. Baker wrote that Eyler stated he and Little had picked up Agan in Terre Haute and that Eyler had "determined Agan was gay" [*TDC*, December 13, 1990: 1]. Baker did not indicate how, or on what factors, Eyler had based his determination. Baker and Pastore reported that Eyler had testified that Agan had willingly accompanied Eyler and Little to the location of his death, and that Agan had agreed to have sex with Little and to engage in a sexual bondage scenario [*TTS*, December 14, 1990; *TDC*, December 13, 1990]. Pastore reported that Eyler stated that Agan "told Little that he had never done anything like that before . . ." [*TTS*, December 14, 1990: A,1]. Both Baker and Pastore reported that Eyler said Little had directed him to stab Agan by saying, "kill the motherf-----. " (Table 6.3). Pastore's article contained two separate references to Little's masturbating and taking photographs (Table 6.3) while Agan was being tied up, and that Little had continued to masturbate as he joined Eyler in stabbing Agan (Table 6.3) to death [*TTS*, December 14, 1990: A,1,6; *TDC*, December 13, 1990: 1]. Baker's article [December 13] made mention of Little's masturbating only once. In addition, Pastore reported that Eyler stated that Little was upset and said, "This went too fast" and after helping Eyler move the body, Little told Eyler to "finish him off," even though Agan was already dead [*TTS*, December 14, 1990: A,6]. In a later article, Pastore wrote that Eyler said, "Little orchestrated the murder, directed it like a theater play and photographed the scene while Agan was being tortured and killed. . . ." (see Table 6.3) [*TTS*, December 16, 1990: A,1].

Baker and Pastore reported that Eyler stated that the photographs taken by Little of the Agan murder were in Little's bedroom when Little's home was searched during the original Agan murder investigation in 1982–1983; however, Baker indicated the Agan photographs ". . . were apparently discovered during a search of Little's Terre Haute home on Saturday" [*TTS*, December 14, A,6; *TDC*, December 13, 1990: 1,4]. On December 17, 1990, Baker and Pastore quoted the Vermillion County Sheriff as saying about Eyler, "Little used him to get his bondage victims" (Table 6.3) and he "believes photos made by

Little of the Agan murder were used to assure Eyler's silence"
(Table 6.3) [*TDC*, 1; *TTS*, A, 1].

It is important to note that neither Baker nor Pastore
reported that Little was not a suspect at the time the initial
search was made in his home. However, Eyler was the only
suspect at that time. Therefore, the search warrant only
pertained to areas of the house that were occupied by Eyler, and
thus, it did not include Little's bedroom.

TABLE 6.3

Prejudicial Statements: Pre-arrest through Trial Stages

Statements	No. Articles in *TTS*	No. Articles *TDC*
1. Little directed Eyler to stab Agan by saying "kill the motherf-----."	6	1
2. Little "masturbated and photographed Agan" as he was being stabbed by Eyler.	16	3
3. "Little orchestrated the murder, directed it like a theater play and photographed the scene while Agan was being tortured and killed."	25	4
4. "Polygraph shows Eyler told truth."	3	4
5. Little "used his influence to control others" and to get others to get "his bondage victims."	10	4
6. Little was involved in "homosexual bondage activities."	4	1
7. Police seized a book in Little's home that had "overtones of child pornography."	4	1

Statements	No. Articles in *TTS*	No. Articles *TDC*
8. Little "stabbed Agan while masturbating."	18	6
9. Little "participated in the killing of Agan."	16	2
10. Agan was killed for Little's "sexual gratification."	5	0
11. Little photographed the Agan murder in order to "assure Eyler's silence."	18	6
12. Photographs seized in Little's home depicted "Little and other men engaged in homosexual acts."	7	4
Total	120	31

Note: *TTS* refers to *The Tribune-Star* and *TDC* refers to *The Daily Clintonian.* (1990).

During his courtroom confession, Eyler also accused Little of killing another man, Danny Bridges, in Chicago, Illinois in August 1984. Eyler had been previously convicted of Bridges' murder and was sentenced to die by lethal injection [Baker, TDC, December 13, 1990: 4]. On December 14, 1990, Eyler's attorney, and the prosecutor and sheriff of Vermillion County were quoted as saying that Eyler "had no reason to name Little as an accomplice" [Pastore, *TTS*, A,6]. Eyler's attorney also stated that Eyler "just wanted to clear his conscience" [Pastore, *TTS*, A,6; Baker, *TDC*, 1]. On December 15, 1990, Pastore reported that law enforcement personnel from Ohio were interested in Little as a possible suspect in a number of unsolved murders in that state [*TTS*, A,1].

Pre-Trial/Trial Stage

Professor Little's arrest and court arraignment occurred on December 18, 1990. He pleaded innocent to the charge of murdering Agan and was placed in jail without bail. Pastore quoted an unnamed woman as saying of Little, "My God, he's just been charged with murder and he's totally emotionless" [*TTS*, December 19, 1990: A,1]. Pastore also reported that Little's attorney would not answer a question about why Little paid for Eyler's apartment in Chicago or why Little paid $25,000 for Eyler's defense in the Danny Bridges' murder case [*TTS*, December 19, 1990: A,1].

On December 19, 1990, Pastore wrote two articles containing information that could be termed as prejudicial toward Little. In an article titled "Polygraph shows Eyler told truth" (Table 6.3), Eyler's attorney advised that Eyler had taken a polygraph examination that indicated Eyler told the truth during his courtroom confession about the Agan murder [*TTS*, A,4]. On December 28, 1990, and January 7, 1991, Baker reported that Eyler had passed a polygraph test concerning his testimony about the Agan murder [*TDC*, 1]. In the article on January 7, Baker reported that Little's attorneys maintained that "statements made concerning polygraph tests were prejudicial to their client" [*TDC*, 1]. Twice during December 1990, Pastore wrote articles in which Eyler or his attorney challenged Little to submit to a polygraph examination regarding his involvement in the Agan murder [Pastore, *TTS*, December 19, A,4 and December 23, A,1].

On January 6, 1991, *The Tribune-Star* published an article by Pastore titled "Few knew alleged seamy side of Little's personality" that could be considered prejudicial in itself. The article contained a number of statements that appeared to be prejudicial toward Little. For example, statements attributed to some of Little's colleagues portrayed him "as a dominant figure who used his influence to control others" (Table 6.3) [*TTS*, A,1]. Two unidentified individuals were attributed as stating that Little was "the nucleus of a young homosexual bondage group" comprised of local university students [*TTS*, A,4]. Pastore quoted a former student as stating he had attended parties at Little's home in which drugs and movies involving homosexual bondage were present, and where guests engaged in homosexual activities involving bondage (Table 6.3) [*TTS*, A,4]. The former student also stated that due to Little's unattractive physical appearance he "used his close friends to meet other young men. They brought them to him" [*TTS*, A,4]. Finally, the Vermillion

County sheriff was quoted as saying he believed "Little moved Eyler to Chicago after police linked him to numerous murders in Indiana. It was getting too hot for Little to keep him in Terre Haute" [*TTS*, A,4].

In an article published during the voir dire stage of Little's trial, Pastore wrote that during a search of Little's home the police had "seized photographs that showed Little performing sexual acts on unidentified males, gay films and videotapes that depicted acts of violence" (Table 6.3) [*TTS*, April 2, 1991: A,3]. In three separate articles published during April 1991, Baker wrote that during a search of Little's home police had seized "photographs of men, including Little and unidentified men, depicting homosexual acts" (Table 6.3) [*TDC*, April 8, 1; *TDC*, April 9, 4; *TDC*, April 10, 1].

On April 6, 1991, Pastore described a request by Little's attorney to get certain evidence excluded from the trial. One such item was a sex education book for parents and children titled *Show Me* that contains photographs in lieu of drawings. Pastore wrote, the book had "overtones of child pornography" (Table 6.3) due to the photographs [*TTS*, A,1]. This appears to be Pastore's personal opinion, as she did not credit anyone else with making the observation.

On March 22, 1991, Pastore reported that a forensic psychiatrist, who conducted a psychological evaluation of Little's accuser, Larry Eyler, wrote in his report that Eyler had surrendered to Little's "perverse demand for destructive and violent action against Steve Agan" [*TTS*, A,4]. Pastore also wrote that the psychiatrist had concluded that Little had urged and directed Eyler to murder Agan [*TTS*, A,4].

On April 12, 1991, *The Tribune-Star* contained an article without a byline titled "Victims' families monitor proceedings." This article contained two quotes that might be considered prejudicial toward Little. Steve Agan's brother was quoted as saying of Little, "I think he did it and should be punished for the crime" [*TTS*, A,3]. The brother of another man, whose murder is still unsolved, was quoted as saying, "I think Eyler is telling the truth. I hope they get Little" [*TTS*, A,3]. In a subsequent article, Pastore quoted an unidentified woman as saying of Little and Eyler, "That is the worst atrocity that's ever been committed in this county. They just killed him for the fun of it" [TTS, April 4, 1991: A,4].

Pastore and Baker both published articles on April 18, 1991, stating that Professor Little had been acquitted of Agan's murder [TTS, A,1; TDC, 1,4]. However, Baker's article contained the following statement, "The verdict was met with disbelief from the spectators who had waited for five days to hear a guilty verdict" [TDC, 4].

Post-Trial Stage

On April 20, 1991, in an article, "Little trial juror uncomfortable with acquittal," Pastore reported interviewing a juror in the Little trial who said, "I feel we set a guilty man free" (Table 6.4) [TTS, A,1]. At that time, Pastore reported that other jurors did not want to discuss the verdict; however, on May 16, 1991, Pastore reported that another juror stated, "I had a gut feeling that he (Little) was guilty" [TTS, A,4]. Both jurors had stated they felt Little had "participated in the Agan murder" (Table 6.4) but the state had not proved its case. Thus, the jury had rendered a not guilty verdict.

Perhaps the most damaging of the post-trial news coverage was the result of conflict among the attorneys involved in the case. These individuals represent the legal system, yet their statements tended to cast doubt on the innocence of Professor Little, even though he had been acquitted of the murder of Agan. For example, Pastore reported that Larry Thomas, the former prosecutor of Vermillion County, had made the following statement about the Little trial: "It's my opinion this was one of the worst jobs of prosecution I've ever witnessed" [TTS, May 16, 1991: A,4]. It was also reported that Thomas had stated that he had spoken to one of the state's trial witnesses, and the individual told him the prosecutor at the trial "didn't ask him the right questions" [TTS, A,4].

TABLE 6.4

Prejudicial Statements—Post-trial Stage

Statements	No. Articles in *TTS*	No. Articles in *TDC*
1. Juror stated, ". . . we set a guilty man free."	2	2
2. Little "participated in the killing of Agan."	2	2
Total	4	4

Note: *TTS* refers to *The Tribune-Star* and *TDC* refers to *The Daily Clintonian.*

On May 9, 1991, *The Daily Clintonian* published a letter to the editor from Eyler's attorney, Kathleen T. Zellner. In her letter, Zellner listed twenty-two questions about the integrity and effectiveness of the Vermillion County prosecutor, the sheriff and at least one juror. Sixteen of the questions cast a shadow on Professor Little's innocence and his ultimate acquittal by the jury. Four of the questions that might be considered the most prejudicial were:

1. Why was the murder trial of Robert David Little left in the hands of a prosecutor with a 0–4 win/loss record . . . and who has never tried, much less won, a major trial?
2. Why did the prosecutor select a juror who, two weeks before the trial, was telling people that he would never vote to convict a college professor . . . ?
3. Why has a juror come forward saying that she thinks they set a guilty man free?
4. Why did the murder victim's mother call me after the verdict to tell me to deliver a message to Larry Eyler that the Agan family believed his confession?

On May 20, 1991, *The Daily Clintonian* published a letter to the editor from Larry C. Thomas, the former Vermillion County prosecutor, which contained two potentially prejudicial statements against Professor Little. Thomas wrote that the Little trial "was one of the worst jobs of prosecution" he had ever witnessed. Thomas also stated that a witness for the state had told him the prosecutor "had never asked him the right questions" during the trial. Both of these statements suggested Little was guilty of the Agan murder and that his acquittal was unjustified.

Discussion

This study was concerned with three basic issues: how the newspaper crime coverage portrayed the accused, whether this coverage could effect an attribution of guilt in the minds of the readers, and if the news coverage contained prejudicial factors against the accused.

These issues were analyzed in the following order: identification of potentially prejudicial factors, how the defendant was portrayed, and the possible effect on attribution of guilt toward the accused. This order was selected because the second and third issues can be logically derived from the first. In other words, prejudicial factors (statements and/or information) are the means by which the newspaper coverage portrayed the accused, and ultimately, both could have a potential impact on the individual reader's attribution of guilt.

Prejudicial Factors

This study was concerned with six potentially prejudicial factors. Each of the newspaper articles pertaining to this case was carefully examined to ascertain if it contained one or more of the six factors. Examples of all six prejudicial factors were found in the combined coverage of the two newspapers.

Factor One: Characterization of the Crime. Table 6.3 contains five statements (1, 2, 3, 8, and 10) that characterize the crime in a potentially prejudicial manner. For example, it was reported on nineteen separate occasions that Little directed Eyler to stab the victim by saying, "kill the motherf-----." (Table 6.3, Statement 1).

This statement could be interpreted as reflecting that the crime was premeditated and carried out with a total lack of remorse.

Perhaps the most damaging factor concerning the crime was the following statement: "Little orchestrated the murder, directed it like a theater play and photographed the scene while Agan was being tortured and killed" (Table 6.3, Statement 3). This statement contains several potentially prejudicial terms and it was repeated a total of twenty-nine times in the two newspapers' combined coverage. The terms "orchestrated" and "directed" indicate the crime was committed in a cold-blooded, callous manner. The word "torture" indicates the crime was particularly heinous and malicious in nature.

Factor Two: Characterization of the Accused. A number of potentially prejudicial factors were found regarding the accused's character. For example, the two newspapers reported on eleven occasions that photographs seized in the accused's home depicted "Little and other men engaged in homosexual acts" (Table 6.3, Statement 12). This statement regarding Little's alleged homosexual activities might not matter in the more cosmopolitan areas of the United States. However, in the highly conservative rural area in which the crime occurred, the statements could be considered highly prejudicial.

Two other statements (Table 6.3, Statements 5 and 6) referred to the accused's involvement in "homosexual" and "homosexual bondage" activities. Here again, the potential harm to the accused's character was increased by the conservative and rural nature of the area and its citizens. Homosexuality and bondage activities might be accepted with greater tolerance in some areas of the United States; however, in Vigo and Vermillion County, Indiana, such activity is rarely discussed, and probably even more rarely observed by their residents.

Perhaps the most damaging blow to the accused's character was the report that he possessed a book which had "overtones of child pornography" (Table 6.3, Statement 7). This statement was repeated a total of five times in the combined newspapers' coverage. With few exceptions (pedophiles) most Americans are offended by the idea of child pornography. This statement had little, or no, bearing on the murder case, but it clearly was prejudicial in regard to the accused's character.

Furthermore, it appears that the book may have had "overtones of child pornography" in the reporter's eyes only, as no other person was credited with making such an observation.

Factor Three: Statements or information that were not allowed in court. The two newspapers combined to publish several statements and items of information that were not admitted in court. The statement "Polygraph shows Eyler told truth," appeared three times in one newspaper and four times in the other (Table 6.3, Statement 4). Two separate articles contained challenges from Eyler and his attorney for the accused to submit to a polygraph examination. However, a polygraph examination of the accused had no legal bearing in this case as polygraph results are not admissible in court.[2]

The Vermillion County sheriff was quoted as saying that he believed "photos made by Little of the Agan murder were used to assure Eyler's silence" (Table 6.3, Statement 11). The two newspapers combined to publish the sheriff's opinion on twenty-four separate occasions.[3] In addition, *The Tribune-Star* quoted Steve Agan's brother as saying of Little, "I think he did it and should be punished for the crime" [April 12, 1991: A,3]. The same article contained the statement of another man who said, "I think Eyler is telling the truth. I hope they get Little" [*TTS*, A,3].

It is important to note that while the statements and/or opinions of the foregoing individuals were correctly reported (the individuals did make the statements), they were inadmissible in a court of law. Furthermore, the alleged photographs were never found, if, in fact, they ever existed. However, the court is concerned only with information and/or evidence that pertains to the legal facts of the matter at hand. Thus, while the newspapers' coverage may have been factual (reporting a person's stated opinion), the statements had no legal bearing on the case.[4]

As previously stated, polygraph results are not admissible in court. So whether the accused submitted to a polygraph examination, or whether Eyler's examination showed he was telling the truth, were irrelevant in the court's attempt to discover the legal facts of the case. Nevertheless, the factual knowledge that the accused did not take a polygraph examination could be interpreted by unknowing readers as an indication of his guilt or, at the least, an indication that he had something to hide. The results were potentially prejudicial toward the accused in either case.

Factor Four: Statements or testimony given untested or unsupported authenticity. This is one of the most difficult factors to analyze for two reasons. First, how does one establish to the satisfaction of all or even a majority of the readers that a statement has not been adequately tested? Second, the same problem exists when trying to establish that a statement lacks authenticity.

Two elements were used in this study in an attempt to assess whether a statement was considered to be untested or to lack authenticity. First, an attempt was made to determine whether the statement maker was identified or not, and whether the statement could be used to establish the legal facts of the case. Second, an assessment was made as to whether or not the statement could logically be classified as opinion or factual in content. With these caveats in place, it is suggested the following statements can be considered as either untested, or as lacking authenticity.

Several unidentified colleagues and two unidentified individuals (former students) were quoted as saying the accused was "a dominant figure, who used his influence to control others" and that he used others to get his "homosexual bondage victims" (Table 6.3, Statement 5). These statements were repeated together or separately on fourteen separate occasions.

The statement that the accused was "dominating" and "influenced others" could be used to describe many university and college professors, as well as many people who are professional, business, or government leaders. These characteristics, in themselves, have little to do with whether or not a person is a murderer.

An unidentified former student was quoted as saying the accused was "unattractive" and used others to "meet other young men." Whether or not a person is attractive is a matter of opinion. The student may have considered the accused "unattractive" but that should not be construed to mean everyone else would have the same opinion.

Finally, the Vermillion County sheriff stated, "Little moved Eyler to Chicago after police linked him to numerous murders in Indiana. It was getting too hot for Little. . . ." This is clearly the sheriff's opinion. There was no legally factual information of this nature presented to the court during the accused's trial. Also, Eyler had resided in the accused's home in 1982. During the original investigation into Agan's murder, the police searched Eyler's room. It is logical to believe that if Little had, in fact, been under suspicion, the police would have searched his possessions too. However, the police only searched the areas of Little's home that were occupied solely by Eyler.[5]

Factor Five: Individuals given untested or unsupported credibility. This area presented difficulties similar to those encountered in the analysis of Factor Four. Therefore, the approach used in assessing the data for Factor Four was also used in this area.

The newspapers in this study gave the greatest unsupported credibility to Larry Eyler, a convicted murderer, who was awaiting execution in Illinois. Six of Eyler's statements against the accused (Table 6.3, Statements 1, 2, 3, 8, 9, and 10) appeared a total of 102 times in the combined coverage of this case by the two newspapers. During the trial, the prosecutor did not produce any physical evidence, or *legally* factual testimony from other witnesses, to support any of six statements made by Eyler concerning the events that took place on the night Agan was killed. The "not guilty" verdict rendered by the members of the jury indicated they questioned Eyler's credibility, and thus, the credibility of the statements he made about the accused.

The publication of opinions voiced by the Vermillion County sheriff also failed the "credibility" test. Due to his position as sheriff, his statements were given a great deal of untested credibility by the newspapers. For example, the sheriff's opinion that the accused photographed the Agan murder to "assure Eyler's silence" (Table 6.3, Statement 11) was repeated a total of twenty-four times in the combined newspapers' coverage of the Little case. However, no such photographs were ever produced in court. Furthermore, the only indication that such photographs ever existed is derived from Eyler's testimony during his confession regarding Agan's murder. Eyler had entered into a plea bargain agreement with the state—a bargain where Eyler agreed to enter a guilty plea and to "testify against any accomplices" in exchange for a sentence of sixty years in prison. This was in lieu of going to trial and possibly receiving the death penalty if found guilty.

Factor Six: Opinions about the guilt of the accused. The combined newspapers' coverage of the Little case was replete with potentially prejudicial statements of this type. For example, Agan's brother and another man were quoted as stating they believed Little was guilty of murdering Steve Agan.

Both newspapers quoted unnamed jurors as stating, ". . . we set a guilty man free" (Table 6.4, Statement 1). The two jurors were also quoted as saying Little had "participated in the killing of Agan" (Table 6.4, Statement 2). This same statement was repeated on eighteen occasions in the combined coverage of the two newspapers during the pretrial and trial stages of the case (Table 6.3, Statement 9).

The former Vermillion County prosecutor and Eyler's attorney were quoted as saying Little's trial had been poorly prosecuted. The former prosecutor stated that a trial witness had told him he had not been asked "the right questions" during the trial.[6]

All of these "opinions" indicate the accused was guilty of the crime. The statements of the jurors and the former prosecutor could be considered especially prejudicial, as they were made after the jury had acquitted Little of the murder charge.

How the Defendant Was Portrayed

The newspapers' coverage, for the most part, portrayed the defendant, Robert David Little, in an unfavorable light. He was portrayed as a man who was involved in, and a leader of, a group of men involved in "homosexual bondage activities" (Table 6.3, Statement 6). He was portrayed as a "dominating individual" who used his influence "to control others," whom he used to get "his bondage victims" (Table 6.3, Statement 5). It was also reported that photographs were found in his home which depicted "Little and other men engaged in homosexual acts" (Table 6.3, Statement 12). This was in contrast to reports that

Steve Agan, the victim, had not engaged in these types of activities.

Little's credibility and innocence were placed into question when it was reported that "Polygraph shows Eyler told truth" (Table 6.3, Statement 4). The newspapers also reported Little would not submit to a polygraph examination, thus indicating his possible guilt or that he had something to hide.

Perhaps the greatest potential for prejudicing the reader's opinion of the accused's character came from the report that police had found a book in his home that had "overtones of child pornography" (Table 6.3, Statement 7). While many people have become more tolerant of alternative lifestyles (homosexuality) and sexual practices (bondage), few of them will tolerate, or condone, the use or possession of child pornography.

Attribution of Guilt

In theory, a defendant's innocence or guilt is supposed to be decided by a court. In theory, when a judge or jury rules that the accused is not guilty, justice has been served. However, as indicated in this case, this may not occur in reality.

The two areas that were potentially prejudicial toward Little with regard to attribution of guilt were the statements made by the jurors and the attorneys. Two of the twelve jurors stated they thought "we set a guilty man free" (Table 6.4, Statement 1), but they believed the state had failed to prove its case. It was also reported that the other jurors would not comment on their decision to acquit.

The newspaper coverage that contained statements by the two attorneys was perhaps the most prejudicial toward the accused. Eyler's attorney stated that one juror was "biased toward the innocence" of Little before being picked for the jury. The former prosecutor referred to the trial as "one of the worst jobs of prosecution" he had ever witnessed. He also stated that one witness told him the prosecuting attorney had failed to "ask him the right questions." The potential result of the attorneys' statements was to cast doubt on the competency of the prosecuting attorney, and the correctness of the jury's verdict.[7] Ultimately, their statements served to throw a shadow of doubt over Little's innocence and, thus, contribute to an attribution of guilt by the newspapers' readers.

Conclusion

Several tentative conclusions can be made from this study. First, the crime coverage in both newspapers tended to be prejudicial toward the accused. Second, the post-trial coverage left a cloud of doubt on the innocence of Professor Little. This doubt could have led readers to attribute guilt to the accused, even though he had been acquitted by a jury. Third, examples were found of all six prejudicial factors listed for the study. Fourth, only two items were found that did not fit the legitimacy, or factual, criterion. They were Pastore's observation that the book *Show Me* had "overtones of pornography" and Baker's reporting that photographs of the Agan murder were found in a search of Little's residence. Both of these observations were apparently unfounded; however, they tended to be very prejudicial toward the accused. Finally, it appears that the two newspapers' crime coverage had little, if any, effect on the jurors' decision in this case.[8] There was considerable coverage and it tended to be prejudicial toward the accused, but in the final analysis the jury found him not guilty based on its interpretation of the testimony and evidence presented during the trial. Nevertheless, most jurors were reluctant to talk to the press about their verdict.

The conclusion reached here is that news media agencies and personnel should report only legally factual information. They should refrain, as much as possible, from reporting opinions and untested observations, whether they be those of others, or their own. This is not meant to imply a desire for censorship. It is a call for responsible reporting of crime news, and for the recognition that the accused is supposed to be "innocent until proved guilty in a court of law."

Furthermore, research has determined that publication of statements and/or information by the news media often result in unwarranted credibility and authenticity being given to those who provided those statements or information. This appears to be the case in this study. Thus it behooves the press to publish only legally factual information if it truly desires to educate and inform the public. To do otherwise in its crime coverage could be tantamount to undermining the criminal justice process.

NOTES

1. This account of the murder was compiled from the Larry Eyler's December 13, 1990, courtroom confession about his role in the murder of Steve Agan.

2. The Supreme Court has ruled that results of polygraph examinations are not admissible in court. Furthermore, it has been reported that polygraph results may be questionable as research studies have found that "correct detections ranged from about 35 to 100 percent" (see Rolando v. del Carmen, *Criminal Procedure: Law and Practice*, Second Edition, 1991:269–270; Pacific Grove, CA: Brooks/Cole Publishing Company).

3. Opinions, with the exception of expert witnesses, are generally not admissible in court. *Ibid*: at 369–370.

4. Many newspaper readers are not familiar with the difference between the concepts of what is "factual" and what is "legal" as they pertain to newspaper crime coverage. There is no reason to question that the reporters were reporting "factual" information; e.g., the statements of opinion were in fact made by the individuals in question. However, "legal" statements and information must meet certain procedural criteria in order to be used in court. Opinions of "lay persons" (those persons not trained in the law, or who are not "experts") are not permitted in court (see note 3, above).

5. The U. S. Supreme Court ruled in Mapp vs Ohio that searches must be based on probable cause and be specific as to who is to be searched, the place to be searched, and what is to be searched for (Mapp vs Ohio, 367 U.S. 643 [1961]). Thus, it would appear the police did not have probable cause to search Little's property in the original investigation of 1982–1983, or they would have done so when they searched the area of Little's home occupied by Eyler.

6. This is hearsay information and is not admissible in a court of law. "The test of oral hearsay is this: If the statement being repeated by the witness is offered to prove the truth of what somebody else has said or other out-of-court statement, the statement is hearsay" (see Rolando v. del Carmen, *Criminal Procedure: Law and Practice*, Second Edition, 1991: 372, Pacific Grove, Ca: Brooks/Cole Publishing Company.) The alleged statement by the witness to Thomas would appear to fit this test and would thus be inadmissible in court.

7. The statements of Eyler's attorney and the former prosecutor served to cast a pall over the accused's trial. In general, most defense attorneys will speak out on behalf of their clients; however, it could be argued that Eyler's attorney exceeded the limits of rationality. Perhaps this can be explained when it is considered she was trying to get Eyler a retrial in Illinois. A conviction of Little in this case could have had a positive impact on her request for a new trial. This was due to the assertion by Eyler that Little had killed the man Eyler was convicted of killing in Chicago, Illinois. The former prosecutor's statements may have been politically fueled. He had just been defeated in a county election. Whatever their reasons, it can be argued that the statements and actions of these two individuals served to discredit the criminal justice system and the legal process they were ostensibly trained, and sworn, to uphold.

8. Limitations in the scope of this study make it impossible to determine the magnitude of impact, if any, the newspapers' coverage had on readers. However, specific coverage from pre-arrest through the post-trial stages of the process tended to cast doubt on the accused's innocence. Perhaps more importantly, some of this coverage occurred after the trial was over—in other words after the accused had been acquitted by the jury. Furthermore, some research has determined that news coverage has the potential to bias readers. For example, one study, in which one group of test jurors was exposed to "prejudicial" news and a control group was not, concluded that "78 percent of the 'prejudiced jurors' voted to convict compared to only 35 percent of the 'nonprejudiced jurors.'" (See David W. Neubauer, *America's Courts and the Criminal Justice* System, 1983: 303, Monterey, CA: Brooks/Cole Publishing Company.)

REFERENCES

Abbott, D. J. and J. M. Calonico. 1974. "Black man, white woman—The maintenance of a myth: Rape and the press in New Orleans." In M. Riedel and T. P. Thornberry (eds.), *Crime and Delinquency: Dimensions of Deviance,* pp. 141–153. New York: Praeger Publishers.

Baker, G. II. 1990. December 13. "Larry Eyler pleads guilty in Steve Agan murder probe." *The Daily Clintonian,* 78: 249, pp. 1, 4.

———. 1990. December 14. "Eyler pleads guilty to clear conscience." *The Daily Clintonian,* 78: 250, p. 1.

———. 1990. December 17. "Hollowell seeks warrant for Little." *The Daily Clintonian,* 78: 251, p. 1.

———. 1991. December 28. "Eyler sentencing set for 2 P.M." *The Daily Clintonian,* 78: 259, p. 1.

———. 1991. January 7. "Little appears in court today." *The Daily Clintonian,* 79: 5, p. 1.

———. 1991. April 8. "Little trial slated to begin in Vermillion court Tuesday." *The Daily Clintonian,* 79: 65, pp. 1, 4.

———. 1991. April 9. "Jury selection begins in trial for professor charged with 1982 murder of Steve Agan." *The Daily Clintonian,* 79: 66, pp. 1, 4.

———. 1991. April 10. "Jury selection continues in murder trial for professor." *The Daily Clintonian,* 79: 67, p. 1.

———. 1991. April 18. "Jury finds ISU's Robert Little 'Not Guilty' of murder charge." *The Daily Clintonian,* 79: 73, pp. 1 and 4.

Cromer, G. 1978. "Character assassination in the press." In C. Winick (ed.), *Deviance and Mass Media,* pp. 225–241. Beverly Hills, CA: Sage Publications.

del Carmen, R. V. 1991. *Criminal Procedure: Law and Practice,* Second Edition, Pacific Grove, CA: Brooks/ Cole Publishing Company.

Drechsel, R. K. Netteburg, and B. Aborisade. 1980. "Community size and newspaper reporting of local courts." *Journalism Quarterly,* 59: 1, Spring 1981, pp. 71–78.

Dulaney, W. 1969. "Identification of race in newspaper crime stories." *Journalism Quarterly,* 46: 3, Autumn 1969, pp. 603–605.

Einstadter, W. J. 1979. "Crime news in the old west: Social control in a northwestern town, 1887–1888." *Urban Life*, 8: 3, October 1979, pp. 317–334.

Fedler, F. and D. Jordan. 1982. "How emphasis on people affects coverage of crime." *Journalism Quarterly*, 59: 3, Autumn 1982, pp. 474–478.

Friendly, A. and R. L. Goldfarb. 1967. *Crime and Publicity: The Impact of News on the Administration of Justice*. Hartford: Connecticut Printers, Inc.

Galliher, J. F. and C. Tyree. 1985. "Edwin Sutherland's research on the origins of sexual psychopath laws: An early case study of the medicalization of deviance." *Social Problems*, 33: 2, December 1985, pp. 100–113.

Humphries, D. 1981. "Serious crime, news coverage, and ideology: A content analysis of crime coverage in a metropolitan monitor." *Crime and Delinquency*, 27: 2, April 1981, pp. 191–205.

Karmen, A. 1978. "How much heat? How much light?: Coverage of New York City's blackout and looting in the print media." In C. Winick (ed.), *Deviance and Mass Media*, pp. 179–200. Beverly Hills, CA: Sage Publications.

Kaufman, S. J. 1990. October 21. "Media could have done more to cover killings." *The Tribune-Star*, Section C, p. 1.

Marsh, H. 1989. "Newspaper crime coverage in the U.S.: 1893–1988." *Criminal Justice Abstracts*, September 1989, pp. 506–514.

———. 1991. "A Comparative analysis of crime coverage in newspapers in the United States and other countries from 1960–1989: A review of the literature." *Journal of Criminal Justice*, 19: 1, January 1991, pp. 67–79.

Neubauer, D. W. 1984. *America's Courts and the Criminal Justice System*. Pacific Grove, CA: Brooks/Cole Publishing Company.

Pastore, P. 1990. December 14. "8-year silence broken with testimony." *The Tribune-Star*, Section A, p. 6.

———. 1990. December 14. "Larry Eyler tells court about night of wild sex acts that led to murder." *The Tribune-Star*, Section A, pp. 1, 6.

———. 1990. December 15. "Ohio authorities interested in Little." *The Tribune-Star*, Section A, p. 1.

———. 1990. December 16. "Eyler tries to shift blame for Chicago killing." *The Tribune-Star*, Section A, pp. 1 and 4.

————. 1990. December 17. "Warrant for Little's arrest may be issued today." *The Tribune-Star*, Section A, p. 1.

————. 1990. December 19. "Calm Little pleads innocent to Agan murder." *The Tribune-Star*, Section A, p. 1.

————. 1990. December 19. "Polygraph shows Eyler told truth." *The Tribune- Star*, Section A, p. 4.

————. 1991. January 6. "Few knew alleged seamy side of Little's personality." *The Tribune-Star*, Section A, pp. 1, 4.

————. 1991. March 22. "Evaluation shows eyler unstable." *The Tribune-Star*, Section A, p. 4.

————. 1991. April 2. "Lawyers want chance at jurors bfore trial." *The Tribune-Star*, Section A, p. 3.

————. 1991. April 6. "Darnell denies Little request." *The Tribune-Star*, Section A, p. 1.

————. 1991. April 12. "Victims' families monitor proceedings." *The Tribune- Star*, Section A, p. 3.

————. 1991. April 14. "Little, his mother expected to testify this week." *The Tribune-Star*, Section A, p. 4.

————. 1991. April 18. "Little acquitted in murder." *The Tribune-Star*, Section A, p. 1.

————. 1991. April 20. "Little trial juror uncomfortable with verdict." *The Tribune-Star*, Section A, p. 1.

————. 1991. May 16. "Juror claims he had help getting basketball." *The Tribune-Star*, Section A, p. 4.

————. 1991. May 16. "Prosecutors at odds over trial successes." *The Tribune-Star*, Section A, p. 4.

Shaffer, R. A. 1986. "Pretrial publicity: Media coverage and guilt attribution." *Communication Quarterly*, 34: 2, Spring 1986, pp. 154–169.

Shelton, P. S. 1965. "Fair trial—Free press: New aspects of an old dilemma." *Issues in Criminology*, 1:1, Fall 1965, pp. 108–122.

Surette, R. 1984. "Media and justice: Summary and future prospects." In R. Surette (ed.), *Justice and the Media* pp. 323–333. Springfield, IL: Charles C. Thomas Publisher.

Wilkie, C. 1981. "The scapegoating of Bruno Richard Hauptmann: The rhetorical process in prejudicial publicity." *Central States Speech Journal*, 32: 1, Summer 1981, pp. 100–110.

CHAPTER 7

Murder and Mayhem in *USA Today:* A Quantitative Analysis of the National Reporting of States' News

Robert A. Jerin
Charles B. Fields

While the public's reaction to crime is impacted by various sources, it seems that the media have the greatest effect on the perception of crime and criminality. Davis (1952), in one of the first and most important studies examining crime and crime news coverage, presented evidence that there is no relationship between official crime statistics and crime as reported in the print media. In fact, this study indicated that the public perception of crime depends almost entirely on what is read in the newspapers. However, this study was conducted before the proliferation of television.

There are several competing schools of thought in this area that provide interesting study. Ericson (1991) feels that most of the previous research on the mass media and crime is deficient because it has focused too much on the effect of the mass media on our perceptions of crime and criminals. He addresses this "effects" tradition by critiquing several widely held assumptions, two of which deserve further attention. The first approach assumes that the mass media (especially television) are the primary sources of our understanding in these areas. It should be noted that some research (Graber, 1979; 1980), however, points out that our knowledge comes from a variety of sources; the media being but one among several.

The second assumption is that the media present erroneous and distorted information about crime. The distortion of the extent of crime and its coverage in the news media is well documented. Studies have focused on the extent of crime as reported in local print media (Cohen, 1975, Meyer, 1975, 1976; Antunes and Hurley, 1977; Graber, 1979; Humphries, 1981; Windhauser, Seiter and Winfree, 1990; Marsh, 1991), the amount on television news reports (Graber, 1979; Surette, 1992), and on comparisons with newspaper coverage of crime in other countries (Marsh, 1991). Marsh (1991: 67–68), in assessing the literature in the area, found that "there is an overrepresentation of violent crimes . . . and the percentage of violent crimes does not match official crime statistics." Additionally, the "emphasis on relatively infrequent violent crimes may contribute to a heightened concern and fear. . . ." While Ericson (1991: 220) admits that discrepancies can be found between the types and amount of crime reported in the media and official reports of crime, why should we expect the "cultural products of mass media to reflect the social reality of crime"?

These are all important areas of inquiry. This exploratory study seeks to ascertain the amount and type of crime news as it relates to individual states as reported in the only national newspaper, *USA Today*, and attempts to discover if there are any differences in the amount, type, or seriousness of the coverage of statewide news in the national daily as compared to official crime statistics (Uniform Crime Reports), and if state population and crime rates are in any way a determining factor.

Methodology

The study is based on a content analysis as reported in *USA Today*'s "Across the USA: News From Every State" section. *USA Today* claims to be the foremost daily newspaper in the United States and is the only source that reports news from every state every day. Using Graber's (1979) differentiation of news topics to establish four general headings, the analysis established the central theme of each news bite in an effort to reduce duplication of recordings. The topics used in the study were: (1) crime and justice, (2) government and politics, (3) economics and social issues and (4) human interest and family.

The crime and justice category was further divided into specific crimes using the Uniform Crime Report (UCR) or the Federal Crime Index along with additional categories including white-collar crimes, corporate crimes, drug-related crimes and an "other" crimes category. This last category included crimes such as vagrancy, gate crimes, vandalism and any others that did not fit the previous categories.[1] An attempt was also made to determine the type of offender for each offense coded.[2]

The analysis covered the full year of 1990 and consisted of 250 different issues being coded. In total, 26,301 news summaries were coded, or an average of just over two stories for each state each day. Of these, 4,236 summaries were crime-related and were further analyzed in additional categories.

The editorial policy of *USA Today*'s "News From Every State" section is reported to be the same as in the general news section. Using the AP news wire service from each state as the source of the news, a regional editor usually selects two news items to be reported each day per state. The news criteria are selected by the regional editors based upon their experience of newsworthiness and public appeal. It is then condensed to a one-to-two sentence news brief and reported under each state's title with the city of origination included (Bacon, 1992).

Analysis

The initial analysis first examined the different types of news and categorized them according to Graber's model. In the "News From Every State," the crime and justice section received the least amount of coverage. The percentage of stories that fell into the crime category was 16 percent (n=4,236). The percentages of additional news categories were government/politics 24.4 percent (n=6,412); human interest/family issues 26.7 percent (n=7,015); and economic/social issues 32.8 percent (n=8,638). A relatively small number of summaries (n=260) that were difficult or impossible to categorize were excluded from the analysis. This balance of issues is unique when compared to Graber's (1979) earlier study in Chicago (see Table 7.1).

However, further analysis in the crime and justice section confirms previous research.

TABLE 7.1

Frequency of News Topics in *USA Today* (1990) and
Chicago Tribune, Sun-Times and *Daily News* (1979)*
(Percent)

Topic	USA Today (N=26,301)	Tribune (N=33,200)	Sun-Times (N=581)	Daily News (N=506)
Crime and Justice	16.1	21.8	28.0	26.7
Gov't and Politics	24.4	41.4	41.5	43.9
Human Interest and Family	32.8	10.6	5.5	7.9
Economic and social issues	26.7	26.0	23.5	21.5

*The primary data included in the table come from a year-long content analysis of *Chicago Tribune*. The other two Chicago daily newspapers were analyzed on a more limited basis. For a more detailed discussion of the methodology, see Graber (1979).

It is perhaps unusual that crime- and justice-related news summaries make up the smallest category of "News From Every State" in *USA Today* while human interest and family summaries constitute the largest. The three papers examined by Graber (1979) all report more news in the areas of government and politics with crime and justice, or economic and social issues ranking second. Human interest and family news ranks last.

The manner in which crime and justice news is reported in the state section of *USA Today* is similar to what was found in earlier research (e.g., Marsh, 1991). The amount of violent index crimes reported is almost 42 percent with murder at 28 percent. Property crimes make up 6 percent of the crime reported, with white collar/corporate crimes totalling about 10 percent. The level of drug crimes is the third highest recorded category with over 8 percent. The "other" crime category constitutes 29 percent of the recordings.

Because of the brevity of the material reported (i.e., two stories per day) the type of crime story that made the news had a uniqueness to it. The material in *USA Today* followed a pattern found in Roshier's work. Roshier (1973: 34–35) identified four sets of factors which seemed to establish why some crimes were selected in preference to others. These factors were:

1. The seriousness of the offense;
2. "Whimsical" circumstances, i.e., humorous, ironic, unusual;
3. Sentimental or dramatic circumstances; and
4. The involvement of a famous or high-status person in any capacity.

Examples of these can be found throughout *USA Today*'s reporting of state events. In many cases a combination of these factors can be observed in the crimes reported. Examples of serious offenses such as murder which combine factors are: *Wisconsin:* "Shanke King, 25, charged with sexual assault, homicide of Kurt Lagoo, 18 months old, was hospitalized in fair condition after hanging self in jail. Autopsy found Lagoo . . . was tortured for week before death" (1/16/90). *Florida:* "Dorothy Dianne Rose, 31, accused of strangling her 2 children with belt, is fit to stand trial June 11, doctors say" (3/16/90).

Examples of combined factors in sexual assault cases include: *Georgia:* "British priest Reverend Anton Mowat could be extradited to USA in 2 weeks to face 10 charges. Indictment charges he molested altar boys at Stone Mountain Catholic Church, state official said" (1/31/90). *Idaho:* "Child sex abuse trial begins today with jury selection for suspended state transportation director, ex-state Senator Kermit Kiebert. He's accused of molesting his daughter, then 12, 4 years ago" (5/14/90). *New York:* "Ex-IBM executive Harold Hotchkiss, 46, pleaded guilty to sexually abusing 11 boys from '84 to '89" (7/17/90).

The combination of factors is even more pronounced when there is a nonviolent offense. The main factor in the newsworthiness of a nonviolent offense seems to be the involvement of a famous or high-status person. Examples of this are: *West Virginia:* "Federal judge denies bail to ex-Governor Arch Moore Jr. pending appeal of his sentencing on extortion, mail fraud, tax fraud, obstruction of justice" (7/21/90). *Tennessee:* "Two candidates for the office of sheriff arrest third candidate on drunk driving charges" (3/21/90). *South Carolina:* "Resignation of Mayor Jerry Dixon—charged February 8 with shoplifting—is being sought by town council" (3/2/90). *Florida:* "State will pursue case of Mayor Bart Hudson—arrested November 5 on charge of masturbating in public restroom" (12/14/90).

Humor is also found in minor offenses. Examples are: *Tennessee:* "Willie Denton—accused of drunk driving while riding a lawn mower—faces April 17 hearing. Police say he refused sobriety test when they stopped him leaving truckstop at 8–10 mph" (3/27/90). *Iowa:* Earl Surette, 29, faces theft charge after police said they found him with three live lobsters in shirt" (4/10/90). *Montana:* "Man pushing motorcycle was correctly convicted of DWI, state supreme court ruled" (8/29/90).

State Comparison

The differences between the states are somewhat difficult to analyze because of the subjective descriptions of crimes reported in each state. Typically, in a brief sentence or two, routine crime-related summaries list the location of the offense, describe the offense itself (perhaps naming the offender and victim) and little else. It is a little easier, however, to determine a subjective category in which to list the offense. Table 7.2 summarizes the state-by-state comparison (selected states) on crime and justice related summaries. The states were selected because of the relatively large (and small) percentage of news topics devoted to law, crime and justice issues.

The highest number of murder-related stories was in Arkansas with fifty-four, New York with fifty, Montana with forty-six, and New Jersey and Wisconsin with forty each. The states with the lowest were Alaska, North Dakota, and Hawaii with six and Nebraska with nine.

TABLE 7.2

State-by-State Comparison
Frequency of Crime- and Justice-Related News Summaries

(Selected Offenses; in Percent)

State	Crime and Justice*	Murder	Drug-Related	White-Collar/Corporate
Top Ten				
Arkansas	26.1	51.6	5.0	13.3
New Jersey	23.1	40.0	6.1	11.1
Wisconsin	22.9	42.9	9.5	3.2
Tennessee	22.1	24.6	7.0	10.5
Missouri	21.5	40.7	22.2	12.9
New York	21.2	32.3	6.2	4.6
Michigan	20.6	24.1	12.1	6.9
Connecticut	20.6	30.8	7.7	7.6
Alabama	20.3	28.6	2.0	18.4
Indiana	20.1	36.7	12.2	12.2
Bottom Ten				
Alaska	7.4	22.2	0.0	5.6
North Dakota	10.2	19.2	19.2	0.0
North Carolina	10.3	22.1	3.7	14.8
Wyoming	10.4	63.3	3.3	6.7
Delaware	10.9	33.3	4.8	0.0
Iowa	11.0	19.4	2.8	8.3
Massachusetts	11.2	24.0	4.0	0.0
Montana	11.3	24.4	9.5	28.6
Rhode Island	11.6	14.3	10.7	7.1
South Dakota	11.7	26.5	5.9	2.9

*Refers to the percentage of the total news summaries devoted to crime and justice topics for each state.

The total number of crime-related stories by state ranged from 38 in Alaska to 152 in New York. Many crime categories had no reportings in some states; these include drugs, rape, and robbery. The population of the state in many cases seems to establish the frequency of the crime reporting more than anything else. An additional concern is the high percentage of crimes fitting into the "other" category. There is a need to redefine this category because of the number of crimes and the important social issues that some address (e.g., hate crimes).

Crime Reporting and Official Crime Statistics

Many studies have dealt with the relationship between the extent of crime reporting and actual crime rates (see, e.g., Antunes and Hurley, 1977; Phillips, 1977, 1979; Fedler and Jordan, 1982). In fact, during periods of decreasing crime rates it seems that, at least in some instances, crime reporting has increased. In an attempt to assess the differences between crime rates and crime reporting, statistics for selected offenses from the Uniform Crime Reports were compared with the same offenses reported in *USA Today*.

Using a ranking system, comparisons between states and official crime statistics (Uniform Crime Reports) offer some interesting information. Table 7.3 ranks the states by their population, U.C.R. Index crime rate, and number and percent of news summaries relating to crime and justice reported in *USA Today*. In addition, four offense categories (murder, rape, drug violations and corporate crime) were examined and ranked according to the reporting rate for each state.

The five most populated states—California, New York, Texas, Florida, and Pennsylvania—are among the states with the highest number of reported crimes (U.C.R., 1990), but while ranked high are not ranked highest in the crime- and justice-related reporting. While this suggests that the number of crime and justice summaries is somewhat related to state population, its proportion when compared to the other categories is not affected by the size of the state.

A comparison of the five states with the highest U.C.R. Index crime rates—Washington, D.C., Florida, Arizona, Texas, and Georgia—and the reporting of more serious crimes offers

TABLE 7.3
State-by-State Comparison

State	Crime Related			USA Today Reporting				
	Population Rank	N	Reporting Rank (%)	U.C.R. Index	Murder	Rape	Drugs	Corporate
Alabama	22	103	9 (20.3)	41	16	8	18	5
Alaska	50	38	51 (7.4)	28	51	24	51	43
Arizona	24	71	29 (14.7)	3	28	13	25	1
Arkansas	33	133	1 (26.1)	31	1	34	2	15
California	1	132	19 (17.6)	7	6	19	21	21
Colorado	26	84	23 (16.5)	13	19	23	22	38
Connecticut	27	103	8 (20.6)	23	15	48	15	6
Delaware	47	55	47 (10.9)	34	33	31	42	51
D.C.	43	62	40 (12.3)	1	39	51	4	29
Florida	4	104	26 (15.6)	2	11	18	6	19
Georgia	11	85	22 (16.6)	5	7	47	14	33
Hawaii	40	63	39 (12.4)	11	49	40	13	32
Idaho	42	66	36 (13.0)	43	31	30	30	49
Illinois	6	82	31 (14.0)	16	8	29	29	14
Indiana	14	102	10 (20.1)	33	17	12	12	9
Iowa	30	56	46 (11.0)	42	47	50	48	36
Kansas	32	76	27 (15.1)	27	22	49	47	24
Kentucky	23	98	12 (19.3)	48	13	3	9	37

State	Crime Related			USA Today Reporting				
	Population Rank	N	Reporting Rank (%)	U.C.R. Index	Murder	Rape	Drugs	Corporate
Louisiana	21	93	18 (18.1)	8	26	46	8	8
Maine	38	69	34 (13.4)	45	29	33	45	35
Maryland	19	67	24 (16.4)	17	43	11	11	50
Mass.	13	57	45 (11.2)	26	40	45	38	40
Michigan	8	105	7 (20.6)	15	21	7	10	20
Minnesota	20	93	15 (18.3)	34	12	6	39	18
Mississippi	31	95	14 (18.9)	44	25	39	23	7
Missouri	15	110	5 (21.5)	29	3	38	1	13
Montana	45	57	44 (11.3)	35	36	44	32	17
Nebraska	36	61	41 (12.0)	39	48	22	44	12
Nevada	39	82	25 (16.1)	12	10	43	24	22
New Hamp.	41	65	37 (12.9)	46	30	42	46	48
New Jersey	9	117	2 (23.1)	22	4	17	26	4
New Mexico	37	63	38 (12.6)	6	45	37	37	11
New York	2	152	6 (21.2)	9	2	10	16	16
N. Carolina	10	52	49 (10.3)	21	42	32	49	31
N. Dakota	48	52	50 (10.2)	49	50	28	28	45
Ohio	7	102	11 (21.0)	32	9	9	35	23
Oklahoma	28	87	20 (17.3)	20	18	16	20	26
Oregon	29	66	35 (13.0)	19	34	27	41	41
Pennsylvania	5	92	17 (18.3)	47	35	15	19	44

| | Crime Related | | | USA Today Reporting | | | | |
State	Population Rank	N	Reporting Rank (%)	U.C.R. Index	Murder	Rape	Drugs	Corporate
R. Island	44	59	43 (11.6)	25	46	36	36	46
S. Carolina	10	70	32 (13.7)	14	38	26	40	3
S. Dakota	46	59	42 (11.7)	50	44	2	43	47
Tennessee	17	112	4 (22.1)	30	20	5	17	10
Texas	3	120	16 (18.3)	4	14	21	2	28
Utah	35	75	28 (15.0)	18	41	14	5	30
Vermont	49	69	33 (13.6)	38	37	25	27	27
Virginia	12	72	30 (14.4)	36	23	35	31	39
Washington	18	86	21 (17.0)	10	27	1	33	34
W. Virginia	34	98	13 (19.1)	51	30	4	34	2
Wisconsin	16	115	3 (22.9)	37	5	20	7	25
Wyoming	51	51	48 (10.4)	40	24	41	50	42

additional insight into crime reporting behavior. None of the states with the five highest crime rates is included in the top five rankings of murder and rape. This difference in reporting may be due primarily to the commonality of major crimes in these states, so that the newsworthiness of serious crimes in these same states may be minimized and other factors (see Roshier, 1973) may play a larger role.

This is in direct contrast to the five states—West Virginia, South Dakota, North Dakota, Kentucky, and Pennsylvania—with the lowest U.C.R. Index crime rates. Three of these states (West Virginia, South Dakota, and Kentucky) are ranked in the top five in rape and rape-related news summaries. This may be due to the perception in the media that certain sensational crimes are more "newsworthy" in states with low crime rates.

Even the states with the highest rankings in terms of *USA Today's* crime-related reporting (Arkansas, New Jersey, Wisconsin, Tennessee, and Missouri) are not states with relatively high crime rates. Only New Jersey is in the top half of the U.C.R. Index offenses (ranked 22nd). The fact that Arkansas is ranked number one in terms of total crime- and justice-related reporting, number one in murder reporting and number two in drug reporting, raises questions concerning the objective reporting of crime-related stories in *USA Today*.

Further analysis of this phenomenon reveals that certain sensational crimes may be responsible for the extensive coverage of serious crime in Arkansas. Examples of this are: *Little Rock*: "Mass murderer Ronald Gene Simmons—in letter to news media—said state attorney Steve Clark is 'incompetent,' shouldn't argue his death penalty case before U.S. Supreme Court. . . . Simmons, who wants to die, said Clark won't argue convincingly for execution" (1/4/90); *Arkadelphia*: "Mary Alice Block, 27, faces arraignment today in death of son Frederick Block, Jr., 9, who was found Monday repeatedly stabbed with butcher knife, authorities said. Police found mother nearby, incoherent" (3/21/90); *Little Rock*: "Judge will rule today on bid by Barry Fairchild, 36, for stay of his September 5 execution, official said. It is widely known in sheriff's office that Fairchild's murder confession was coerced, ex-Pulaski County deputy James testified Tuesday" (8/29/90). Additionally, combinations of Roshier's (1973) typologies discussed earlier are found in these examples.

While statistical comparisons between official crime rates and the extent of crime related reporting in *USA Today* may be problematic, there are at least some preliminary indications of a relationship between the reporting of certain crimes and crime rates (see Table 7.4).

TABLE 7.4

Simple Correlations Between Uniform Crime Reports (1990) and Crime and Justice Reporting in *USA Today*

(Selected Offenses)

	Crime and Justice Reporting				
	All Offenses	Murder	Rape	Drugs	Corporate
U.C.R.					
Index	.0193	−.0032	−.2346*	.3663**	.1742
Violent	.2313	.1731	−.1166	.3884**	.1830
Murder	.0743	.0259	−.2215	.3699**	.1071
Population	−.6598***	−.1141	−.2557*	−.4250**	−.0935

*   p < .05
** p < .01
*** p < .001

When correlations between rape as reported in *USA Today* and the U.C.R. Index are examined, it seems that those states with high crime rates were less apt to have rape-related summaries during the year. There is, however, a strong positive correlation between drug-related reporting and official crime rates. No relationship was found between reporting of corporate/white-collar offenses, murder, and all offenses combined and official crime statistics. Furthermore, *USA Today* had more drug-related news summaries and total crime-related summaries for small states (in terms of population) than for larger states.

Conclusion

The reporting of news events across the United States follows previous patterns found in regional newspapers. The print media sensationalize certain crimes and ignores many others. Many times lesser crimes are reported not because of the event, but because of the notoriety of the individuals involved or the humor that is present. However, the breakdown of crime news in comparison to other areas of interest does not seem out of proportion.

The data seem to suggest that the reporting of major crimes is not based on official crime statistics or state populations. Furthermore, the media reporting of a few sensational crimes in low crime rate states can distort the true amount of crime in those states. This study has also found that a major factor in a crime's being reported by the media is not the crime itself, but the circumstances surrounding the crime, the public nature of the offender or victim, or the humorous nature of the incident. This is especially true with minor offenses. It seems that the accuracy of the reporting of criminal acts will always be compromised by the "newsworthiness" of the incident.

Notes

1. The offenses coded were: murder/non-negligent homicide, sexual assault/rape, robbery, aggravated assault, burglary, theft, arson, white-collar, drug-related, drunk driving, corporate, domestic violence, child abuse, and other.

2. The offenders coded were: elected government official, law enforcement, family member, stranger, acquaintance, and unknown.

REFERENCES

Antunes, G. E. and P. A. Hurley. 1977. "The representation of criminal events in Houston's two daily newspapers." *Journalism Quarterly,* 54: 756–60.

Bacon, J. 1992. Personal Communication (2/15).

Cohen, S. 1975. "A comparison of crime coverage in Detroit and Atlanta newspapers." *Journalism Quarterly,* 52: 726–30.

Davis, F. J. 1952. "Crime news in Colorado newspapers." *American Journal of Sociology,* 57: 325–30.

Ditton, J. and J. Duffy. 1983. "Bias in the newspaper reporting of crime news." *British Journal of Criminology,* 23: 159–65.

Ericson, R. V. 1991. "Mass media, crime, law, and justice." *British Journal of Criminology,* 31 (3): 219–249.

Fedler, F. and D. Jordan. 1982. "How emphasis on people affects coverage of crime." *Journalism Quarterly,* 59: 474–78.

Graber, D. A. 1979. "Is crime news excessive?" *Journal of Communication,* 29: 81–92.

———. 1980. *Crime News and the Public.* New York: Praeger.

Hans, V. P. and J. L. Dee. 1991. "Media coverage of law: Its impact on juries and the public." *American Behavioral Scientist,* 35 (2): 136–149.

Humphries, D. 1981. "Serious crime, news coverage, and ideology: A content analysis of crime coverage in a metropolitan paper." *Crime and Delinquency,* 27: 191–205.

Marsh, H. L. 1991. "A comparative analysis of crime coverage in newspapers in the United States and other countries from 1960–1989: A review of the literature." *Journal of Criminal Justice,* 19: 67–79.

Meyer, J. C. Jr. 1975. "Newspaper reporting of crime and justice: An analysis of an assumed difference." *Journalism Quarterly,* 52: 731–34.

———. 1976. "Reporting crime and justice in the press." *Criminology,* 14: 277–78.

Phillips, D. P. 1977. "Motor vehicle fatalities increase just after publicized suicide rates." *Science,* 196: 1464–65.

————. 1979. "Suicide, motor vehicle fatalities and the mass media: Evidence toward a theory of suggestion." *American Journal of Sociology*, 84: 1150–74.

Roshier, B. 1973. "The selection of crime news by the press." In S. Cohen and J. Young (eds.), *The Manufacture of News*. Beverly Hills, CA: Sage, pp. 29–39.

Schlesinger, P., H. Tumber and G. Murdock 1991. "The media politics of crime and criminal justice." *British Journal of Sociology*, 42 (3): 397–420.

Shoemaker, P. J. and S. D. Reese. 1990. "Exposure to what? Integrating media content and effects studies." *Journalism Quarterly*, 67: 649–652.

Surette, R. 1992. *Media, Crime and Criminal Justice: Images and Realities*. Pacific Grove, CA: Brooks/Cole.

Windhauser, J. W., J. Seiter, and L. T. Winfree. 1990. "Crime news in the Louisiana press, 1980 vs. 1985." *Journalism Quarterly*, 67: 72–78.

CHAPTER 8

Patrolling the Facts: Media, Cops, and Crime

Renée Goldsmith Kasinsky

In recent years the police have taken a proactive strategy in mediating and negotiating their public image in the media in addition to their proactivity in defining crime. The news has become a significant part of the material and ideological realities of police work where crime definition and crime control are central themes. Fast-breaking crime stories remain the staple of the police reporter's beat. Known in the trade as "bang-bang" reporting, crime stories are high interest and stereotyped. Every crime story is a "whodunit." There is always a victim with whom the public can identify, and an alleged perpetrator to be feared or reviled (Powers and Kasinsky, 1993).

The average police officer has become a knowledge worker. This reshaping of their traditional role allows their organization to maintain legitimacy in a society where knowledge is power. In order to look at the question of control and power I will examine the culture and ideology of police in general as well as the police organization, and the influence of "news texts" and sourcing. The following are some questions I will consider. How do the police and the media view their own enterprises in terms of functions and ideology? What is the interaction between the police and news media representatives? How is knowledge about crime or a policing event represented as known? What is presented as a credible news source? Is there a disjunction between our public images and the realities of police work? Using the concept of textual mediated reality I will examine information published about two celebrated police incidents in which the interpretations of media texts were central. I will argue that the interests of the police operate simultaneously with those of the media to become part of our society's policing apparatus.

In this chapter I will examine the process of interaction between the news media and the police in the context of the larger mass media's portrayals of both of these institutions. That is to say, I am locating newsmaking criminology in the context of other media that shape, reflect, and interact with how the police and journalists see their work. Easily capturing the media spotlight on a daily basis enables the police to "sell themselves" more easily than most organizations. However, it also makes them more vulnerable to immediate public scrutiny and criticism, especially when their actions are in violation of normative standards. The conflict generated from this situation is central to the interaction of police and media.

Critical Interactive Perspective

My analysis lies within the critical tradition of media studies. The critical approach means thinking critically about things which are usually taken for granted. This can entail re-examining anything from Walt Disney Donald Duck comics to the concept of "objectivity." Much recent media research has been based upon a "dominant ideology" thesis (Abercrombie, Hill, and Turner, 1980). Those who use either a neo-Gramscian theory of hegemony (Hall, Critcher, Jefferson, Clarke, and Roberts, 1978), or a "propaganda model" (Herman and Chomsky, 1988), have argued that the power of politically and economically dominant groups in the society defines the parameters of debate. Their power ensures the privileged reproduction of their discourse, and by extension, largely determines the contours of the dominant ideology—that which is socially thinkable.

Although most critical media theorists would agree with major portions of this dominant ideology thesis, some theorists have pointed out that inadequate attention has been paid to the communication process as a whole, and to the ongoing conflictual processes both inside central institutions and within the media themselves (Schlesinger, Tumber, and Murdock, 1991).

In this chapter I suggest a more complex model of the media, encompassing this critique, which integrates the dominant ideology thesis within the framework of symbolic interactionism. It views both the organizations of the media and the police profession as a "textually mediated reality" (Smith, 1990). We are constantly engaged in textually mediated forms of action which affect our perceptions and influence our actions in society. We engage with textual materials daily as we read the newspaper or watch television (Smith, 1990). The news and TV do not merely monitor the events of the real world, but rather they construct representations and accounts of reality based upon the conventions, ideologies, and the organization of journalism and news bureaucracies (Chibnall, 1977).

Power and Mediated Discourses

Textual discourse of the mass media presents the world as a textual construct, in which belief is a commitment to one construct rather than another. Dorothy Smith, analyzing two different texts, illustrates how a textual account translates actual police practices into the public textual discourse of the mass media through which they become known and interpreted to citizens (Smith, 1990). It tells us how an event becomes represented as known, and is closely related to how we as the public evaluate the credibility of a piece of information.

Smith contrasts two accounts of a classic event, a confrontation between police and street people, that took place in Berkeley, California, in the 1960s. The first account, written by a professor who observed, appeared as a letter in an underground newspaper in 1968. The second account is a response from the mayor of Berkeley claiming, on the basis of an internal investigation, that the police acted properly. It presents an alternative account of the events, redescribing them as proper police procedure.[1] The two texts articulate the discourses of the local political struggle between the anti-Vietnam countercultural "movement" and the local representatives of law enforcement to the wider public.

The first text is a letter, published in the underground newspaper, which is written from the standpoint of an actual experience—a man who was on the margins of the events tells his story as he saw it. He accuses the police of attempting to provoke the people on the street in order to justify harassing and arresting them, describing what he saw as a brutal and arbitrary use of police force. What he tells is restricted by what he has seen and heard from where he saw and heard it. It is not connected to previous events or to later ones. His version enters textual time when it is published in the newspaper but does not itself depend upon a textual reality constituted independently of it (Smith, 1990).

The official text from the mayor's office is markedly different from that of the professor's text. The standpoint is organizational; it is based upon an inquiry conducted by the chief of police with unnamed police officers and reported to the mayor. It is presented as the product of an official inquiry, grounded in the observations of police officers in their official capacity and by their anonymity as specific subjects.

There is little disagreement between the two accounts on the particulars of the story. However, the official version reconstructs the witnessed events as moments in extended sequences of institutional action, locating them in textual time, dependent on textual realities already institutionally accomplished. The mayor's version subsumes the professor's version and converts it into an organizational version. It claims retroactively that the professor's observations were causes of properly mandated police action. Smith concludes that this process imbues the mayor's letter with "the privileged textual practices of the ruling apparatus" (Smith, 1990: 214).

Ideology and the Police

Traditionally, the police have adopted a reactive approach to news communication. In the past few decades the police profession has become much more involved with the news media, which has been accompanied by an increase in their political power, personnel, and fiscal power. They have made an effort to control their environment through a proactive strategy of selectively disclosing knowledge about organizational activities and of defining their public image. The police believe that in relation to a particular incident, a proactive approach to the news media is useful in controlling the version of reality that is transmitted, sustained, and accepted publicly. The rationale for a public relations department within the police department was the control of reporters and their news accounts, according to some police (Ericson et al., 1989).

The police are the primary definers of crime and its control to the public: they delineate the phenomena they subsequently control. They develop the system of classification concerning what constitutes crime, crime rates, and case clearance. They account for their work in these terms, both within the law-enforcement system and to the public. The police expend a considerable proportion of their resources on knowledge control, to achieve accountability in the legal system and the public culture. Police chiefs are both sources and critics of crime news. Although they deplore the emphasis of news stories on crime, they nevertheless seek to manage crime information (Skolnick and McCoy, 1984). They have an elaborate system of internal reporting to the point where officers become "paper police." They spend more time writing accounts of their investigative activity than on actually doing the investigative work (Ericson et al., 1989).

For their part, police recognize that in all of their communications, knowledge is power. In relation to the news media, power entails offensive and defensive strategies that maximize helpful news and minimize hurtful news. Viewed as a strategic commodity, news as knowledge is not considered for its truth value, but rather for its value to the policing mandate. In the eyes of the police information officer, news is but another commodity in the social control business (Ericson et al., 1989). The police attempt to maximize their ability to "sell the police" to the media, and therefore to the public. They attempt to mobilize the media to help them accomplish their occupational goals. Thus they see the media as a resource for handling emergencies, investigations, and crime prevention, and enhancing police resources. The media also serve the police at the level of organizational and occupational ideology, helping to create a positive image of the police, and thereby mobilizing popular support (Ericson et al., 1989).

Police-citizen transactions are structured and carefully controlled as to which accounts will be made public communications and which will remain private. The main task of the employees in public relations is to produce news releases about crime that police officers have selected as newsworthy. The facts to be reported are only those circumscribed and channelled into the grooves of the major-occurrence news-release form. Excluded, for example, is any account from the victims, witnesses, and suspects involved in the crime incident. For the purpose of public knowledge, public-affairs employees settle on the facts of crime, and in the process give these facts their "performative character" (Fishman, 1980). That is, the information about a crime is constituted not as it happened, but as the police force bureaucracy wants it understood publicly. As Wheeler (1986: 15) summarizes in his observations of the public affairs unit, "[T]he purpose of the occurrence report is to construct the occurrence as criminal, thereby making the police action seem sensible, proper, and officially authorized." In this way, the account provides "the procedures for not knowing certain events," namely those events that are not relevant to the bureaucratic organizations (Smith, 1990: 63).

The dominant view reflected in the literature on media is that the police-reporter relationship is asymmetrical, in favor of the police. This view has been grounded in the perspective of journalists (Chibnall, 1977; Fishman, 1980). By failing to ground their knowledge in the police perspective, researchers have ignored the ways in which the police experience constrictions on news discourse, just as reporters are limited by police discourse. I contend that police-reporter transactions are interdependent and that there are controls on each side.

The police are also restricted and controlled to some degree by the media. They strive to avoid negative coverage that might tarnish their image or hurt a specific operation. Police officers believe that they need to respond to news media to avoid negative coverage and denial of future news access. The feelings of dependency and loss of control are vividly real to those experiencing them. Ironically, the techniques journalists use to compel police to respond are the familiar ones police use routinely to interrogate citizens (Ericson et al., 1989). The journalist visualizes a news context for the news text, that often has little relation to the source's own social context. Journalists exercise control through their editing of the text. They can bias a text by selecting or emphasizing one source, having obtained multiple sources of information. They can collapse many interviews into one interview, and manipulate the content as well as the meaning of the text. They can edit out material that doesn't correspond with their point of view, and present partial truths. The resultant textually mediated discourse is a product not only of the reporters' individual biases but also the organizational context in which the media are produced.

The police can be considered to be narrative agents who mediate the margins of "otherness," the world of the deviant that both threatens and defines the world of the everyday. However, both police as well as journalists can also be perceived as "other" from the standpoint of the public attempting to understand how their world is constructed. I suggest that police and the media reinforce each other's organizations through their exercise of power and control in their joint construction of mediated texts for the public.

Ideology and Organization of the News Media

In the eyes of the police, both crime-incident reporting and the reporting of instances of police deviance are part of the news media's bias toward the dramatic and sensational, based on their orientation toward selling newspapers and performing well in broadcast markets, regardless of what they themselves try to do to introduce other considerations. Criminologists and police think that other distortions may also result from the media's focus on an individual case.

Reporters continually press for what the police regard as premature disclosure due to the fact that they face constant deadlines. The police have a different sense of timing; they would prefer to carry out a thorough investigation and reveal the facts only when it has been firmly decided what they are. The reporter's goal is to get the facts with no investigation, and worries little if things have changed or require correction for a later news bulletin. The executive director of the Police Chiefs (PERF), Gary Hayes, asserted that the public misses the complexities of major criminal justice policy issues because newspapers adhere to a practice of simplistic crime reporting (Skolnick, 1984). The media emphasize the role of the police as "crime fighters" rather than as "public servants." Even though this flies in the face of empirical data on police activity, the police go along with this practice because it serves their own goals as well.

Sociologist Gaye Tuchman claims that both "newsworkers and news organizations present themselves as the fourth branch of government [in the sense that they believe] they act as gadflies to insure that government serves the people" (1978: 157). This can be an argument for the media placing controls on the police as they do on other powerful public organizations. Some sociologists, criminologists, and lawyers have argued that the police "patrol the facts" and control how crime and policing are portrayed in the media. Criminologists are routinely placed in the position of being secondary definers of crime, having to address crime as it is first classified by police. Publics wishing for knowledge about crime and police activities are therefore placed in a dependent position. The media often work within the parameters of police discourse about crime.[2]

However, the role of the media is often an uncritical, "don't-rock-the-boat" approach. Herman and Chomsky (1988), among others, show how the media serve a propaganda function. They argue that there are structural relationships that filter out information and limit what can become news in the U.S. One important filter is "sourcing," the issue of what constitutes a credible source. The dominant sources tend to flood the market. Government sources, including local police departments, the Pentagon, and the State Department, can saturate the media with information or disinformation, because information from these sources is considered official and carries with it the assumption of credibility. In a recent British study of the media, judges, lawyers, and court officials appeared in national daily newspapers as the second highest source of news, followed by police and law enforcement sources, whereas social workers, such as probation and prison workers, were the least utilized as a source of news (Schlesinger, Tumber, and Murdock, 1991).

In addition to sourcing there are several other important considerations in the selection and filtering of information that are built into the organizational structure of the media. They are constraints of available time, resources, and geography; "news" decided on by the tradition of news value or television value (for example, visual impact); and most importantly, this cultural air we breathe, the whole ideological atmosphere of our society (Glasgow University Media Group, 1980). This cultural air tells us that some things can be said and others are better left unsaid. For example, the mainstream press or television will never present an alternative view that the police should be disarmed, or the view that the U.S. needs female police stations like those started in Brazil. It will not argue that social workers should take a vow of poverty, or the view that social workers should rise up on behalf of their clients.

The political functions of the police, both instrumentally and symbolically as a political instrument for the control of conflicts (Van Outrive, and Fijnaut, 1983: 53–54), have parallels in how the news media institution sees its own enterprise. Instrumentally, the media have had a similar political concern, embodied in their fourth-estate mandate. They are centrally involved in designating deviance and advancing control remedies, and they do so in the name of the "general good" or "public interest." At the symbolic level, the primary significance of the police in newspaper ideology lies in their physical and symbolic role as representatives and defenders of the established consensus and its institutions. Given that the notion of responsible reporting entails the promotion of the public interest, it follows that it also entails the promotion of police interests (Chibnall, 1977). The news media and police therefore have an "instrumental affinity in reproducing order and an ideological affinity in acknowledging order" (Ericson et al., 1989: 92).

Journalists need to communicate in terms of the common sense, which has already been established by the police monopoly on public discourse about crime. This dependency among journalists is accentuated by their need to "fix" quickly on their stories, and to provide daily reports of police activities. Therefore, they depend on police news releases about major crime, routinely furthering the crime discourse of the police by rewriting police releases as news items. Thus police news is transformed into crime news: crime news reflects the most traditional assumptions of the treatment of news. These are spelled out by Todd Gitlin: "News concerns the *event*, not the underlying condition; the *person*, not the group; *conflict*, not consensus; the fact that *'advances the story,'* not the one that explains it in general: the archetypical news story is a crime story . . ." (1980: 28).

In this context, the police department offers the reporter the fundamental facts to write the story as well as suggestions and opportunities for visual presentation of the facts. To the extent that any analysis of the facts is appropriate, the public relations officer can offer that to the reporters as well. Finally, she can provide statements by police concerning the development of the case. This type of reporting lends itself to journalists depending on public relations professionals as sources of news. This dependence is heightened in the instance of crime stories because there is no question that such stories sell newspapers. The journalist is always in an inferior negotiating position: the reporter who cannot get information is out of a job, whereas the policeman who retains it is not. It has often been stated that the reporter's world is drawn toward that of the policeman rather than vice versa (Chibnall, 1977; Fishman, 1980). Reporters know they need the police. I would add that the police are equally dependent on the reporter in carrying out their work. Both the reporter and the police produce public textual discourse that structure communication for public consumption.

Disjunction: Mediated Images and Public Perceptions

The way that police officers are construed by Americans is influenced by our dominant cultural images, which are filtered through our mass media.[3] These images appear in the mediated images that have helped to shape our view of the profession of police work. Newswriters and television play an important part in constructing these images. As Gitlin reminds us, our society's public cultural space is "saturated with mass media" and the "routines of journalism normally and regularly combine to select certain versions of reality over others" (1980: 4). Michael Parenti explains the process this way:

> The social institutions of capitalist society are the purveyors of its cultural myths, values and legitimating viewpoints, and to the extent that news producers—from publishers to reporters—are immersed in that culture, they may not be fully aware of how they misrepresent, evade, and suppress the news. . . . Devoid of the supportive background assumptions of the dominant belief system, the deviant view sounds just too improbable and too controversial to be treated as news, while the orthodox view appears as an objective representation of reality itself. (1986: 240)

Lippmann (1922) coined the intriguing phrase "the pictures in our heads" to identify our pictures of social reality we receive through the media. An example will show how familiar media images help contribute to the pictures we hold in our heads of police officers and many other occupational groups.

First, think about Pictures-in-the-Papers of police.
- Police Officers Driving in their Cruisers: a law enforcement image
- Police Gathered for a Fellow Officer's Funeral: a "hero" image, died in the line of duty
- Uniformed Officers Handcuffing a Suspect: a law enforcement image

Next, think about Pictures-in-our-Heads of police.
- Police Officers Delivering Bad News to Families: a human services image, a frightening idea
- Police Cars Piling up in a Chase Gone Awry: a "fool" image, featured in motion pictures
- Police Coercing Suspects into Confessions: a "villain" image, based on experience or movies

Neither of these sets of pictures may be "reality" for our own community. To say this, however, is not to say the reservoir of images is insignificant. Each reader or viewer will draw upon it as he or she encounters future media coverage of police (Powers and Kasinsky, 1993).

Klapp (1962) argues that there are three major categories that penetrate the popular consciousness: praise, condemnation, and ridicule; he uses popular archetypes of the hero, villain, and fool to represent these dimensions of social control and order in any society. Whereas the heroes are positive role models, the villains represent negative models of evil to be feared, hated and ridiculed. These models are utilized in the mass media to control persons as well as to put on "significant dramas and rituals" (16–17). Typing also defines "emergent roles" and helps the process of "professionalization" (18, 21).

According to Parenti (1992), television drama has influenced public perceptions of the police and the legal system. The more time people spend watching television and movies, the more their impressions of the world resemble those of the "make-believe media." The high visibility of policing as a high-action profession lends itself to cop shows becoming a major staple of network television entertainment. Television continues to be the major mediated image for most Americans.

For more than forty years prime-time television dramas have presented allegories about police and detectives as well as lawyers and criminals. Almost one-third of all prime-time entertainment shows since 1958 have been concerned with law enforcement and crime (McNeil, 1980), and nearly a third of all the characters on prime-time television are involved in either the enforcement or violation of the law (Dominick, 1973).

Television shows of crime-fighting heroes both reflect and shape public opinion. In the forties with Sergeant Joe Friday in "Dragnet," the police were big heroes. Throughout the fifties and sixties, the police were no longer the central heroes; the detectives and lawyers became more prominent. By 1968 the police were again legitimate heroes in the guise of "Mod Squad." Television producers had found new ways to channel the rebelliousness of the era into popular new dramas, without damaging perceptions of either the police or their work. They were "cool" and, by implication, so was their work; as Todd Gitlin (1983: 258) wrote, "to the law-and-order minded of all ages who saw in the kids' plain clothes not simply hand-loose garb of the young but the disguises of effective law enforcement."

In the 1970s a new type of policeman appeared—the blue-collar ethnic cop. This crime fighter was tougher, as well as more violent. Kojak personified the response to changing perceptions of crime. Television from this era up to the nineties has made a conscious effort to solidify "crime control" values in the American culture. In the eighties and nineties, however, the major image change for police is that they are depicted more like social workers on shows such as "Cagney & Lacey" and "Hill Street Blues." They are women, warm, vulnerable, "real" people (Stark, 1987).

Not only have televised portraits changed public attitudes, they can even alter the way police act. "Time was when officers of the law were dull, plodding Sergeant Fridays—sober, simply doin' a job folks," critic Robert Lewis Shayon wrote during the 1950s. "Now, after a generation of broadcasting, cops are highly competent, alertly tempered, debonair, even witty gentlemen. This modification of behavior could have come about only because of the relentless pervasive influence of dial cops on the real thing" (Stark, 1987: 258).

In turn, real-life dramas and television dramas have often blended together in eerie ways, influencing public attitudes as well. For example, television viewers' images of the Stuart story in Boston revolved around the brutal footage of the discovery of the Stuarts by the police and photographers from a CBS cop show "911" that was in Boston when the actual shooting occurred. The footage has been repeatedly shown on news and

feature programs and was made available for promotional
purposes for a CBS movie on the Stuart case. We will analyze
this case in more depth below.

There is a clear disjunction between public images of the
police and the reality of police work conveyed by social scientists
and shared by the police. Police agree as well with the fact that
the media image of crime is a gross distortion. Most of their time
is spent in routine administrative or clerical work, or in attempts
to locate and interview victims on cases that experience has
shown will never be solved. Police officers are often upset when
the media images of themselves do not seem to match their
professional image. However, Ericson et al. (1989) found that
police were most concerned with whether the media positively
reflected the force's image rather than with providing an
accurate understanding of crime, police organization, and their
occupation. Distortions of police based on their "crime-fighting"
role served their organizational image and therefore did not
seem to upset them.

Celebrity Media Cases Portraying Police

As is common in media stories, portrayals of occupations
are usually broad strokes without fine distinctions or
explanations. They are frequently snatches of human interest
stories or interesting visuals. For every in-depth feature article
there are scores of news flashes. Critical media studies writers
such as Gitlin (1983) talk about journalistic conventions and the
concept of news as drama. For example, a story is more likely to
be about a prison uprising than about prison literacy efforts. This
drama is so familiar that it has a name: "Who's To Blame?"
Recurring media coverage patterns such as the blame theme are
important in discerning bias and the filtering process.

If news is drama, how are police officers cast as characters?
The analysis presented here will utilize provocative news stories
that are not necessarily typical, but are illustrative of the
interaction between police and journalists. They illustrate the
filtering process that patrols and mediates "the facts." These
stories speak to the everyday conflicts between the police and

journalists as they carry out their routine work within the context of their organizations. I will analyze the active ways in which texts organize their discourses and create a textually mediated reality. The first case is that of the Stuart murder, which captures the dominant cultural images of policing in North American culture. The Rodney King story, a more atypical, deviant case, serves as a counterpoint. The texts are mainly taken from the *Boston Globe*, the *Los Angeles Times*, and the *New York Times* as well as various commission reports.

The Stuart Murder

Many studies have commented on the extent to which violent crime fills the pages of both national and local newspapers. The Stuart murder is a typical story of violent homicide, but some atypical aspects helped it become the focus of national media attention. Two years after the initial story it was still newsworthy. The changing media frames portraying police as heroes, fools, and villains can give us some insight into how the media creates public textual discourse (Kasinsky, 1991). How did police and media collaborate in filtering out information that led them to the wrong suspect? The interaction between police and media, as well as how the media select information sources, will provide us with some major clues.

The story first appeared in the Boston dailies on October 23, 1989. Headlines on page one read, "Couple Shot After Leaving Hospital; Baby Delivered." According to initial news reports, the Stuarts, driving home from Brigham and Women's Hospital in downtown Boston after a child-birthing class, had been shot in their car by an unknown African-American gunman who fled the scene. With his seven-month pregnant wife slouched beside him, dying from a gunshot wound, Stuart dialed an emergency number on his cellular car phone, reaching state police headquarters. The state police dispatcher, who directed police units to the couple's car, became known as a hero. The police detectives on the case were also portrayed in the media as heroes.

Shortly thereafter, hundreds of police searched the site of the crime, the Mission Hill area, and identified a "prime suspect" who fit the initial description that Charles Stuart gave to the police. The suspect, William Bennett, was thirty-nine and was identified in the press as an unemployed African-American man, an ex-con who had spent the past thirteen years in prison for crimes that included shooting a police officer. The major Boston papers reiterated all these stereotypes in many articles along with the Stuart story, emphasizing the black face of urban violence. The media prematurely publicized the details of evidence of only the main police suspect at an inconclusive point in the investigation to the exclusion of contradictory evidence as told by other key witnesses. The media all too eagerly had cooperated with police in accusing of murder an innocent African-American who had been set up by the police; and they had in the process implicated the predominantly African-American community of Mission Hill. A serious travesty of justice took place, affecting the above individuals as well as the public who had a right to full knowledge of all the evidence when the investigation had been properly concluded.

In a unexpected twist of events less than three months later, on January 5, 1990, Charles Stuart became the number one suspect. Large bold headlines on page one of the *Boston Globe* read, "Stuart Dies in Jump off Tobin Bridge After Police Are Told He Killed his Wife." Throughout January, bold headlines on the front pages of the *Boston Globe* covered the Stuart story and suggested motives. "Probers Suspect Stuart Killed Wife to Collect Insurance, Start Restaurant." The formerly heroic detectives who got their suspect were now cast in the media as bungling fools. According to *Boston Globe* reporter Reid, "Dispatcher's Pride has Turned Sour." A photo of the dispatcher, Gary McLaughlin, portrays him as a "crestfallen, bewildered man" when he received the news after Stuart's death: "I've become a part of a very bizarre thing." [*Boston Globe*, 1990, Jan. 5, A19].

The police and prosecutors' sense of urgency to find a suspect had led them to the wrong person. With this dramatic turnabout, the media now portrayed the police in a shrill tone, as villains with racist motives. William Bennett was released, and the African-American community now expressed its indignation with the police *vis-à-vis* the media. In articles discussing the reaction of the African-American community of Mission Hill, the police were vilified by the media. The following headlines capture their angry tone: "Black Leaders Demand that [Mayor] Flynn Apologize" [*Boston Globe*, 1990, Jan. 6, A1], "Black Leaders Denounce Handling of Investigation" [*Boston Globe*, 1990, Jan. 6], "Black Leaders Ask Review of Stuart Probe" [*Boston Globe* 1990, Jan. 7, A1]. The Boston police force's stop-and-frisk policy for suspected drug dealers and gang members, centering in Boston's primarily African-American communities of Roxbury and Dorchester, had raised the ire of leaders and African-American youth in these communities. The presence of police and detectives in the Mission Hill area immediately after the murder, stopping and frisking hundreds of suspects, added fuel to the earlier conflict between Boston's minority community and the police: "Mission Hill Tries to Heal the Pain. 1,000 area residents hold prayer service" [*Boston Globe*, 1990, Jan. 8, A7].

A few days later Mayor Flynn devoted a major portion of his State of the City address to the black community's reaction to the police handling of the Stuart murder in the context of its threat to race relations in the city of Boston [*Boston Globe*, 1990, Jan. 10, A20]. Then, in December 1990, more articles appeared on the heels of the release of the attorney general's own investigation that concluded that the Boston police department "engaged in improper and unconstitutional conduct in the 1989–90 period with respect to stops and searches of minority individuals in the Roxbury, Dorchester, and Mattapan communities" (Shannon Report, 1990: 60). Special feature articles appeared in the *Globe* for the rest of January; for example: "Evidence Against Bennett was Tainted Lawyers Say." "In City Newsrooms, Cynics were Believers." "Chuck wanted His Name Up in Lights," by popular columnist, Mike Barnicle. "Legacy of the Stuart Murder," "An Image of a Trusting Wife Linger," by Matthew Brelis [Jan. 21] and the same day, "Poll: Stuart Case Hurt Race Relations," by Peter Howe. Additional articles appeared on the Stuart case with the investigation of the grand jury. "Stuart Grand Jury Probe Residents' Charges" [*Boston Globe*, 1990, Oct. 21, A1, A32].

The following year, the end of September 1991, almost two years after the murder of Carol Stuart, the case of the brother-in-law and a friend appeared before the criminal courts, "New Chapter in Boston Murder Case," "Suspect's Brother, Friend Indicted" [*Boston Globe*, 1991, Sept. 28].

An examination of the filtering process operating in the Stuart case is key to our understanding of the way it was investigated and reported in the newspapers. From the outset, the police pursued William Bennett as the main suspect and did not seriously consider alternative avenues of investigation. The print media collaborated with the police in presenting a textually mediated account which underlined police sources and omitted any alternative information which might have led to other possible theories. Before January 5, newswriters and columnists alike, such as Mike Barnicle of the *Boston Globe*, wrote multiple stories decrying the black face of violence and pointing the finger at Bennett as the murderer. None of the major Boston newspapers, neither the *Boston Globe* nor the *Boston Herald*, pursued interviews with police informants who claimed that the police coerced statements from at least three young witnesses, who were coached to point the finger at Bennett. It was only more than one year after the murder that an official investigative report of the attorney general comments upon the malpractices of the Boston police department in the Stuart case. The report cautiously acknowledges that based on the statements of the witnesses, "repeatedly the police appear to have threatened, coerced, and offered favors to obtain testimony that would implicate Willie Bennett" (Shannon, 1990: 64).

The issue of "sourcing" is relevant here. A young woman reporter, Michelle Caruso from the *Boston Herald*, had an alternative theory that Stuart was the main suspect, and attempted to convince the prosecutor to pursue this avenue of investigation. On November 11, 1989, she sounded the only cautionary note among all the major dailies, which named Bennett as the key suspect although he had not yet been charged with the crime. Her interview source was a police informant who charged that "the police are pressuring her to implicate Bennett though she denied to them seeing him on the night of the shooting" (58). Caruso was well trained in the importance of having a legitimate source to back up her point of view. As Caruso described it, "The bottom line was, we came an inch away from writing a story about all the doubts I had. I needed an expert in law enforcement, or a forensic guy to say, 'This case is not what it seems'" (Caruso, 1991: 58). A reporter still needs a source, "A reporter can't write her own opinions." At the time, Caruso did not consider her female police informant to be a sufficiently legitimate source; she dared not pursue her own investigative line far enough because it was contrary to the line of investigation being pursued by the homicide unit and contrary to what had become the dominant textually mediated reality. In the Stuart case, Caruso, a trained police reporter, suspended confidence in her own experience as an investigator and instead relied on the organizational representation of police texts as the authoritative interpreters of what was really going on. Media norms of what constituted legitimate sources took precedence, precluding an alternative textual account which challenged the police account.

The Rodney King Beating

In the American press it is not common for police officers to be portrayed as villains. The Rodney King story of police abuse was carried by the newspapers and other print media for at least a month as a headlined story. Like the Charles Stuart case, it featured interpersonal violence. However, in this case the police were portrayed as the major perpetrators of the violence. Another similarity with the Stuart case was the racial harassment theme that was repeatedly mentioned in the King story. In this case the victim, Rodney King, was African-American and all twenty-seven of the police officers on the scene that night were white.

In this section, the following questions will be explored: How did this event become constructed by the media? What were the competing images and texts presented by the media and police? Did public perceptions favor the dominant police interpretation of the event as an "isolated event" or the media's interpretation of "widespread police brutality?" Ever since the

Rodney King beating, the subsequent acquittal of the police by a Simi Valley jury, and the federal trial of four police officers, the topic of police violence has been a major topic of discussion in the print mass media, television, radio and legislative hearings. According to Skolnick and Fyfe (1993: xvii) in their recent book on police violence, "both the content and the results of this [media] attention show a tendency to oversimplify, rather than to analyze with any depth or meaning."

The Rodney King incident occurred in Los Angeles on March 3 at 12:30 A.M. However, the first major news of the Rodney King beating was a visual account of the beating by the amateur cameraman George Holliday, who happened to capture the event on his personal camcorder. The videotape had high visibility as it was first broadcast on Channel 5 in Los Angeles the night after the event, followed by repeated showings on CNN and all the major TV networks. This independent source was the mediated electronic reality upon which the mainstream media constructed their subsequent stories. This graphic image of many policemen beating a citizen was etched into the minds of the public as it was played repeatedly.

Three different Los Angeles commissions produced competing textual accounts of the King beating: an internal investigation by the Los Angeles Police Department, a report by the Police Commission, and another by an independent commission appointed by the mayor and the police chiefs, referred to as the Christopher Report, headed by Warren Christopher, a Los Angeles attorney. This independent commission refers to the conflicting, competing versions and emphasizes the importance of the independent videotaped account.

> Our Commission owes its existence to the George Holliday videotape of the Rodney King incident. Whether there even would have been a Los Angeles Police Department investigation without the video is doubtful, since the efforts of King's brother, Paul, to file a complaint were frustrated, and the report of the involved officers was falsified. Even if there had been an investigation, our case-by-case review of the handling of 700 complaints indicates that without the Holliday videotape the complaint might have been adjudged to be "not

sustained," because the officers' version conflicted with
the account by King and his two passengers, who typically
would have been viewed as not "independent."
(Christopher Report, 1991, ii)

The first print story in the *Boston Globe* appeared on March
7, "A Home Videotape of a Dozen LA Police Officers Beating
and Kicking on an Unarmed Black Man—Increased Racial
Tensions in the City." A profile of the victim described him as an
"unemployed construction worker," released from prison, "a
parolee," having served six months of a two-year sentence for
second degree robbery. Only a few negative descriptors were
presented.

Four days later the official police response was delivered
by Chief Darryl Gates at a Los Angeles press conference in the
presence of seventeen TV cameras and over seventy members of
the news media. All newspapers covered the story. The *Boston
Globe* caption read "LA Chief Wants 3 Charged in Beating" [1991,
Mar. 8, A12]. According to the *Los Angeles Times*, Chief Gates
announced four officers would face criminal charges and that the
others who watched and did nothing could face administrative
punishment. In the conference Gates preached that police
academy graduates need a "reverence for the law." He
continued, "What they should have done, if they really loved
their brother officers [was to] have stepped in and grabbed them
and hauled them back and said, 'Knock it off!' That's what the
sergeant should have done [and] that's what every officer there
should have done" [1991, Mar. 8]. The subtext of the conference
was that the behavior of the police was an "aberrant," "isolated"
event that would be officially punished.

The news conference was contested by many of the media
persons present who expressed by their questions their
skepticism of Chief Gates' sincerity based on his past record. The
questions reflected a particular mistrust of the Los Angeles
Police Department and other Southern California law
enforcement agencies on the part of persons of color and their
representatives whose personal experiences confirmed a
different reality. Gregory Boyle, a Jesuit priest and pastor of
Dolores Mission Church, whose membership consisted of black,
Hispanic, working-class, and poor people from East Los Angeles,

criticized Gates' interpretation of the incident. His counter-interpretation was that "Most people of color can recall such an incident happening to them or to a family member or neighbor" (Boyle, 1991).

Most Los Angeles residents and especially persons of color polled by the media were found to distrust the police. Eighty-six percent said they had seen the videotape and said they agreed with King's version that he had cooperated with police instructions, rather than the police version that he "acted menacingly." Only two percent of black respondents believed the police account. Ninety-two percent of all respondents thought the arresting officers had used too much force against King [*Los Angeles Times*, March 10, 1991].

These two versions on the issue of cooperation and the use of police force were not, however, the only ones being contested. In this case, different law enforcement observers both challenged and verified King's account textually represented by the videotape.

In the initial news stories of the Rodney King incident there was some mention of contradictory accounts of the incident; the police account differed from those of Rodney King and his two passengers. A full police report was not released to the media. Most of the news accounts did not probe the contradictory details. Accounts of other law enforcement officers witnessing the event disagreed with the official police version, but were not reported in most newspapers, including the *Boston Globe*. At least two of the many officers present acknowledged the use of police force, supporting the textual reality presented in the video. Officer Melanie Singer of the California Highway Patrol said she believed King was trying to comply with the officer's commands when he was beaten. She said that "King did not aggressively kick or punch the officers; he was merely trying to get away from the officers." Officer Ingrid Larson also contended that "King did not appear to be combative, but merely used his arms to block the baton strikes." Paramedics on the scene also testified that King was not acting violently (Christopher Report, 1991, 13).

The night of the beating, verbatim accounts of radio conversations on the police computer network created an additional text at variance with the official police version. Sergeant S. Koon, the supervising officer that night, joked to the commander of his watch, knowing that his conversation was being recorded, that: "U(patrol unit) just had a big time use of force . . . chased and beat the suspect of CHP pursuit, big time" [Mydans, 1991, Mar. 19, A1]. The response from the police station was, "Oh well, I'm sure the lizard didn't deserve it, HA HA I'll let them know, OK" (Christopher Report, 1991, 14). These officers acted with little concern for censure of their comments or behavior by the higher police authorities. They expected the chief to back them up, as he had done in the past. But the public showing of a citizen's videotape precluded the "business-as-usual" course of action.

Media-created public opinion gave credibility to the view that police brutality was not an "isolated event." The *Boston Globe* and the *New York Times* gave a high profile to a presentation by two members of the Congressional Black Caucus urging a wider inquiry on police brutality and harassment of minorities. Responding to the media framing of the event, Attorney General Thornburgh ordered a national inquiry on police brutality. A front page *Boston Globe* headline, "Thornburgh Orders Nationwide Inquiry on Police Brutality," was accompanied by a photo of Rodney King [*Boston Globe*, 1991, Mar. 15, A1]. The media's image of police brutality in Los Angeles framed as institutionalized racism became a national problem rather than an isolated incident. The phrase "police brutality" become the major theme in many news stories, often coupled with the subthemes of racial discrimination and harassment.

These larger themes of racism and police brutality became more muted with time. After a couple of weeks the focus of the media shifted to the conflict between Chief Gates and his adversaries, the mayor and leaders in the minority community. Chief Gates became the political scapegoat as both the Los Angeles mayor as well as the community of color exercised their political clout to remove him as chief—a "quick-fix" problem resolution. Only a few op-ed columns and stories by special interest groups continued to present the text that police brutality is a systematic and widespread practice in California and elsewhere, especially used against persons of color. For example, the *New York Times* ran a special story headlined, "Videotaped Beating by Officers Puts Full Glare on Brutality Issue," with the subheading, "Details Heighten Sense That it Was No Aberration" [March 18, A1]. The *Boston Globe* carried a similarly headlined story. The *New York Times* on March 19 carried an op-ed piece, "L.A. Cops, Taped in the Act."

The Rodney King case was framed by the media as being more than an isolated case of police brutality. Rather, the use of brutality by the L.A. police department upon the minority community was presented by the media as representative of a widespread phenomenon. The use of an initial independent source allowed the media to be more critical than usual of excessive police force. However, the critical capacity of the mainstream media did not extend to a serious exploration of the underlying causes of police brutality and racism. They did not print the full texts of the police reports, including full verbatim accounts of police radio conversations and full texts of witnesses including other law enforcement officers who contradicted the official police account of the incident. These additional texts would have provided readers with additional information to make an independent judgement as to whether or not excessive police force was used by police on Rodney King. In their absence, the videotape, repeatedly shown, was for the majority of the public the most compelling text which condemned the Los Angeles police actions.

Conclusion and Implications

In this chapter I have suggested a framework for understanding both the organizations of the media and the police profession as a textually mediated reality. The media and policing organizations, based upon their own organizational demands, have collaborated in constructing texts which in turn have legitimated the privileged reproduction of their discourses. Through their use of filtering devices and procedures such as overdependence upon police and other official sources, the media have become part of the policing apparatus of our society.

An interactive approach focuses on specific contestations of power between the police and the media and within these institutions. This approach can be an important one, especially for marginalized and oppressed persons who need to know not only how to deconstruct the powerful images of the textual reality, but how to create new versions of mediated reality with which to empower themselves.

The media help legitimate our society's current ideological system with images and themes that propagate private enterprise, personal affluence, individual acquisitiveness, consumerism, and racial and sexual stereotyping (Parenti, 1992). Both broadcast and print media tend to sensationalize street crime and crime fighting, to the exclusion of much meaningful consideration of other crimes, especially corporate crime, wife and child abuse, and other crimes committed against oppressed groups.

Moreover, police interests operate simultaneously with those of the media. The police have recognized the fact that they will grow and be nurtured if they are perceived as crime-fighters, but not if the public recognizes their inability to protect people against crime. The public is presented with images in the frame of existing sociopolitical orthodoxies. Themes that would raise questions about the existing arrangements of wealth and power are, with rare exceptions, not included. The broader, systematic causes of social problems are also ignored, although the symptoms may be bemoaned. Problems are shown as solved by individual efforts within the system, rather than collective efforts against it. In both the Rodney King and Stuart cases, racism and police brutality are named, but the systematic underlying causes for them are not examined.

Police and media interactions in both the Stuart and King cases suggest distinctive approaches. In the Stuart case the media's reactive approach led to their collusion with the police by relying on their version of textually mediated reality. In this role they exercised little independence and investigative functions, whereas in the King case an independent videotaped account enabled the media to take a greater proactive role. The police and other observers' texts were not subsumed into the police chief's organizational text due to the power of the videotaped image as well as the media's presentation of the alternative texts from the alliance of both the mayor and the communities of color. The media's role in both of these cases had very different consequences. In the Stuart case the media contributed actively not only to condemning an innocent person but also to exercising stereotyped judgment against an entire community of persons of color. In the King case the media's proactive stance educated and pressured authorities in Los Angeles and Washington to take a more active role in investigating and acting against institutional racism.

Gramsci (1971) noted that the capitalist class achieves hegemony not only by propagating manipulative values and beliefs, but by actually performing vital social functions that have diffuse benefits.[4] The media try to invent reality but they must also sometimes admit realities. For example, they took the lead in the Rodney King story by exposing the way in which police brutality is used oppressively against racial minorities. They led the clarion call for reform. If the media are to maintain legitimacy in a democratic society, they must maintain their democratic appearances and occasionally give in to popular demands[5] (Parenti, 1992).

This suggests a more daring role for the media that goes beyond simply maintaining their legitimacy by serving as a major watchdog institution over police activities. As the fourth branch of government, the media can act as a gadfly to insure that government works for its citizens. Rather than "patrolling the facts" by presenting carefully selected images of crime and police, the media could begin to take their critical, investigative role more seriously. They could begin to police the police.

NOTES

1. The immediate context was a local history of confrontations between movement people and the police. Shortly before the publication of the professor's letter in the underground newspaper,

Berkeley Barb, a rally had been held without permit and the police had been ordered by city council to disband it. The resulting resistance led to the imposition (requested by the police) of a curfew on the city. Enforcing it produced many complaints of harassment and the excessive use of force. When this problem was raised in city council, a majority voted to condemn police behavior. The mayor was strongly opposed to the motion. Thus there was already polarization on the issue and the response of the public was of importance to the mayor and chief of police. See Darrough, W., "When versions collide: Police and the dialectics of accountability," *Urban Life,* 7(3): 379–402, 1978.

2. The term "culture work" has been used to refer to the role crime data play in shaping what we perceive to be the reality of crime. Michalowski notes that only those institutions like the FBI and local police departments produce official statistics (the Uniform Crime Report) of the common index crimes: murder, rape, robbery, assault, burglary, larceny, auto theft and arson, which are then publicly disseminated for popular consumption by the media (see Michalowski, R., *Order, Law and Crime,* New York: Random House). There is no comparable release of statistics on white-collar crimes such as injuries and deaths due to violations of worker safety standards, consumer fraud, price-fixing, corporate kickbacks or illegal stock manipulations. Corporate violations are for the most part not treated as worthy of media attention. This selective generation and dissemination of data on social harms in America serves to shape our image of crime as primarily an individualistic working-class phenomenon. See Renée G. Kasinsky, *Crime, Oppression and Inequality,* Needham Heights: Ginn Press (Div. of Simon Schuster), 1991:3–4.

3. It is important to recognize to what extent the printed media are different from television. Print media are also internally differentiated and distribute their attention between different kinds of discourse. For example, the "popular" and tabloid newspapers give far greater play to the opinions and perspectives offered by the victims of crime and their relatives and by those suspected or convicted of crimes. They are more oriented to "common-sense" thinking and discourse, and less to professionalized debate and the evaluation of policy. On the other hand, the quality newspapers offer space for the views of experts, elites and pressure groups. Similarly within television programs, there is no uniformity of images. "There is no such thing as the mass media image of law, lawyers and justice," says Suzanne Frentz (1992: 9), who points out that at the start of the 1991 television season there were twenty-three programs on law, lawyers, and justice, representing a spectrum of portrayals. See Frentz, S., *Staying Tuned: Contemporary Soap*

Opera Criticism, Bowling Green, OH: Bowling Green State Univ. Popular Press, 1992.

4. Feminist theorists expanding upon the works of Gramscian theory have coined the term "counter-hegemony." Models of cultural hegemony often reinforce views of working-class persons and women as passive recipients of cultural messages. Feminist scholars have questioned this view, offering a more complex picture of cultural change as a multi-dimensional set of interactions in which hegemonic intentions are accommodated, resisted, and reshaped in a variety of ways. They have focused on the experience of women and other marginal groups in their resistance to oppressive conditions. The particular ways hegemonic control is being contested have produced contradictions and new dilemmas, but they have also led the way to new possibilities for further resistance to oppressive conditions.

5. Gitlin in his popular book, *The Whole World is Watching: Mass Media in the Making and Unmaking of the New Left*, Berkeley: Univ. of California Press, 1980, p. 11, believes that oppositional groups can be effective contributors in the media-movement process and in policy reformulations. He asserts that "groups out of power—radical students, farm workers, feminists, environmentalists, or homeowners groaning under the property tax—can contest the prevailing structures of power and definitions of reality." Charlotte Ryan gives examples of how victims and advocates can challenge unfair media frames and use the media to promote change (p. 14). See Charlotte Ryan's informative book, *Prime Time Activism*, subtitled "Media Strategies for Grassroots Organizing," Boston: South End Press, 1991.

REFERENCES

Abercrombie, N., S. Hill, and B. S. Turner. 1980. *The Dominant Ideology Thesis*. London. Allen and Unwin.

———. 1986. *Sovereign Individuals of Capitalism*. London: Allen and Unwin.

Bennett, W. Lance. 1983. *News; The Politics of Illusion*. New York: Longman.

Bittner, E. 1990. *Aspects of Police Work*. Boston: Northeastern Univ. Press.

Boston Globe. 1990, Jan. 5. Stuart dies in jump off Tobin Bridge after police are told he killed his wife, A1.

————. 1990, Jan. 6. Black leaders demand that Flynn apologize, A1.

————. 1990, Jan. 6. Black leaders denounce handling of investigation.

————. 1990. Jan. 7. Black leaders ask review of Stuart Probe, A1.

————. 1990, Jan. 8. Mission Hill tries to heal the pain, 1,000 area residents hold prayer service, A7.

————. 1990, Jan. 10. Article on Mayor Flynn State of the City Address, A20.

————. 1990, Oct. 21. Stuart grand jury probe resident's charges, A1, A32.

————. 1991, Mar. 7. A home videotape of a dozen L.A. police officers beating and kicking on an unarmed black man—Increased racial tensions in the city.

————. 1991, Mar. 8. LA chief wants 3 charged in beating, A12.

————. 1991, Mar. 15. Thornburgh orders nationwide inquiry on police brutality, A1.

————. 1991, Sept. 28. New chapter in Boston murder case.

————. 1991, Sept. 28. Suspect's brother, friend indicted.

Boyle, Gregory J. 1991, March 11. Defenseless, the poor are also voiceless. *Los Angeles Times.*

Brelis, M. 1990, Jan. 21. An image of a trusting wife. *Boston Globe.*

Caruso, M., footnote in Lydon, C. 1991. The Boston hoax: She fought it, He bought it. *Washington Journalism Review,* p 58.

Chibnall, S. 1977. *Law-and-Order News.* London: Tavistock.

Christensen, T. 1987. *Reel Politics.* New York: Basil Blackwell.

Christiansen, J., J. Schmidt, and J. Henderson. 1982. The selling of the police: Media, ideology and crime control. *Contemporary Crisis,* 6, 227–239.

Christopher, Warren, et al. 1991, July 9. *Report of the Independent Commission on the Los Angeles Police Department.* Christopher Report.

Darrough, W. 1978. When versions collide: Police and the dialectics of accountability. *Urban Life,* 73: 379–402.

Dijk, T. A. 1988. *News As Discourse.* Hillsdale, NJ: L. Erlbaum Assoc.

Dominick, J. 1973. Crime and law enforcement on prime-time television. *Public Opinion Quarterly,* 37, 241–50.

Ericson, R. V. and C. D. Shearing. 1986. The scientification of police work. In Böhme, G. and Stehr, N., (eds.), *The Knowledge Society: The Growing Impact of Scientific Knowledge on Social Relations.* Dordrecht: Reidel, 129–59.

Ericson, R. V., P. M. Baranek, and J. B. L. Chan. 1989. *Negotiating Control: A Study of News Sources.* Toronto: Univ. of Toronto Press.

Fishman, M. 1980. *Manufacturing the News.* Austin: Univ. of Texas Press.

Frentz, S. 1992. *Staying Tuned: Contemporary Soap Opera Criticism.* Bowling Green, OH: Bowling Green State Univ. Popular Press.

Gitlin, T. 1980. *The Whole World is Watching: Mass Media in the Making and Unmaking of the New Left.* Berkeley: Univ. of California Press.

———. 1983. *Inside Prime Time.* New York: Pantheon.

Glasgow University Media Group. 1980. *More Bad News.* London: Routledge and Kegan Paul.

Gramsci, A. 1971. *Selections from the Prison Notebooks.* Ed. and translated by Hoare, Q., and Smith, G. N., New York: International Publishers.

Hall, S., C. Critcher, T. Jefferson, J. Clarke, and B. Roberts. 1978. *Policing the Crisis: Mugging, the State, and Law and Order.* London: MacMillan.

Herman, E. H., and N. Chomsky. 1988. *Manufacturing Consent: The Political Economy of the Mass Media.* New York: Pantheon.

Howe, P. 1990, Jan. 21. Poll: Stuart case hurt race relations, *Boston Globe.*

Kasinsky, R. G. 1991. *Crime, Oppression and Inequality.* Needham Heights, MA: Ginn Division of Simon Schuster.

Klapp, O. 1962. *Heroes, Villains and Fools: The Changing American Character.* Englewood Cliffs, NJ: Prentice-Hall.

Kramer, Michael. 1991, April 1. *Newsweek*, 15.

Lippmann, W. 1922. *Public Opinion.* New York: Harcourt, Brace and Co.

Los Angeles Times. 1991, March 8.

———. 1991, March 10.

Manning, P. K. 1977. *Police Work: The Social Organization of Policing.* Cambridge: MIT Press.

———. 1992. Technological dramas and the police: Statement and Counterstatement in organizational analysis. *Criminology*, 303: 327–346.

Michalowski, R. 1985. *Order, Law and Crime*, New York: Random House.

New York Times. 1991, Mar. 18. Videotaped beating by officers puts full glare on brutality issue, A1.

McNeil, A. 1980. *Total Television: A Comprehensive Guide to Programming from 1948 to the Present*. 2nd ed. New York: Penguin.

Mydans, Seth. 1991, March 19. In messages, officers banter after beating in Los Angeles. *New York Times*, A1.

Parenti, Michael. 1986. *Inventing Reality: The Politics of Mass Media*. New York: St. Martin's Press.

———. 1992. *Make-Believe Media: The Politics of Entertainment*. New York: St. Martin's Press.

Powers, P., and R. G. Kasinsky. 1993. "It ain't just a question of misunderstood": A framework for studying media frames. Forthcoming in *Progressive Human Services*.

———. 1993. Media depictions of police work and social work. Forthcoming in *Social Work Education Journal*.

Reid, B. 1990, Jan. 5. Dispatcher's pride has turned sour. *Boston Globe*, A19.

Ryan, C. 1991. *Prime Time Activism*. Boston: South End Press.

Sahin, H. 1980. The concept of ideology and mass communication research. *Journal of Communication Inquiry*, 61, 3–12.

Schlesinger, P., H. Tumber, and G. Murdock. Sept. 1991. The media politics of crime and criminal justice. *British Journal of Sociology*, 423, 397–420.

Shannon, J., S. Jonas, M. Heins. 1990. *Report of the Attorney General's Civil Rights Division on Boston Police Department Practices*. Shannon Report, 72 pp.

Shayon, R. L. 1966. July 30. Morality building with the FBI. *Saturday Review*, 42.

Skolnick, J. and C. McCoy. 1984. Police accountability and the media. *American Bar Foundation Research Journal*, 521–557.

Skolnick, J. and J. Fyfe. 1993. *Above the Law: Police and the Exessive Use of Force*. New York: Free Press.

Smith, D. E. 1990. *Texts, Facts, and Femininity: Exploring the Relations of Ruling*. London: Routledge.

Stark, S. 1987. Perry Mason meets Sonny Crockett. *University of Miami Law Review*, 42: 229–283.

Toch, H. and J. D. Grant. 1991. *Police as Problem Solvers*. New York: Plenum Press.

Tuchman, G. 1978. *Making News: A Study in the Construction of Reality.* New York: Free Press.

Wheeler, G. 1986. *Reporting Crime: The News Release as Textual Mediator of Police/Media Relations.* MA dissertation, Centre of Criminology, Univ. of Toronto.

Van Outrive, L. and C. Fijnaut. 1983. Police and the organization of prevention. In Punch, M. (ed.), *Control in the Police Organization.* Cambridge: MIT Press, pp. 47–59.

PART III

Reconstructing Crime News

CHAPTER 9

Newsmaking Criminology: Reflections on the Media, Intellectuals, and Crime*

Gregg Barak

Although academicians in criminology and criminal justice have come to appreciate the importance of the media in constructing ideological images of crime and punishment, apparently they have not considered how to use mass communications for the purposes of informing, interpreting, and altering those images to reflect more realistically the social, political, and economic conditions of crime and social control. Students of crime and crime control, recognizing that significant relationships are involved in constructing criminal images and in setting public policy agendas, likewise have devoted their time and attention to the study of mass media and its presentation of criminal activities (Cohen and Young, 1973; Fishman, 1978; Humphries, 1981). Yet in spite of all the discussions about the importance of the media in presenting popular portrayals of crime and justice (Bohm, 1986; Box, 1983; Hall, Critcher, Jefferson, Clark, and Roberts, 1977; Pepinsky and Jesilow, 1984; Walker, 1985; Wright, 1985), nobody has suggested ways of using the media expressly for participating in the mass construction of those portrayals. Beginning with an analysis of the relationships among the developing political economy of the mass media, intellectuals, and conceptions of crime and justice, I shall suggest a criminological practice capable of taking advantage of the opportunities in the production of crime news, which I call *newsmaking criminology*.

Newsmaking criminology refers to criminologists' conscious efforts and activities in interpreting, influencing, or shaping the presentation of "newsworthy" items about crime and justice.[1] More specifically, a newsmaking criminology attempts to demystify images of crime and punishment by locating the mass media portrayals of incidences of "serious" crimes in the context of all illegal and harmful activities; strives to affect public attitudes, thoughts, and discourses about crime and justice so as to facilitate a public policy of "crime control" based on structural and historical analyses of institutional development; allows criminologists to come forth with their knowledge and to establish themselves as credible voices in the mass-mediated arena of policy formation; and asks of criminologists that they develop popularly based languages and technically based skills of communication for the purposes of participating in the mass-consumed ideology of crime and justice.

A newsmaking criminology invites criminologists and others to become part of the mass-mediated production and consumption of "serious" crime and crime control. It requires that they share their knowledge with the general public. Accepting such an invitation implies first of all that criminologists understand the role of mass communications within the hegemony of bourgeois capitalism.

Hegemony, Mass Communication, and Bourgeois Capitalism

According to Marxist thought, one clear meaning of hegemony (and the meaning generally accepted today) refers to domination. The other meaning refers to leadership authority and legitimacy, implying some notion of consent. At the time of the Russian Revolution both the Mensheviks and Lenin used the term to "indicate political leadership in the democratic revolution, based on an alliance with sections of the peasantry" (Bottomore, 1983: 201).

Gramsci (1971) is usually credited with developing the Marxist concept of hegemony most fully. He also used both meanings of the word in his writings. In his pre-prison period (before 1926), he used the term in the older sense to refer to a working-class strategy. Initially Gramsci's hegemony referred to the necessary organization of alliances that the working class needed in order to overthrow the bourgeois state and to represent the social basis of the workers' democratic state. While in prison, Gramsci introduced a new meaning when he applied the term to the manner in which the bourgeoisie establishes and maintains its control over the proletariat. This second meaning of hegemony—domination—is used most commonly today by social and behavioral scientists, Marxist and non-Marxist alike.

During the advanced stages of capitalism, argues Gramsci, bourgeois domination consists of a variety of manifestations, including organized force, moral leadership, intellectual persuasion, and political compromises with opposition blocs of interest that represent a basis of consent for a given social order. Thus Gramsci's notion of hegemony is not one of economic determinism or of ideological rigidity, but one in which the dominant or ruling class is created and recreated constantly in a network of institutions, social relations, and ideas. Gramsci's definition or view of the bourgeois state goes well beyond those definitions of the state as an instrument of capitalist domination, and his conception of hegemony cannot be reduced simplistically to issues of legitimation, false consciousness, or manipulation.

In accordance with Gramsci's approach to hegemony, a fully extended analysis of media, intellectuals, and crime assumes that the prevailing orders of the political economy depend on both the passive and the active consent of the governed, and on the collective will of the people in which various groups within society unite and struggle. In other words, hegemony includes not only the ruling classes' world views but also the world views of the masses. These views are composed of a variety of elements and experiences, some of which may actually contradict the dominant ideology without disturbing or delegitimizing the prevailing social order. In the everyday construction of social reality, the role of mass communications is central to the contradictory relations of hegemonic domination.

In the modern age of ideology and technology, mass communication—literature, audio, video, and research—is integral to accumulation, legitimation, and repression in capitalist society (Gouldner, 1976; Mosco, 1986). At the same time, however, it represents an essential framework for social and political struggle. Regarding the former application, mass communication has been used increasingly by the state to manage and mitigate the consequences of the widening conflicts and contradictions of monopoly and multinational capitalism. "Disinformation" campaigns are an obvious illustration of the way in which state-mediated conceptions of official reality are used to "distort" social reality. In the area of crime and crime control, for example, police wires (or news dispatches) are released daily, and the FBI officially collects and disseminates the rates for various crimes.

As for the latter application, at least since the 1960s, both the Left and the Right have been made aware of the significant role that mass communication plays during periods of legitimation crisis and mass conflict. Struggles involving the poor and the working classes, women, blacks, homosexuals, and other powerless groups, opposition to domestic violence and to nuclear energy, and the support of peace agendas and the protection of the environment all reflect the complex relationships between political conflict and the mass media. These social movements demonstrate the importance and the value of extending one's message and analysis, whether left or right. As a consequence, unfortunately, only a very small fraction of intellectuals have begun to use mainstream (mostly alternative) media to promote their ideological point of view. In addition, the Left and the Right alike have learned from interacting with the media that both co-option and internal disruption are possible outcomes (Mosco, 1986). The two sides disagree strongly, however, about the relationship between mass communications and hegemony.

Mass communications research with a leftward, critical, or Marxist orientation tends to focus on the political economy or on the content and culture of media (Mosco, 1986). Studies emphasizing the political economy are concerned with questions of ownership and control of media institutions, with processes of media production, distribution, and reception, and with analyses of the various links between media and the wider capitalist system. Studies that emphasize content and culture are concerned with analyzing the impact of content and form on consciousness and on ideological production, and with linking the production of media to the wider ideological apparatus of capitalist society.

An overview of leftist research reveals some formidable obstacles to a newsmaking criminology. First, certain U.S.-based firms such as AT&T, GE, Westinghouse, RCA, CBS, and ABC have been able to build huge commercial media empires and, with the aid of close state connections, to frustrate successive attempts to establish publicly controlled broadcasting stations and networks. One outcome of this "privatization" of the media has been the nearly complete integration of the mass-consuming audience into the bourgeois value system (Smythe, 1981). A second related problem is that the two-sided nature of discourse is becoming increasingly one-sided and popularized; fewer and fewer people are doing the speaking and more and more are doing the listening. The transnationalization of capital, for example, has not only accentuated the exchange value of mass communication over the use value; in the process, the takeovers of media firms by international conglomerates, whose principal interests lie elsewhere than in nurturing pluralistic discourse, already have caused significant reductions in the ratio of public service programs to private-time programs (Aufderheide, 1987).

The Left argues that the legitimation of various forms of state and corporate activity are commonly reinforced by a mass-mediated consciousness whose objective has become the selling of a particular bourgeois way of life. The Left also maintains that the prevailing ideas, meanings, and mass interpretations of marketing, culture, and information create images of private property, free enterprise, individual acquisitiveness, militarism, sexism, and racism conducive to both the ideological and the material reproduction of capitalism worldwide (Schiller 1973; 1976). In the words of the dean of the graduate school of journalism at the University of California at Berkeley, the United

States now has a "private ministry of information and culture" (Schiller, 1987). The Left argues further that because great media combines have increasingly absorbed thousands of newspapers, magazines, radio stations, and television channels, it appears that cultural pluralism is taking a beating. In addition, during this era of merger capitalism, in which nonmedia corporate giants are taking over major networks and in which other efforts are directed at economizing news coverage and increasing profitability, the future of true dialogue does not look very bright. Moreover, the 1980s have witnessed deregulation; the Federal Communications Commission has reduced the number of television and radio hours that broadcasters previously devoted to public service time, children's noncommercial programming, news, and public affairs (Aufderheide, 1987). The big winner in mass communications is entertainment, where objective reality is most obscure.

Whereas the Left is concerned about the monopolization and privatization of the mass media, right-wing and mainstream media critics are more concerned about the internal dynamics of control. Right-wing and liberal analyses alike assert that media and the business elites are not necessarily the close-knit allies that the Left suggests. The Right has gone so far as to argue that even though business elites of the private sector own the media, they still lack ideological control. Reed Irvine (1987), chairman of Accuracy in Media and editor of the *AIM Report*, argues that Laurence A. Tisch, president of CBS, and Thomas S. Murphy, chairman of Capital Cities/ABC, have become servants, not masters, of their staffs. Irvine refers specifically to Dan Rather's savage attack on Tisch for ordering personnel cuts at CBS News and to Peter Jennings' claim that the staff at ABC regarded Murphy's takeover as if it were the Nazi occupation of France. As Irvine wrote in "Notes from the Editor's Cuff":

> The owners of the big media companies have by-and-large been brainwashed into accepting the idea that they have no right to criticize the way their staffs report the news. It is both amusing and disheartening to see men who can throw around billions of dollars to acquire ownership of businesses kowtow to their hired help, apparently for fear of being criticized if they don't. (1987: 3)

The research efforts of those in the middle of the political and ideological spectrum suggest an alternative to the "capitalist-dominated media" and the "media-dominated capitalist" positions. The liberal-pluralistic orientation to mass communications regards both the national media and the business elites as major, but not dominant, forces in the marketplace of competitive ideas. Although these elites are among the strongest forces in mass communications, they are surrounded by unions, minorities, feminists, consumers, and intellectuals. The latter groups are viewed as representing forces with which media and business groups alike must reckon. As laissez-faire liberals argue, the rise of a relatively autonomous media elite has hardly gone unnoticed: "Some hail them as the public's tribunes against the powerful—indispensable champions of the underdog and the oppressed. Others decry them for allegiance to an adversary culture that is chiseling away at traditional values" (Lichter and Rothman, 1981: 60).

Media Bias—Left or Right?

To try to answer the question "Is the media biased to the left or to the right?" I will review the survey findings of a certain study of media and business elites. During 1979 and 1980, as part of a larger study on elites, S. Robert Lichter and Stanley Rothman of the Research Institute on International Change at Columbia University directed the interviewing of members of the national media elites, composed of leading print and broadcast journalists. For purposes of comparison they also interviewed executives at several major corporations.[2] The objective of the study was "to discover [the] backgrounds, attitudes, and outlooks [of the media elite] toward American society and their own profession" (Lichter and Rothman, 1981: 42). This study may be interpreted as demonstrating that the media elite tends to lean to the liberal Left.[3] Lichter and Rothman concluded:

> The pointed views of the national media elite are not mere wishes and opinions of those aspiring to power, but the voice of a new leadership group that has arrived as a

major force in American society. Cosmopolitan in their
origins, liberal in their outlooks, they are aware and
protective of their collective influence. (1981: 60)

I believe, however, that one could interpret the findings
more accurately to reflect the fact that the media elite, which in
general supports the values of bourgeois capitalism, actually
serves the conservative Right by helping to sustain the structural
relations of privilege and inequality in America. Whether more
people hail or decry the views of the media elite, the collective
viewpoint of the mass media is closely collateral to the
hegemonic relationships existing in advanced capitalism. In
short, I would argue that both mass communications and the
media elite are subordinate to the hegemonic values of the
political economy. My contention is supported by the findings of
Lichter and Rothman.

Demographically, the media elite is composed mainly of
white males in their thirties and forties. Only one member in
twenty is nonwhite; one in five is female. The media elite
consists of highly educated, well-paid professionals, a strong
majority of whom grew up in socially privileged backgrounds. A
substantial number come from big cities in the northeastern and
north central states.

Ideologically, 54 percent of the leading journalists
described themselves as left of center; only 19 percent chose the
right side of the political spectrum. With respect to social and
political attitudes generally, one of the more predominant
characteristics of the media elite is its secular outlook: 50 percent
declared no religious affiliation; only 8 percent attended church
or synagogue weekly; 86 percent seldom or never attended
religious services. Moreover, a large majority of the media elite
opposed government regulation of sexual activities, upheld a
pro-choice position on abortion, and rejected the notion that
homosexuality is wrong. Most members of the media elite were
also strongly supportive of environmental protection, affirmative
action, and women's and gays' rights.

In party affiliation, the media professionals favor the
Democrats over the Republicans. With respect to presidential
elections from 1964 to 1976, journalistic support for the
Democratic candidate never dropped below 80 percent. Between

1964 and 1980, less than one-fifth of the media elite ever supported a Republican presidential candidate. Furthermore, the Democratic margin among elite journalists was 30 to 50 percent greater than among the entire electorate during this period.

Although few members of the media elite were "outright socialists," to use the authors' own words, they revealed a strong preference for welfare capitalism, a belief in guaranteed employment, and support for income redistribution as a means of assistance for the poor. On the other hand, most of the journalists believed that free enterprise gave workers a fair shake, that deregulation of business was good for the country, and that people with greater ability should be entitled to higher wages than those with less ability. Similarly, only one in eight supported public ownership of corporations, while two-thirds opposed the idea strongly.

Despite their acceptance of the capitalist economic order, many of the journalists were dissatisfied with and critical of the social and cultural systems. Forty-nine percent agreed with the statement that "the very structure of our society causes people to feel alienated"; 28 percent agreed that America needs a "complete restructuring of its basic institutions." It also appears that the journalists' systemic critique spilled over into the international arena, especially regarding the relationship of the United States with Third World countries. In fact, most members of the media elite typically voiced the same criticisms that were raised in the Third World: 56 percent agreed that American economic exploitation had contributed more than its share to Third World poverty, 57 percent regarded America's heavy use of natural resources as "immoral," and 75 percent rejected the counter-argument that Third World nations would be even worse off without assistance from the United States and other Western countries.

With respect to the subject of hegemony, the most interesting and most informative responses came from efforts to discover how the media elite deals with the "big picture" and to learn what goals they think the United States should pursue in the future. Using a list of choices and a classification scheme developed by political scientist Ronald Inglehart, Lichter and Rothman measured whether an individual subscribed to "instrumental" and "acquisitive" values or to "expressive" and "post-bourgeois" values. They found the following:

> Substantial segments of the media elite endorse the "postbourgeois" value orientation that Inglehart calls a "silent revolution" transforming the political culture of advanced industrial society.... Only one in eight business leaders picks any of the "expressive" values as America's pressing concern. By contrast, one in three journalists deems citizen participation, a humane society, or a society less oriented around money as our most important goal— more important than either economic well-being or national defense. (1981: 46)

I have serious doubts about the transformation of the political culture through some kind of "silent revolution." As for the comparative differences between the media and business elites, I am neither impressed nor convinced by the fact that the archetypal representatives of a bourgeois society made one-third of the liberally dominated media appear "post-bourgeois." The fact remains that two-thirds of the media elite examined by Lichter and Rothman subscribed to the hegemony of bourgeois capitalism.

Ideology, Mass Media, and Public Knowledge of Serious Crime

One can argue that mass communications in general and news production in particular, whether privately or publicly owned, are withholding or censoring systems engaged in value-laden and interest-specific concerns. Furthermore the news-producing system, like the capitalist political economy, contains its own contradictions. On one side it is asked, "what major newspaper will risk running an exposé of a corporation's illegal operations next to that corporation's full-page advertisement?" General Motors, Parke-Davis, Merrill Lynch, and other corporate giants spend more than 100 billion dollars annually to advertise; car thieves, prison rioters, muggers, and welfare cheats do not. On the other side it is argued, "street criminals, especially violent ones, and suite criminals who are caught in scandal and intrigue make for very good copy." We can recall the stories of such upper-world "criminals" as John Delorean, Jean Harris and Ivan Boesky. Yet the social construction of mass-mediated depictions of serious crime goes beyond mere interests and corporate profits.

To be sure, the mass media allow for contradictory treatment of crime and criminals; they present a variety of crimes, punishments, and exercises of justice. More important, perhaps, the study of ideology, serious crime, and news coverage reveals that "the mode of explanation permits a wide range of interpretations of the crime problem and its solutions" (Humphries 1981: 205).

Although I agree with Humphries (1981: 205) that stories about serious crime are ideological in the hegemonic sense that their "presentation conforms to the way of life and thought that predominates in and is diffused throughout society in all its manifestations," I believe that historically, mass communications have portrayed dangerous crime in a distorted or one-dimensional fashion. Although bourgeois capitalism does not require that this should be the case, Culhane, Hills, and others tell how it occurred.

Culhane illustrates vividly how mass media coverage has contributed to the construction of one-dimensional images of crime and criminals when she states: "Outcries about muggers who slug elderly women do not include a description of the same elderly woman who may be surviving in a cold room, undernourished and frail, because a corporation deprived her of her pension. One crime is visible and condemned; the other is invisible and ignored" (see Burtch, 1986: 141–42). Similarly, in his examination of the political economy of corporate violence, Hills (1987: vii) exposes the one-dimensionality of crime consciousness when he acknowledges the grave need to "heighten awareness of the vast scope of serious harm caused by the illegal acts of 'respectable' business executives who impersonally kill and maim many more Americans than street muggers and assailants."

Moreover, the whole province of crime news coverage has been a captive of politicians and law enforcement officials alike.

From the President and the U.S. Attorney General to the local mayor and district attorney, conversations about serious crime repeat the same themes. During the first six years of his administration, for example, President Reagan spoke tirelessly about welfare cheats, child molesters, and dope dealers. When he addressed the International Association of Police Chiefs in 1984, he discussed the "criminal subculture" in America. His list of outlaws included the usual street criminals, drug pushers, and corrupt local officials and police officers. The President's list, however, omitted his numerous political appointees who violated federal and international law; corporations that fix prices, causing the public to pay inflated sums for products, defense contractors who defraud the government out of millions of taxpayers' dollars through overcharges and fraudulent billings; the presidents of companies whose safety violations and hazards result in injury or death to large numbers of employees; and the CEOs of large corporations who dump chemicals and other pollutants into the environment, endangering or impairing the lives and health of millions of people (Clinard and Yeager, 1980; Cullen, Maakestad, and Cavender, 1987; Ermann and Lundman, 1978; Frank, 1985; Hills, 1987; Ofari, 1985).

Outside the news arena, television shows and films generally distort the picture of crime and crime control. They not only exaggerate the incidence of street violence (Davis, 1952; Roshier, 1973) but also project criminal stereotypes (Klapp, 1962; Simmons, 1965) and crime myths (Box, 1983; Pepinsky and Jesilow, 1984; Wright, 1985). At best, the mass media provide what Reiman (1984: 37) terms a "carnival mirror," which presents a "distorted image of the dangers that threaten us—an image created more by the shape of the mirror than by the reality reflected." Films and television even depict so-called middle-class and affluent citizens as engaging in crime, but instead of showing such everyday crimes as those committed in American workplaces and executive suites, they tend to depict these persons as being guilty of street crime. The message is clear: powerful and powerless members of society break the same laws and commit the same crimes. Reiman (1984: 46) sums up the situation nicely when he argues that the mass media project a "double-edged message that the 'one-on-one' crimes of the poor are the typical crimes of all and thus not uniquely caused by the pressures of poverty; and that the criminal justice system pursues rich and poor alike—thus when the criminal justice system happens mainly to pounce on the poor in real life, it is not out of any class bias."

Discussions and representations of suite crime are fewer, more subdued, and less threatening than those associated with street crime. Similarly, descriptions of political criminals and the seriousness of their violations are influenced largely by whether the action in question advances or retards the legitimacy of the dominant political and economic arrangements. In both cases the message is usually clear that the danger of "real criminals" comes from below, not from above (Reiman, 1984). This message is as true for the Wall Street scandals as for the Iran-Contra affair.

More fundamentally, all three types of crime—index, corporate, and political—are portrayed primarily as individual rather than social phenomena. The mass production of serious crime has been "diagnosed" as having little or no relationship to the capitalist political economy. Not only is the presentation of crime and crime control severed from its underlying socioeconomic conditions; it is also disconnected from its own historical development. Hence the mass-mediated construction of crime and justice remains preoccupied with alienated and isolated offenders rather than with organized, structural, and institutional wrongdoers.

In sum, mass-mediated ideology about crime and punishment is more than a question of profits and debits or of individual versus institutional analyses. Criminal and penal ideology also involves news production and occupational status; both elements are related to questions of political autonomy and to the larger legitimization crisis. As I will argue in the next section, the possibility for developing a newsmaking criminology exists precisely because of the contradictions in the business of news production.

Criminologists, Mass Media, and Thematic Crime

Criminologists and others know that the mass media play
a critical role in shaping and reinforcing discussions of crime and
justice, but they (we) have not considered seriously how to
become part of the social construction of public opinion. With
few exceptions, criminologists and other social scientists leave
the construction of mass-mediated themes of crime and crime
control to the journalists and the film and television writers. In
short, academicians and other intellectuals have not bothered to
use their professional knowledge for popular consumption.

Fishman (1978) states that "crime news" involves the
formation of a restricted class of crime themes in interaction with
the overlapping news judgments of media organizations, whose
reporters and editors depend primarily on law enforcement and
politicians for their crime news stories. He argues further that
the mass-mediated construction of crime and crime control is the
product of ideologically "acceptable" or "favorable" news
themes. As a result, crime news has served to reify ideologically
a bourgeois rather than a post-bourgeois orientation to crime and
justice. Yet there is nothing fixed or immutable about this
bourgeois orientation to making crime news. Certainly there are
obstacles—occupational, bureaucratic, political—to developing a
newsmaking criminology, but no absolute barriers exist to
prevent criminologists and others from participating in the
formation of crime themes. In other words, within the
contradictions of news production and within the hegemony of
advanced capitalism, popular conceptions of crime or "thematic
crime" can be altered scientifically and ideologically by
newsmaking criminologists. By participating specifically in the
newsmaking process as credible spokespersons, criminologists
can work to redefine the parameters of acceptable or favorable
themes about crime and justice.

The contradictions within mass communications reveal an
environment in which professional journalists of the news-
producing community and the intellectual-cultural elites are not
only competitors and adversaries but also allies. Although the
technocrats of the news-producing industry may have a greater
economic affinity with the bourgeois values of the political status

quo than with the values of change-oriented criminologists, other members of the news-producing community share more than the common ideological ground of pluralistic thought and free expression. They also hold in common the occupational norms of fairness, objectivity, and public service. These values of "professionalism" are supposed to allow "the facts" and discourses of rationality to prevail over special interests and popular emotionalism. To appear too biased, especially during institutional crises, threatens the occupational status or legitimacy of these professions and others (Cullen et al., 1987). Nevertheless academicians—especially those with leftist or progressive politics—generally view themselves as ideological adversaries of the "capitalist-dominated media" and pit their critical or post-bourgeois values against the prevailing mainstream or bourgeois values.

If criminologists would take the time to develop relationships with those media people who share the values of a post-bourgeois future, they could come to appreciate the possibilities of a newsmaking criminology. Opportunities for such a criminology exist within the contradictions of news production—between the ability to report news and the ability to make news. As one editor and publisher said, "There's not enough news—not enough to go around . . . that's the reason what you read in the newspaper and hear on TV tonight is the same news you'll get in the morning papers and in broadcasts all through the day. Our capability to report news has outstripped our ability to make news" (Murray, 1986).

Newsmaking Criminology and Crime Themes

Within the contradictions of advanced bourgeois society, the success or failure of a newsmaking criminology will depend on the inclinations or the abilities of criminologists and others to develop relationships with the people and the processes internal to news production. Gaining access to mass communications networks, local or national, is problematic, but without direct access, criminologists will not be able to participate in the mass construction of "serious" crime and crime control. As suggested above, material schisms exist between the personnel of the consciousness industry and those of the cultural apparatus, and those schisms must be traversed. Of course social schisms also exist between the cultural elites and the masses.

As introduced here, a newsmaking criminology is similar to Gouldner's (1976) notion of a newspaper sociology; the latter refers to sociologists who participate in the public sphere, who receive public recognition for doing so, and who thus play a role as public persons. A newsmaking criminologist can become a credible public voice, capable of participating in the struggle over which moral rules and which definitions of social reality will prevail. As Gouldner notes:

> Social struggle in part takes the form of contention over What Is and what should be done about it. Since the latter comes to be defined as grounded in the former, political struggle increasingly takes the form of contention among competing versions of reality, through the mutual undermining of adversary versions of reality, and by the development of articulate "methods" or epistemologies as rhetorical recommendations for the versions of reality offered. (1976: 34)

Fishman's discussion of ideology and crime themes is useful here. He begins with the assumption that "all knowledge is knowledge from some point of view, resulting from the use of procedures which people use as a means not to know" (1978: 531). Fishman then demonstrates how routine news gathering and editing involve "procedures not to know." In his study of mass-mediated stories of "serious" crime, the selective information provided by law enforcement officials and by politicians represents such procedures. On the basis of "their interactions and reliance on official sources, news organizations both invoke and reproduce prevailing conceptions of 'serious crime'" (1978: 531). In the course of news production, news organizations develop and report small groups of stories with common themes such as crimes against the elderly, youth crimes, or black-on-black crimes. In sum, Fishman concludes that the production of crime news, like the production of news generally, is highly selective and involves a glut of possible stories, only a few of which will ever be presented. Therefore the identification and sorting of individual news items according to possible themes is a very useful way of ordering news work.

A newsmaking criminology must appreciate that the basic portrayals of serious crime and crime control served up by the mass media are the products of ideological construction or of the development of selective crime themes and of procedures not to know. These themes not only de-emphasize and ignore some harmful behavior; they also remove most incidents of criminality from their historical and structural contexts. Only partially representative of serious crime and torn from their material foundations, these crimes are relocated in a symbolically and culturally created construct, the news theme:

> Because newsworthiness is based on themes, the attention devoted to an event may exceed its importance, relevance, or timeliness were these qualities determined with reference to some theory of society. In place of any such theoretical understanding of the phenomena they report, newsworkers make incidents meaningful only as *instances of themes*—themes which are generated within the news production process. Thus, something becomes a "serious type of crime" on the basis of what is going on inside newsrooms, not outside them. (Fishman, 1978: 536)

Fishman's analysis is only partially correct. I would argue that he overstates his case because the inside of the newsroom is never fully autonomous, nor is it a self-contained, closed system. In addition to the primary exchange of crime themes across newsrooms, there is the fundamental interaction between people working inside and outside newsrooms. In addition, community activists and public interest groups alike are conducting social movements against (for example) corporate greed and crime and for social and economic justice. Accordingly, the challenge of a newsmaking criminology is to locate crime and justice in their political, structural, and historical contexts. By participating in the newsmaking process, criminologists cannot only provide a different background for crime news but can strive to alter the prevailing news themes that help to reproduce popular conceptions of crime and justice.

In keeping with both the critical and the reflexive sociological traditions, I agree with others (Box, 1983; Pepinsky and Jesilow, 1984; Reiman, 1984; Walker, 1985; Wright, 1985) that many of the popular conceptions about crime and justice are distortions of the hegemonic relationships within bourgeois capitalism. Spread by mass media, governmental officials, and criminologists, these distortions, myths, or crime themes at best prevent rational approaches to crime control and social justice; at worst they threaten human existence and life itself (Reiman, 1984). To challenge the established crime themes and to establish rational alternatives to the prevailing policies of bourgeois crime control, these themes of mass communication must change.

Recent history suggests that crime themes, at least those expressed by criminologists, do change. For example, the dominant crime themes of the 1960s had an individualistic orientation and focused on labeling, social interaction, and juvenile delinquency. Over the past two decades these themes have been modified to accommodate a structural orientation and to focus on complex organizations, corporations, and the state. Beginning with Schwendinger and Schwendinger's (1970) classic statement on the subject, crime themes have been developing which argue that institutional and structural relations are not only responsible for imperialistic wars, cultural and physical genocide, organizational violence, systemic racism and sexism, the manufacturing of unsafe products, and the maintenance of dangerous and unhealthy working conditions, but that these "crimes against humanity" or "crimes of exploitation" are also at least partially responsible for street crime. These themes, which were peripheral to all but radical criminology less than twenty years ago, have become prominent in the works of critical and mainstream criminologists alike. Among the topical themes at the 1988 annual meeting of the American Society of Criminology were such themes as "The Political Economy of Crime and Crime Control," "Crimes By and Against the State," "The Definition, Patterns, and Control of Corporate Crime," and "Comparative and International Perspectives on Crime and Justice."

These emerging and developing crime themes call for alternative policies to "crime control." They incorporate analyses whereby systems of social control are viewed as inseparable from the developing political economy. According to these themes, systems and strategies of crime prevention require public policies that do not involve merely the activities of the criminal justice system, but, more importantly, those of other political, economic, and social sectors as well (Barak, 1986; Currie, 1985). Yet despite these changes in the academic arena, the mass media remain preoccupied with the same old themes. With the exception of Ralph Nader and other public-interest activists, few individual and no systematic attempts have been made to interject any structural analyses into the mass media. Until such attempts are made, popular conceptions of "serious" crime will continue to serve the interests and the hegemony of bourgeois capitalism.

Newsmaking Criminology Exemplified

I have argued that the contradictory relationships within news production reveal social forces operating both against and for newsmaking criminology; the hegemonic relations within the political economy of advanced capitalism determine "free-market" constraints and "free-expression" opportunities. There is no one-dimensional or monolithic ideology or interpretation but rather a number of prevailing and conflicting points of view. Yet this is not to say that bourgeois capitalism is not the dominant ideology. Rather, the hegemony of capitalist ideology is in a constant state of creation and re-creation, reflecting the changing political economy on the one side and the opposing ideologies of a post-bourgeois capitalism on the other. Finally, these contradictory relationships involve actual newspeople with varying perspectives and ideologies, who have been exposed to the occupational norms of fairness and objectivity as well as to the technocratic norms of efficiency and expediency. Hence newsmaking criminology depends on the abilities of criminologists and others to tap the available opportunities within the mass media.

With some effort, criminologists can be credible spokespeople, can make criminological news, and can participate in the popular construction of images of crime and crime control. Like law enforcement officials and politicians in general, they can occupy the position of the professional source in the mass-mediated production of crime news. Moreover, newsmaking criminologists need not be limited to the role of information source; they can also venture into "producing" crime themes. Individual criminologists can play only a minimal role, but networks of newsmaking criminologists have the potential for changing themes of crime, violence, and justice.

For the sake of clarification and illustration, I would like to describe some of my own experiences as a newsmaking criminologist. These and other samples of newsmaking criminology are not meant to exhaust the mass-mediated possibilities, nor do they conform exactly to the methodological proofs of the experimental model. Nevertheless they represent attempts to explore empirically one type of criminological newsmaking. I do not argue that a newsmaking criminologist can alter or modify crime themes per se, but that he or she can participate as a credible public voice, offering a variety of theoretically enriched analyses that challenge the prevailing crime myths and enlarge the popular discourse on crime and justice.

The particular mode of newsmaking criminology that I have employed involves networking with people who converge in the overlapping spheres of the state, the community, and the mass media. To begin with, I have developed professional relationships with persons responsible for the management and administrative functions of various justice bureaucracies. I have also identified myself publicly with leftist ideas and causes. More specifically, I have aligned myself politically with all kinds of progressive agendas and organizations.

I moved to Montgomery, the capital of Alabama, in September 1985. In a relatively short time, primarily because of my numerous newspaper editorials and commentaries, which have appeared throughout Alabama, I developed my role both as a newsmaking criminologist and as a social and political critic. In turn, this media and political exposure facilitated my participation in a number of community-based events and projects (e.g., Conference on Incarcerated Mothers, SCLC's Poor People's Crusade, Alabama Prison Project). My practice of newsmaking criminology also helped me to secure selective governmental appointments such as general advisor to the

Alabama Attorney General's Task Force on Victims and advisory council member to the Alabama Department of Corrections. As a result of this activity, I now serve as consultant to media-related productions. As a consultant I not only help journalists to develop their perspectives on covering crime news, but also provide the media with story ideas and with contacts. Recently I participated in the making of a video documentary on black-on-black crime, written and directed by a black media specialist.

The two illustrations of newsmaking that follow revolve around the social, racial, and economic ideologies of the Deep South. They are also part of the conflict between the instrumental and the expressive values found in the contradictory relationships between crime and control and between inequality and privilege, whether the newsmaking involves police-community relations, black-on-black crime, or the injustice of wealth and poverty in America.

Relations between Montgomery's black community and the police have been strained as far back as the early nineteenth century, when the institution of policing was born locally for the express purpose of controlling slaves. Police assaults and homicides involving blacks as victims can be recalled *ad infinitum* by black Montgomerians; the most recent public hearings on the alleged abuses by the Montgomery Police Department (MPD) were nothing new. This was the second set of public hearings, however, in what had become, by the summer of 1986, a three-year investigation conducted by the Alabama Advisory Committee to the U.S. Civil Rights Commission.

The findings from the first set of hearings, held in the winter of 1983–84, were deemed unacceptable by Republican officials in both Washington and Montgomery. Charges of covering up and racism were heard from both sides. So much time had passed without the findings being released by Reagan's Civil Rights Commission that a second set of hearings was agreed to, allegedly to reflect the changed relationships between police and community. The editorial page editor of the *Montgomery Advertiser*, the "liberal" daily newspaper, suspected that the hearings were nothing more than a theatrical production. He supported my idea of running a three-part commentary on the op-ed page of his paper. In addition to the hearings themselves, background meetings were held with some of the principals in Montgomery's police-racial tensions. These "news stories" about law enforcement and police-community relations provided me with a unique newsmaking opportunity.

An allowance of some 4,300 words gave me the space to critique (and to support selectively) black and white community leaders, the MPD, the investigation, the hearings, the findings, and the recommendations. It also allowed me to present an analysis of the problem and the solution. My analysis, of course, differed from the perspectives of the police and of both the white and the black politicians. Even so, the credibility or legitimacy of my perspective was verified by several invitations to address public audiences on crime and justice issues and to write other issue-related pieces for mass consumption.

If black-on-black crime is one of contemporary America's media themes, it plays well in Dixie, where the New South is still plagued by the racism of the Old South. As the mayor of Montgomery and chairman of the Alabama Republican Party said in reference to Montgomery's 10 percent increase in crime during 1985, "If you look behind the numbers, you'll see the major problem is still black-on-black crime." As a result of the controversy about this crime theme, Alabama Public Television's "For the Record" devoted one of its nightly shows (April 29, 1986) to the topic.

I was one of three guests on the program; the other two were a black civil rights attorney and local community leader and Montgomery's (white) chief of police. This newsmaking opportunity permitted me to influence the focus and the direction of the program, partly because of my input while information was being gathered for the development of the host's line of questioning. My influence was also due in part to an arrangement made before the show, whereby it was agreed that typically I would respond after the other two guests. The net effect of this newsmaking episode was that the familiar news themes about a racist criminal justice system, the subculture of violence, and morally weak individuals were augmented by themes that emphasized the historical and structural relationships within racial and social inequality. More important, perhaps, the whole discussion of black-on-black crime was placed into the wider contexts of crime and social justice. Participating in these and other newsmaking experiences established me as an "Alabama Voice," to use the name of the column of one newspaper where one of my statewide-distributed articles on wealth and poverty appeared. Yet attempts at newsmaking criminology do not always succeed. With time, however, one can learn which newspapers and other media outlets are and are not receptive to particular ideologies. Sometimes newsmaking efforts bring mixed results, especially as one moves away from crime and criminal justice per se and toward a critique of the hegemonic relations of bourgeois capitalism and the free enterprise system. Sometimes, too, as with the other contradictions of advanced capitalism, "nothing succeeds like failure."[4]

Conclusion

In keeping with the research and findings of Ericson, Baranek, and Chan (1987: 364), my reflexive-empirical experiences have revealed that "while the news-media institution is effectively closed to most citizens . . . a limited range of sources can pry it open and sometimes harness its power to advantage." Although it is exceedingly difficult for nonmembers of the deviance-defining elite to penetrate the media's airtight circle, the fact remains that newsmaking crime and crime control are based on information obtained by organizations. Consciousness about crime, punishment, and justice, like all news stories, is derived from and subject to interpretation in context and to journalists' judgments and interpretations in various organizational contexts or systems as they work to transform the specialized, bureaucratized knowledge of sources into common sense. Therefore the tasks of a newsmaking criminology are not only to provide the specialized sources of knowledge and to gain entry into the various bureaucratic channels, but also ultimately to develop its own vehicles of mass communications.

As most media analysts agree, penetration of the mass media is difficult because "those who control the media of public communication, and especially the news media, are part of the central institutions of social control, and join with key sources from the other central institutions of social control to effect hegemony" (Ericson et al., 1987: 362). Furthermore, because journalistic knowledge of crime and justice is based for the most part on inward-looking, self-referential, and partial knowledge, newsmaking criminologists represent nearly the only significant alternative source for defining crime and justice. Accordingly, in this chapter I call on criminologists, especially critical and progressive criminologists, to participate in the social construction of crime and crime control as a means of bringing about social change and social justice.

Finally, I have argued implicitly, if not explicitly, that the role of a newsmaking criminologist is possible because journalists' values and practices are not fixed rigidly but are rather fluid. The newsmaking process involves not only the ongoing negotiations and conflicts among newsroom personnel at all levels but also the interaction of newspeople with newsmaking sources, both elite and non-elite. In sum, I agree with Ericson et al. (1987: 352) that journalists do not display the great normative consensus that many recent academic analysts have claimed: "In spite of the fact that the knowledgeability of journalists is severely circumscribed, we see more openness, equivocality, and choice in the news" than others perceive. Hence one may ask, will academic criminologists and criminal justice educators remain spectators of the mass-mediated construction of crime and crime control or will they engage actively in producing crime themes for public consumption?

NOTES

* This essay is reprinted with permission from *Justice Quarterly*, 5, 4, December 1988: 565–567; with permission of the Academy of Criminal Justice Sciences.

1. As introduced here, newsmaking criminology presupposes that there is no such thing as "objective" news reporting and interpreting. The presentation of crime and violence in the mass media, for example, cannot be disconnected from the prevailing ideologies of the day. Without discussing the pros and cons of partisan and value-free scholarship, I note that the neglect of newsmaking criminology, particularly by leftist criminologists, is especially interesting in light of their preferences both for partisanship and for alternative public policies.

2. Hour-long interviews were conducted with 240 journalists and broadcasters at such media outlets as the *New York Times, Washington Post*, the *Wall Street Journal, Time, Newsweek*, and *U.S. News and World Report*, and with national news departments at CBS, NBC, ABC and PBS, as well as at major public broadcasting stations. Interviews also were conducted with 216 management-level employees at seven *Fortune 500* companies, including a multinational oil company, a major bank, a public utility, and a nationwide retail chain.

3. Discussions of media bias, like discussions of "serious" crime, cannot be separated totally from ideological convictions. In the words of Alexander Cockburn (1987: 17), syndicated writer for *The Nation* and for *In These Times:* "When right-wingers like Reed Irvine press forward with astounding claims that the mainstream media are populated by ultra-liberals and even crypto-Bolsheviks, chances are they will cite studies by Robert and Linda Lichter. A few years ago the Lichters, wallowing in the usual mush of social scientific 'objectivity,' conducted surveys proposing the view that most of the reporting elite are only a couple of steps to the right of Trotsky. The truth, as anyone capable of turning on a TV set or opening a newspaper knows well, is that reporters maintain about the same revolutionary profile as Sen. Bill Bradley." In any event, when I contacted Accuracy in Media, the findings of Lichter and Rothman were cited and a copy of their article was mailed to me. Even if their methods were flawed (Gans, 1985), and even if their conclusions were ideologically biased, I found their study useful for providing a sense of where professional journalists stand.

4. An example of a newsmaking experience that simultaneously failed and succeeded is an article of mine on the injustice of wealth and poverty in Alabama, which was distributed statewide. This article discussed economic inequality, the shrinking middle class, and the plight of the poor. More specifically, I launched an attack on Alabama's wealthiest corporate landowners and their political cronies, who are responsible for the fact that Alabama has the lowest property tax in the nation (66 percent lower than 49th-ranked Mississippi). My additional critique of America's military priorities and of Alabama's ultraregressive taxing system was more than the editorial page editor of the *Mobile Press Register* could tolerate. On Sunday, June 28, 1987, Ralph Poore devoted his entire editorial, "Fallacies That Might Hurt," to critiquing my piece, which had not been published within 150 miles of Mobile. Whether or not Poore's remarks were correct is beside the point; his very response legitimized to some degree the themes of exploitation and repression that I was raising. Although he did a hatchet job on my argument and was less than convincing even on his own terms, the fact remains that the news themes of a post-bourgeois ideology had found their way onto the *Press*'s editorial pages. Such are the contradictions in newsmaking America.

REFERENCES

Aufderheide, P. 1987. "Media beat." *In These Times*, June 24–July 7, p. 20.

Barak, G. 1986. "Feminist connections and the movement against domestic violence: Beyond criminal justice reform." *Journal of Crime and Justice*, 9: 139–62.

Bohm, R. 1986. "Crime, criminal and crime control policy myths." *Justice Quarterly*, 3, 2: 191–214.

Bottomore, T., (ed.). 1983. *A Dictionary of Marxist Thought*. Cambridge, MA: Harvard University Press.

Box, S. 1983. *Power, Crime and Mystification*. London: Tavistock.

Burtch, B. 1986. "Interview with Claire Culhane." *Crime and Social Justice*, 26: 135–50.

Clinard, M. B. and P. C. Yeager. 1980. *Corporate Crime*. New York: Free Press.

Cockburn, A. 1987. "Ashes and diamonds." *In These Times*, July 8–21, p. 17.

Cohen, S. and J. Young (eds.). 1973. *The Manufacture of News*. Beverly Hills: Sage.

Cullen, F. T., W. J. Maakestad, and G. Cavender. 1987. *Corporate Crime under Attack: The Ford Pinto Case and Beyond*. Cincinnati: Anderson.

Currie, E. 1985. *Confronting Crime: An American Challenge*. New York: Pantheon.

Davis, F. J. 1952. "Crime news in Colorado newspapers." *American Journal of Sociology*, 57: 325–30.

Ericson, R. V., P. M. Baranek, and J. B. L. Chan. 1987. *Visualizing Deviance: A Study of News Organization*. Toronto: University of Toronto Press.

Ermann, M. D. and R. J. Lundman, (eds.). 1978. *Corporate and Government Deviance: Problems of Organizational Behavior in Contemporary Society*. New York: Oxford University Press.

Fishman, M. 1978. "Crime waves and ideology." *Social Problems*, 25: 531–43.

Frank, N. 1985. *Crimes against Health and Safety*. Albany: Harrow and Heston.

Gans, H. J. 1985. "Are U.S. journalists dangerously liberal?" *Columbia Journalism Review*, November/December, pp. 29–33.

Gouldner, A. 1976. *The Dialectic of Ideology and Technology: The Origins, Grammar, and Future of Ideology*. New York: Seabury.

Gramsci, A. 1971. *Selections from the Prison Notebooks*. New York: International.

Hall, S., C. Critcher, T. Jefferson, J. Clarke, and B. Roberts. 1977. *Policing the Crisis: Mugging, the State and Law and Order*. New York: Holmes and Meiser.

Hills, S. L., (ed.). 1987. *Corporate Violence: Injury and Death for Profit*. Totowa, NJ: Rowman and Littlefield.

Humphries, D. 1981. "Serious crime, news coverage, and ideology." *Crime and Delinquency*, 27: 191–205.

Irvine, R. 1987. "Notes from the editor's cuff." *Aim Report*, June, p. 3.

Klapp, O. E. 1962. *Heroes, Villains, and Fools*. Englewood Cliffs, NJ: Prentice-Hall.

Lichter, S. R. and S. Rothman. 1981. "Media and business elites." *Public Opinion*, October/November, pp. 42–60.

Mosco, J. 1986. "Marxism and communications research in North America." In B. Ollman and E. Vernoff (eds.), *The Left Academy: Marxist Scholarship on American Campuses*. Volume 3. New York: Praeger, pp. 237–62.

Murray, J. 1986. "There's not enough news today." *The Montgomery Advertiser*, October 8, p. 12A.

Ofari. 1985. "The mugging of America." *Ofari's Bi-Monthly*, special summer edition, 1, 6: 1–12.

Pepinsky, H. and P. Jesilow. 1984. *Myths That Cause Crime*. Cabin John, MD: Seven Locks.

Reiman, J. 1984. *The Rich Get Richer and the Poor Get Prison: Ideology, Class and Criminal Justice*. New York: Wiley.

Roshier, B. 1973. "The selection of crime news by the press." In S. Cohen and J. Young (eds.), *The Manufacture of News*. Beverly Hills, CA: Sage, pp. 29–39.

Schiller, H. 1973. *The Mind Managers*. Boston: Beacon.

———. 1976. *Communication and Cultural Domination*. White Plains, NY: International Arts and Sciences Press.

———. 1987. "Information: Important issue for '88." *The Nation*, July 4–11, pp. 1, 6.

Schwendinger, H. and J. Schwendinger. 1970. "Defenders of order or guardians of human rights?" *Issues in Criminology*, 5: 113–46.

Simmons, J. K. 1965. "Public stereotypes of deviants." *Social Problems*, 12: 223–32.

Smythe, S. 1981. *Dependency Road: Communication, Capitalism, Consciousness and Canada*. Norwood, NJ. Ablex.

Walker, S. 1985. *Sense and Nonsense about Crime: A Policy Guide*. Pacific Grove, CA: Brooks/Cole.

Wright, K. 1985. *The Great American Crime Myth*. Westport, CT: Greenwood.

CHAPTER 10

Becoming a Media Criminologist: Is "Newsmaking Criminology" Possible?

Cecil E. Greek

Introduction

In a 1988 *Justice Quarterly* article, Gregg Barak proposed that criminologists offer their expertise to the media rather than avoid interviews. His hope was that a more realistic image of crime and the criminal justice system could be presented to counter the media's sensationalist treatment of such issues. This essay tests that proposition based on the author's extensive interaction with the news media in Oklahoma City, Oklahoma, and Tampa, Florida. Comparisons are made of newspaper interviews, remote television interviews, live "on air" interviews, and live television and radio talk shows. The problems encountered by the author in each of these types of situations are detailed. A review is made of the literature produced by professional media consultants whose goal it is to help people get their messages across through these various media formats. The essay questions whether an adequate communication of criminological research is possible within currently established media formats.

The Goals of "Newsmaking Criminology"

Barak (1988: 566) has defined "newsmaking criminology" as follows:

> a newsmaking criminology attempts to demystify images of crime and punishment by locating the mass media portrayals of incidents of "serious" crimes in the context of all illegal and harmful activities; strives to affect public attitudes, thoughts, and discourses about crime and justice so as to facilitate a public policy of "crime control" based on structural and historical analyses of institutional development; allows criminologists to come forth with their knowledge and to establish themselves as credible voices in the mass-mediated arena of policy formation; and asks of criminologists that they develop popularly based languages and technically based skills of communication for the purposes of participating in the mass-consumed ideology of crime and justice.

Barak argued that in the past criminologists have not considered how to use mass communications for the purposes of informing, interpreting, and altering media images to reflect more realistically the social, political, and economic conditions of crime and social control. By participating directly in the newsmaking process as credible spokespersons, criminologists can work to redefine the parameters of acceptable or favorable themes about crime and justice. For example, Barak (1988: 574) suggests that criminologists attempt to counter the media's focus on "street crimes" by "alerting the public to the vast scope of serious harm caused by the illegal acts of respectable business executives who impersonally kill and maim many more Americans than street muggers and assailants." In addition, while academics have changed the way they think about crime— e.g., by adopting Marxist, structuralist, or institutional models— news media personnel, according to Barak (1988: 581), remain preoccupied with the "same old themes."

Barak (1988: 582) also has suggested participation in organizations that seek to influence policy as another way to do "newsmaking criminology." One reason this is important is that the media typically search for "official spokespersons" of various organizations for quotes while compiling stories (Altheide, 1976: 22; Fishman, 1980: 85).

The Problems Related to Trying to Communicate Criminology Through the Media

Is it possible to adequately communicate the complexity of criminological concepts, research, and theory through the media? Can traditional media formats such as news and talk shows clearly reflect criminological concerns or will they distort the message? In addition to criminologists, a number of other social scientists have discussed these issues and most have expressed dissatisfaction with the majority of media coverage of social science (e.g., Baker, 1987; Barrile, 1984; Benderly, 1989; Ericson, 1991; Fishman, 1980; Wong and Alexander, 1991). As Weiss and Singer (1988: 3) have documented:

> When reporters move social science from the domain of the disciplines into the domain of news, they strip it of certain features, such as complex statistics, and recast it in terms compatible with the norms and procedures of journalism. They provide a "news peg," a handle to hang the story on, and cast it into a narrative form that corresponds with the modes in which news is written.

As a result, media coverage of social science research is not just a shortened and simplified version of an academic product. "It is a different creation, crafted by different professionals according to different norms to serve a different purpose" (Weiss and Singer, 1988: 2).

Language becomes a key issue here, opening up the possibility of misinterpretation. For example, given that social scientists use terms such as "significant," "consistent," or "power" in ways that journalists assume the general public will not understand, journalists feel compelled to translate such terms into everyday speech (Cohn, 1989).

Statistics create another problem. When journalists misinterpret statistical data they usually err in the direction of "overinterpretation." According to Cohn (1989: 3), "The reason for this professional bias is self-evident; you usually can't write a snappy lead upholding the negative," e.g., that the viewing of pornographic materials has by itself little impact on behavior. Furthermore, when a study merely suggests that something might be the case reporters sometimes present the results in a more black-and-white style. Finally, the fact that a study may be preliminary is on occasions omitted (Cohn, 1989: 4).

In the worst case scenario, the reporter knows what story he or she wants to write in advance and uses social scientists and their research simply to support a preconceived idea. As social scientists have acquired prestige as knowledge experts in our society, journalists sometimes seek to use them to enhance their own credibility. McLaughlin (1986: 116) believes broadcast journalists are more likely than print journalists to have a preconceived story line while print journalists more frequently allow a story angle to develop out of the facts, because broadcast journalists have less time to work on individual stories.

Another issue that must be dealt with is the fact that some journalists believe that only social scientists with an ideological point to make would seek publicity for their research. According to journalist Cohn (1989: 4), reporters "tend to rely most on 'authorities' who are either most quotable or quickly available or both, and they often tend to be those who get most carried away with their sketchy and unconfirmed but 'exciting' data—or have big axes to grind, however lofty their motives." For this reason journalists believe that experts cannot be used over and over again. There is also a fear among reporters that experts will become too familiar to the public if they are called upon too often.

The case of Lawrence Sherman illustrates some of the problems being discussed here. Sherman was principally responsible for the now well-known Minneapolis spouse abuse study. Cognizant of the fact that press coverage helps justify continued or increased funding for research, Sherman sought out maximum press coverage for his study through the following publicity techniques: (1) He shot and distributed documentary footage so that any television news agency could use it. (2) Sherman negotiated with the *New York Times* which agreed to publish an exclusive story on his preliminary findings. One hundred and seven newspapers picked up the article and ran it. (3) The final report was released to the media on one of the slowest newsdays of the year in order to receive optimal exposure (Sherman and Cohn, 1989: 119–120). However, the media latched on to one finding regarding the impact of a pro-arrest program on spouse abusers. As a result of the publicity many police departments around the country adopted pro-arrest policies. Sherman himself was taken aback by these results as he stated later that his findings were not pro-arrest but pro-research (Sherman and Cohn, 1989: 121). At the same time Sherman was heavily criticized by other criminologists for releasing his findings without first doing replications. While this may be a valid criticism, it is also indicative of the type of response social scientists who attempt to inform the public of their work will receive from their colleagues.

Personal Experiences with the Media

In 1988 I first read Barak's article. Having previously done only a few media interviews, I found Barak's discussion of trying to "inform" the media about criminology fascinating and decided to make myself available to the media more frequently. What follows is a brief report of my experiences.

I attempted to increase my contacts with the media by developing a good working relationship with the university's public relations office. There I was welcomed because the university desires positive media attention. I received several types of assistance. The first was to develop a number of press releases that were sent to all the local news media. These typically employed "teasers": quotes attributed to me that expressed opinions or angles the media may not have yet considered—or so we thought—about criminological "news" topics in the immediate area. The second avenue of exposure was through the university's media guide. After I received a copy of the page proofs of the newly revised media guide which listed my name once, I had my name added under a number of topic areas including: pornography, free speech and censorship; prisons, jails, community corrections programs; juvenile justice;

and occult crime; all areas in which I have done research or extensive teaching. I also wrote a short description of what I could discuss under each topic and these were incorporated into the guide. In addition to collaborating with the university's media affairs office, I invited reporters assigned to cover the police and court beats to address my classes and as a result established some personal contacts. These efforts produced results: I was interviewed by newspaper and television news journalists, asked to make appearances on radio and television talk shows, and had my speeches or statements made at public forums covered by the media.

Following up on Barak's (1988: 582) suggestion that one participate in organizations that seek to influence policy as another way to do "newsmaking criminology," I was able to join the local boards of both the American Civil Liberties Union and another free speech organization, the Friends of the First Amendment. As a result of these efforts I increased my media contacts from one or two a year to between ten to twenty a year.

Most of the interviews for which I was contacted dealt with two broad topics: censorship/pornography and community corrections. Since the news media are fascinated with stories concerning sex and crime (Zoglin, 1992), it is not surprising that this would be the result.

The probation/parole stories typically featured either a case of a convict who received an "early" release and committed a new horrible crime or concerns over whether new community corrections programs would lead to similar incidents. Sometimes there were other interviewees present such as spokespersons for victims' rights groups such as Mothers Against Drunk Driving. (On one occasion I was seated on a couch next to a disabled victim of a drunk driver, and my own emotional reaction severely undercut my ability to discuss community-based alternatives to prison for such offenders.) The position I typically supported was that these programs are successful cost-effective alternatives to prison, but that they do require careful screening of offenders.

Given that a number of controversies have arisen regarding pornography, sexual expression, and nudity in Florida in recent years—ranging from the 2 Live Crew trial, the removal of centerfolds displayed at the workplace, crackdowns on adult entertainment establishments, ordinances about T-back bathing suits and hot dog vendors, couples having their sex lives taped by nosey neighbors, to the arrest of Pee Wee Herman—I received a number of calls from television, radio, and newspapers asking for my opinion. My ACLU affiliation helped generate some of the interest in my thoughts, as the media likes to include a "civil liberties" statement in most of its stories on these topics.

Certainly the issues of pornography and sexual expression beg for a publicly reasoned discussion of the issues. Stereotypes of pornography abound, so much so that the Meese Commission could simply reify them without even examining the content or themes of these forms of sexual expression (Nobile and Nadler, 1986). In addition, there is little public understanding of why civil libertarians and attorneys are willing to defend the rights of producers, distributors, sellers, and consumers of pornography. I thought I might be able to "enlighten" the public through media interviews on these topics. I appeared on a number of radio and television talk shows and shared the camera/microphone with such disparate guests as adult porn actresses, distributors of pornography, anti-pornography feminists, ministers, and state leaders of the American Family Association (a national Christian organization founded by Donald Wildmon and dedicated to eliminating all pornography and "cleaning up television"). I came prepared on all of these occasions to talk about the First Amendment, the need to protect civil liberties, the actual content of typical pornographic materials, the nature of the adult film industry, the religious and feminist objections to pornography, as well as the many studies that have been done regarding the effects of exposure to pornographic materials. Obviously there was not enough time to take up all of these issues each time.

To my surprise, not all of the interviews went as I had envisioned. I made a number of "mistakes" and walked into several media "ambushes," largely as a result of my desire to agree to do as many interviews as possible. Without public relations training I learned by "experience." The type of mistakes differed, often depending on the media format involved—live interviews presented different problems from canned interviews and from talk shows. (Some of my mistakes were simply stupid, such as wearing brightly colored socks and hiking shoes to a television interview, thinking my feet would certainly never be on camera.) Unfortunately I was placed on a couch with another interviewee and several full body shots were shown on the air.

One of the worst "ambushes" occurred during the taping of a half-hour program called "Pro and Con" on which I was the only guest. I had agreed to come on the show to discuss the debate over NEH's funding of controversial art such as the Robert Mapplethorpe exhibit and the obscenity trial in Cincinnati when the photographs were displayed there. However, after ten or fifteen minutes of discussion on these topics the host switched to what I perceived as "baited questions" to launch an attack on the ACLU as the party responsible for removing prayer and Bible-reading from the public schools and as the defender of homosexuals in the military. Though not prepared on these topics, I proceeded to discuss them anyway, but finally requested that we move the questioning back to the original topics. I should have anticipated the interviewer's questioning style since prior to my interview I had watched him grill two St. Petersburg police officers as if they were responsible for the Rodney King beating in Los Angeles when they were there solely to discuss community-oriented policing.

Another program that went awry was a television talk show on pornography featuring the Florida head of the American Family Association. Since the producers were concerned about the potential volatility of the issue (other guests included a minister and an adult videostore owner), a pre-broadcast meeting was held with all participants to go over ground rules. The AFA guest was corrected on several of his facts (e.g., he claimed a proposed ordinance was already law), and all agreed not to discuss the red herring of child pornography. On the program itself the AFA guest misstated the very same facts on which he had been corrected thirty minutes earlier and kept talking over my comments about civil liberties by shouting, "The ACLU supports child pornography!" My response was to directly point out that the issue was a red herring and state my opposition to the manufacture and sale of child pornography.

Some of my other experiences have been similarly frustrating. When interviewed regarding pornography and sexual expression, I have found my statements regarding civil liberties, for example, used as a voiceover with nude dancers as the visual backdrop on television news segments. On other occasions, public speeches I have given were quoted out of context by newspaper columnists who wanted to paint a negative picture of my willingness to share a podium with someone in the adult entertainment business. Articles published in university publications describing the type of research I do have resulted in negative letters written to university administrators. Magazines have simply printed the "teasers" sent out in press releases without bothering to call for an interview to amplify the statements. However, on the whole, I still feel positive about my efforts and will continue to attempt to raise awareness of these issues.

I did not find significant differences in the way the news media operated in Oklahoma City versus Tampa. The journalistic method is apparently very similar nationwide as journalism education is quite standardized (Tuchman, 1978). In addition, the constant pressure to seek high ratings appears to have led to the homogenization of American television journalism.

The Advice of Expert Media Communicators on How to Handle the Various Media Formats

After a number of contacts with the media I began to notice certain patterns to the questioning, the ways in which my interview statements were spliced into an edited news segment, etc. I also consulted the literature produced by public relations professionals who help their clients better get their message across as a way to gain additional insight on how I could become a more effective communicator (see Hilton and Knoblauch, 1980; Blythin and Samovar, 1985; Brady, 1977; McLaughlin, 1986; Rafe, 1991; Ailes, 1988; Cohen, 1987; Schmertz, 1986; Robinson, 1987). These texts provide a great deal of general knowledge about how to manage television, radio, phone, and newspaper interviews and specific information about how to handle live "on air" interviews, canned television interviews, and television talk shows. What follows is a summary of their suggestions along with some of my own advice.

The differences between phone, radio, newspaper, and television interviews are important and should be kept in mind when participating in them. Phone interviews are frequently done by newspaper journalists looking for facts, background information, or a quick quote or comment. Some press relations guides suggest not doing the actual interview on the first call, but promising to do a little research on the topic the journalist is calling about and to call back (Rafe, 1991: 127–128). Then, you should call back promptly—recognizing that journalists all work under deadlines—after preparing yourself with facts, background, and quotes.

I found that I, like a number of other experts, do not particularly like phone interviews and tend to disclose less information over the phone (Killenberg and Anderson, 1989: 178). Worries about being misquoted appear to be greatest in phone/press interviews because reporters have absolute control over how the information will be used (McLaughlin, 1986: 95). Unlike a television interview, there is no way to discern the demeanor of the quoted individual or the tone of their conversation when it appears in print. Also, many experts feel that if the reporter truly thinks the information you have to give is valuable they will take the time and trouble to schedule a person-to-person interview. However, one must recognize that deadline pressure and breaking stories often dictate calling for quotes. Planned stories, on the other hand, have more forethought, are usually longer, and require a scheduled interview. Nevertheless, I often found myself using circumlocution or speaking in vague generalities during telephone interviews in which I wanted to avoid being quoted. However, this method can backfire, leaving reporters with the impression that one is inept or uncooperative, and therefore should not be called again. In fact, a better practice would be to directly inform the reporter of your reluctance to speak on a particular issue, but hasten to add that you'll be glad to help them in the future on other stories regarding your field of expertise—then name a couple of specific topics.

However, in all fairness to newspaper journalists, it must be pointed out that they are in general better prepared than their electronic media counterparts to interview experts. The former are usually more thorough than television journalists because they are typically given more time to prepare stories and don't cover as many different topics in a day as television reporters (Killenberg, 1992; Schmertz, 1986: 40). Continuously being assigned to the same beat also allows newspaper reporters to be better informed about their stories.

Radio interviews, like phone interviews, offer the interviewee one possible advantage over television exchanges; the interviewee can concentrate solely on what he is going to say while not having to be concerned about all the visual and staging problems associated with live or taped television interviews. However, radio is a strange medium to work in given that it presumes to have a fickle audience—even more fickle than television viewers armed with remote controls—which tunes in and out continuously (Hilton and Knoblauch, 1980: 3). Therefore, talk radio interviewers spend a considerable amount of time rehashing so that those who have just tuned in can be quickly brought up to speed. As a result one does not always get the opportunity to make all the points one would like to make. In addition, phone callers often ask questions which are not directly relevant to the issues being discussed. In comparison to talk radio formats, interviews done by community radio or National Public Radio are usually much more in-depth and professionally handled.

Television interviews and talk shows are more difficult to handle than radio or phone interviews because you must communicate your message visually as well as aurally. Those who appear on television must recognize that the television camera has fundamentally changed public speaking (Ailes, 1988; Postman, 1985). In a lecture hall or auditorium few if any people have a close up view of your face. On television "a close-up can move a person's face to an electronic distance physically equivalent to a nose-to-nose confrontation" (Hilton and Knoblauch, 1980: 9). As a result, television viewers receive clues to a person's attitudes and state of mind that are hidden at ordinary physical distances. Similarly, "broadcast talk" is based on the belief that one is addressing the audience as individuals not members of a crowd (Scannell, 1991: 3). In effect, the television camera presumes a face-to-face encounter or co-presence but paradoxically the encounter is one with a faceless nonpresent mass audience (Goffman, 1981: 138).

Public relations professionals have attempted to offer solutions to the new problems associated with "public speaking" on camera. Their suggestions are largely twofold: advance preparation and what Erving Goffman (1959, 1967) would refer to as "self management"—making sure that your on-camera "demeanor" is appropriate.

Because of the risks involved in appearing on camera one should be cautious in accepting requests for interviews. Prior to agreeing to do a television interview one should ask a reporter the following type questions: (1) What is the purpose of the interview? (2) What type of interview will it be? e.g., live or taped? Will the videotape be edited or broadcast in its entirety? (3) Why have I been selected? (4) Who will be conducting the interview? (5) What is the technical and physical setting of the interview? (6) How long will the interview be? (7) Who will the audience be? (Blythin and Samovar, 1985: 180). It is not inappropriate to ask the interviewer to agree to ground rules. If you do not feel comfortable with the situation it might be best to pass on the opportunity. A bad television interview can decrease an expert's social status more so than a radio or newspaper interview (Cohen, 1987: 26). Reporters select experts based not only on what they know but how they look and how effectively they can communicate their knowledge (Cohen, 1987: 115). Those who perform poorly the first few times they are called upon by the media are unlikely to be asked again.

Preparation would include finding out who the other interviewees/guests will be and their perspectives, preparing answers to all questions you think you might be asked (it is not inappropriate to ask an interviewer what questions they intend to ask), rehearsing your answers and videotaping your responses, if possible, and having someone critique your performance.

If you are not familiar with the interviewer you must expect any type of questioning, including the following: false facts, reinterpretation of your response, putting words in your mouth, false assumptions or conclusions, hypothetical premises, baiting you into accusations, leading questions, multiple-part questions, forced choice questions, and loaded questions. On talk shows other guests may try to use these techniques against you if they disagree with your position. Rafe (1991: 102–104) gives examples of each of these questioning styles and suggests responses for them. For instance, if given a hypothetical question it is acceptable to respond with something like: "Since that's a hypothetical question, we really don't know what would happen." Then, go on with your response. When faced with a multiple-part question Rafe suggests simply picking the part you choose to answer since one is under no obligation to try to respond to every part. If faced with false facts or a reinterpretation of your response, one must avoid the tendency to respond as if the interviewer's statements are accurate; instead, graciously correct the interviewer, and then make your own statement.

One must keep in mind that the broadcast news media are interested in "conflict." Lively discussion or debate is much preferred over the droll lecturing style of some professors. Talk shows generally put entertainment success ahead of informational success (Cohen, 1987: 30). The best broadcast communicators present their information in a lively and entertaining way. Snappy one-line answers and sound bites are essential, according to analysts of the broadcast media.

Many of the media relations books offer tips on how to dress for television, sit properly, make proper use of microphones, and effectively use gestures and eye contact to reaffirm your statements (Blythin and Samovar, 1985: 145–148; Rafe, 1991: 47–49,77,82; Armes, 1988). Roger Ailes (1988: 3) argues that when on camera the first seven seconds are crucial to establishing your credibility and rapport with the home audience. Behaviors to avoid on television—in the first seven seconds and throughout the interview—because they will distance you from the audience include: failing to establish initial rapport with viewers; stiffness or woodenness in the use of body;

presentation of material that is intellectually oriented; forgetting to involve the audience emotionally; appearing uncomfortable because of fear of failure; poor use of eye contact and facial expression; lack of humor; speech direction and intent unclear due to improper preparation; inability to use silence for impact; lack of energy, causing inappropriate pitch pattern, speech rate, and volume; and the use of boring language and lack of interesting material (Ailes, 1988: 9).

While criminologists certainly must present intellectually oriented material, when they appear in the media their message will have to be articulated in such a way that it can be communicated to the greatest number of people. Blythin and Samovar (1985: 188–193) suggest the following techniques for media presentation: (1) Start with your main point first. (2) Be brief. (3) Relate to your audience. (4) Be accurate. (5) Don't flaunt your expertise. (6) Don't be evasive. (7) Stay calm—even during difficult moments. (8) Make effective use of language. (9) Try to establish and maintain your personal credibility.

If the situation turns into a debate or heated discussion between you and the interviewer or other panelists, the following suggestions may prove helpful:

1. Be quick to identify which questions are being used to bait you and which are legitimate.
2. Never allow incorrect statements to stand. Respond to them immediately. Otherwise the audience will believe they are true.
3. Avoid debating. Be the rational and calm one. Use "defusers" to cool down heated questions (e.g. "If I were in your position, I might be inclined to agree").
4. Don't repeat negative questions. Make only positive points.
5. Be very cautious in the use of statistics. Try not to use more than two statistics per utterance, and make them of the same "denomination."

Statistics are best used for points of comparison, in a set of two (Blythin and Samovar, 1985: 198–199; Rafe, 1991: 86, 97; Hilton and Knoblauch, 1980: 100).

Schmertz (1986) goes even further and advocates "creative confrontation" as the appropriate style for media interviews. By this he means making sure you go first in a possible debate situation, being very well prepared, and "grabbing all the good points for yourself."

The differences between live and taped interviews are also important to recognize. Taped interviews are particularly problematic because what you have said in a typical ten- to thirty-minute taped television "news" interview is likely to be edited to one or two ten-second sound bites leaving you with little control over the context of your remarks. You can ask to have your prerecorded answers kept intact, but I have found that such promises are frequently broken by reporters. The only solution I know of is to offer one or two juicy sound bites in your responses that typify your position, hoping the story editor will choose those. For example, whenever I was interviewed regarding pornography I found that mentioning the First Amendment, civil liberties, and "the need to protect the most objectionable materials in order to keep 'censors' out of schools, museums, and libraries" was usually too tempting for reporters to edit out. On the other hand, avoid parenthetical discussions or long segues between portions of your key responses to a question because you never know when such "bits" might be used because they make a point the reporter wishes to make.

Live interviews can be more effective in communicating your message than taped ones because of the sense of immediacy created as a result of the fact that the speech act is taking place in real time. However, any mistakes that are made cannot be edited out. The most important preparation in such a situation is anticipating what types of questions you will be asked. Without such information you can very easily end up looking quite foolish. At first I was reticent to ask reporters what they were after—thinking I was somehow infringing on the rights of journalists. However, most proved quite willing to clue me in on what questions would be mine if I asked. On the other hand, journalists are often taught not to discuss the actual questions with broadcast interviewees in advance because the interviewees may not want to repeat their answers again (McLaughlin, 1986: 165).

As a communication style for live interviews it is most important to answer questions directly and simply, beginning with the main point you want to make and attempting to get in as many ancillary statements supporting your main point as possible before you are cut off by other guests or the host. When asked questions to which you do not know the answer it is better to say "I don't know" than to use gobbledygook or long evasive answers (McLaughlin, 1986: 94). The latter will only make you appear worse. In such circumstances I usually say something like, "I am not up to date on that subject," and quickly switch the topic back to the previous question and make additional points about it.

Conclusion

Is "newsmaking criminology" possible? My experience and that of others leads me to conclude that trying to use the media to bring the findings of criminological research to a larger audience and enlighten the public is a more difficult task than originally envisioned. It requires an understanding of how the media operate, knowledge of how to communicate successfully in a variety of formats and circumstances, and advance preparation.

Criminologists and other social scientists have found it extremely difficult to communicate the complexities of social scientific research through a media format such as a television talk show which is principally concerned with attempting to "entertain" an audience. At best it appears that only coverage of major points or the use of short quotes are possible given most contemporary news media formats. If criminologists hope to communicate through the media they must tailor their findings to these various formats.

However, as long as criminologists remain outside of rather than part of the media they will always be subject to the biases of reporters, editors, news bureau chiefs, etc. With little or no control over how your statements are edited the risk of being misunderstood is indeed great. One solution to these problems would be for criminologists to seek permanent ongoing relationships with the press. In particular, criminologists should strive to become consultants with the ability to provide input over story editing, whom to interview, or even which stories to cover. However, the expert will first have to convince the news organization that linking up with them will make the station's crime news coverage well-rounded and more accurately reflect reality. I believe that only under these conditions will genuine "newsmaking criminology" be possible.

REFERENCES

Ailes, Roger (with Jon Kraushar). 1988. *You Are the Message: Secrets of the Master Communicators.* Homewood, IL: Dow Jones-Irwin.

Altheide, David. 1976. *Creating Reality: How Television News Distorts Events.* Beverly Hills: Sage Publications.

Armes, Roy. 1988. *On Video.* New York: Routledge.

Baker, Mary, et al. 1987. "The impact of a crime wave: Perceptions, fear, and confidence in the police," *Law and Society Review.* 17, 2: 319–335.

Barak, Gregg. 1988. "Newsmaking criminology: Reflections on the media, intellectuals, and crime," *Justice Quarterly.* 5, 4: 565–587.

Barrile, Leo. 1984. "Television and attitudes about crime: Do heavy viewers distort criminality and support retributive justice?" In Surette, Ray (ed.) *Justice and the Media.* 141–159 Springfield, IL: Charles C. Thomas.

Benderly, Beryl. 1989. "Don't believe everything you read . . . A case study of how the politics of sex-difference research turned a small finding into a major media flap." *Psychology Today.* November, 67–69.

Blythin, Evan and Larry Samovar. 1985. *Communicating Effectively on Television.* Belmont, CA: Wadsworth.

Brady, John. 1977. *The Craft of Interviewing.* New York: Vintage Books.

Cohen, Akiba. 1987. *The Television News Interview.* Beverly Hills: Sage Publications.

Cohn, Victor. 1989. *News and Numbers.* Ames: Iowa State University Press.

Ericson, Richard et al. 1991. *Representing Order: Crime, Law, and Justice in the News Media.* Toronto: University of Toronto Press.

Fishman, Mark. 1980. *Manufacturing the News.* Austin: University of Texas Press.

Goffman, Erving. 1959. *The Presentation of Self in Everyday Life.* New York: Doubleday.

———. 1967. *Interaction Ritual.* Garden City, New York: Doubleday.

———. 1981. *Forms of Talk.* Philadelphia: University of Pennsylvania Press.

Hilton, Jack and Mary Knoblauch. 1980. *On Television! A Survival Guide for Media Interviews.* New York: AMACOM.

Killenberg, George M. 1992. Personal interview. February 13th.

Killenberg, George M. and Rob Anderson. 1989. *Before the Story: Interviewing and Communication Skills for Journalists.* New York: St. Martin's Press.

McLaughlin, Paul. 1986. *Asking Questions: The Art of the Media Interview.* Toronto: International Self-Counsel Press Ltd.

Nobile, Philip and Eric Nadler. 1986. *United States of America v. Sex: How the Meese Commission Lied About Pornography.* New York: Minotaur Press.

Postman, Neil. 1985. *Amusing Ourselves to Death.* New York: Viking.

Rafe, Stephen. 1991. *Mastering the News Media Interview: How to Succeed at Television, Radio, and Print Interviews.* New York: Harper Business.

Robinson, James. 1987. *Winning Them Over: Get Your Message Across by Dealing Successfully with the Media.* Rocklin, CA: Prima Publishing and Communications.

Scannell, Paddy (ed.) 1991. *Broadcast Talk.* Newbury Park, CA: Sage Publications.

Schmertz, Herb, with William Novak. 1986. *Good-bye to the Low Profile: The Art of Creative Confrontation.* Boston: Little, Brown and Company.

Sherman, Lawrence and Ellen Cohn. 1989. "The impact of research on legal policy: The Minneapolis domestic violence experiment." *Law and Society Review.* 23, 1: 117–144.

Tuchman, Gaye. 1978. *Making News.* New York: Free Press.

Weiss, Carol and Eleanor Singer. 1988. *Reporting of Social Science in the National Media.* New York: Russell Sage Foundation.

Wong, Linda and Bruce Alexander. 1991. "'Cocaine-related' deaths: Media coverage in the war on drugs." *The Journal of Drug Issues.* 21, 1: 105–119.

Zoglin, Richard. 1992, February 17th. "Prime time lively." *Time.* p. 8.

APPENDIX A

Radio/TV/Newspaper Interviews and Appearances

1988

a. April 4. I was featured on a half-hour program taped and broadcast by KCSU-TV in Oklahoma City. The program on "Church and State" featured a political science professor as well.

b. May 12. television news interview on TV 5 in Oklahoma City. I was allowed to make a comment about a program on television evangelism that had just been broadcast by Ted Koppel on ABC. My live comment dealt with financial improprieties and criminal acts by television ministers such as Jim Bakker.

c. November 14. Television news interview on TV 9 in Oklahoma City. News feature was called "School Halls to Prison Walls." My statement was edited out of context to make it appear I agreed with the proposition that juvenile crime is much more serious today.

1989

a. January 21. I was interviewed by TV 9 in Oklahoma City regarding the popularity of talk radio. Only one sound bite from the edited interview was used and I had considered it a throw-away line, not an important comment.

b. October 24. I was interviewed by WTKN-AM in Tampa on the topic of forfeiture as a criminal penalty, particularly discussing Florida's felony forfeiture laws. I was the sole guest on a one-hour broadcast.

1990

a. July 5. Television interview by Reggie Roundtree of TV 10. Topic: Gov. Martinez's decision to change the rules regarding D.O.C. work-release inmates. Broadcast on the same date.

b. August 17. Newspaper Interview: *Tampa Tribune.* Interviewed by Neil Cote concerning censorship. Article appeared on August 20th, page P-1.

c. August 17. Television interview by TV 10 concerning censorship and the formation of the local chapter of Friends of the First Amendment. Also featured was X-rated film actress Barbara Dare.

d. August 17. Television interview by TV 8 concerning censorship and the formation of the local chapter of Friends of the First Amendment. Also featured was X-rated film actress Barbara Dare.

e. September 12. Radio talk show. WMNF-FM. Discussion with USF professor Ruth Whitney concerning pornography and feminism. Broadcast live.

f. September 13. Television talk show *Eye on Tampa Bay,* television 13. Discussion with David Caton of the American Family Association concerning pornography and religion. Also present were an adult bookstore owner and a minister. Broadcast live.

g. November 15. *Tampa Tribune* columnist Neil Cote covered a speech concerning censorship given by me at St. Petersburg Junior College. Article appeared on November 19th, p. P-1. Cote accused me of being a spokesperson for the pornography industry.

h. November 15. Television interview by TV 44 concerning censorship. Broadcast on same date.

i. November 30. Television appearance. Appeared live on TV 8 News at noon to discuss the new Florida Parole Commission's early release policies. The other guest was a local MADD spokesperson who had been crippled by a drunk driver.

1991

a. January 4. Television interview by Reggie Roundtree of TV 10. Topic: A USF student was not permitted to show pornographic films as a part of his multi-media art exhibit. Parallels to the Mapplethorpe case were drawn.

b. Winter. "Pornography is the 'Big Lie,' Professor Says," *Bayboro Briefing.* Vol. 8: 1. This interview discussing my research was done by the university's public relations officer, Deborah Kurelik.

c. Spring. "Pornographic Liberties: Even the Unpopular Deserves Protection under the First Amendment," *USF Magazine*. Vol. 33: 1. This interview discussing my research was done by the university's public relations officer, Deborah Kurelik.

d. May 9. Television appearance. Appeared as the sole guest on "Pro and Con," a Paragon Cable talk show hosted by John McCarthy. Topics included Cincinnati Mapplethorpe trial and continued NEA funding of controversial art. The program was rebroadcast a number of times.

e. July 5. Television interview by TV 10. Topic: Arrest of Tony Alamo, a minister who physically abused children. Broadcast on same date.

f. August 19. My remarks were featured in a *Tampa Tribune* article entitled "Privacy issues exposed: What is legal?" written by Jennifer Tucker, pp. B-1, 3. Topics included the Tampa "Sex, Blinds, and Videotape" incident.

g August 23. "Sex, Blinds, and Videotape, Part 1," *Eye on Tampa Bay*. TV 13. I was on the show to discuss the legal implications of this incident. Lee Adler, who videotaped a couple having sex in their bathroom, was the other guest.

h. August 26. "Sex, Blinds, and Videotape, Part 2," *Eye on Tampa Bay*. TV 13. I was on the show to discuss the legal implications of this incident. The couple who were unknowingly videotaped were also guests.

i. September 9-12. "Pushing the Limits," TV 8. I was interviewed as part of this three-part series on sex and violence on television. I was credited only as ACLU although I had asked to have my academic position recognized.

1992

a. April 1. I was the sole guest on the Jones Cable public access program "First Freedom." The topic was "Operation Looking Glass," the sting operation run by the U. S. Postal Inspection Service aimed at purchasers of child pornography.

** In addition to these appearances, I was called on a number of other stories in which my comments were not used. On other occasions, I acted as a consultant and gave the names of other experts who could be called.

CHAPTER 11

Newsmaking Criminology as Replacement Discourse

Stuart Henry

Any account of social life is necessarily partial. We selectively and systematically omit in order to sharpen and differentiate. To focus on a topic is to enhance by elimination. The one begets the other. Journalists are professional account makers, skilled at purposive elimination, tuned to resonant enhancement. They reflect what they describe, therein constituting that described as at once real, real again, real in fact. Through their media, journalists' accumulated constitutive work permeates the very relationships they purport to describe, giving it sustenance, form and shape.

Nor are criminologists inactive in this process. Our assent to communicated truths is emergent through our silences, these too, accumulated and constitutive of the real. As Michel Foucault (1978) has reminded us, silences are strong tools in the construction of reality. So in considering crime, itself a socially constructed category, journalists form alliances with agents of social control, vocal public commentators, interest groups, offenders and victims, to co-manufacture crime events, crime patterns and crime trends and, ultimately, to constitute the substance that is criminological phenomena (Cohen and Young, 1980; Chibnall, 1977).

To transcend our passive contribution to such socially constructed and publicly consumed crime truths, it is necessary for criminologists to actively intercede in the constitutive process. As can be seen throughout this book, there are many

ways to accomplish intercession. The focus of this chapter is on
some of the ways that have been described as "newsmaking
criminology" (Barak, 1988). Newsmaking criminology consists of
criminologists actively challenging silences, identifying
omissions, and of resurrecting the eliminated through
participating in the making of news stories about crime.
Elsewhere I have described this process as one dimension of
"replacement discourse" (Henry, 1987; Milovanovic and Henry,
1991; Henry and Milovanovic, forthcoming). Here, then, we are
concerned with newsmaking criminology as replacement
discourse.

Making Crime News

In challenging silences through replacement discourse the
aim is to "interrupt the smooth passage of 'regimes of truth,' to
disrupt those forms of knowledge about crime which have
assumed a self-evident quality, and to engender a state of
uncertainty in those responsible for servicing the network of
power-knowledge relations" (Smart, 1983: 135). Before
criminologists embark on such a critique it is necessary to be
clear about the outcome to be achieved. This requires
understanding of what replacement discourse is and what it is
not.

Replacement discourse is not the same as oppositional
discourse, even though both may result in public challenges to
prevailing crime truths. Oppositional discourse is as constitutive
of existing reality as is supportive discourse since each
addresses, and therein reproduces, the prevailing conceptions
and distinctions while disputing their content. For example,
while Selva and Bohm (1987) have emphasized that, in many
respects, an oppositional legal discourse which utilizes the
existing structure of legal discourse may prove productive and
liberating, this downplays the significance of the constitutive
effects of "liberating" practices in law. A no more graphic
example of this process is oppositional adolescent reaction to
school by working-class kids. While they "resist" and reject the
system that rejects them, it is this reaction formation (Cohen,

1955) that subsequently consigns them to the bottom of the very hierarchy they despise (Willis, 1977).

Replacement discourse, in contrast, is directed at the dual process of deconstructing prevailing structures of meaning and displacing these by new conceptions, distinctions, words and phrases, which convey alternative meanings. The critical component of replacement discourse resides in the criminologist's ability to deconstruct that which is established truth, while at the same time providing the replacement aspect to claim any newly created space with its own internally generated alternatives. Perhaps the classic example of a criminologist successfully interjecting replacement discourse into the popular culture is Sutherland's call through his writing (1940; 1941) and public addresses as president of the American Society of Criminology, for an expansion of the definition of "crime" to include the concept of "white collar crime." Drawing attention to "a large area of criminal behavior that had been neglected by criminologists" he insisted that "white collar crime is 'really' crime" because, like offenses against criminal laws, violations of regulatory laws have both the key elements: "legal definition of an act as socially injurious and legal provision of a penalty for the act" (Sutherland, 1949: 511; 1945). In spite of its controversial birth, "white collar crime" has become an accepted dimension of the public consciousness, with surveys reporting between 80 and 90 percent of the public believing that white collar offenders deserve prison for their crimes (Newman, 1968; Gibbons, 1969; Braithwaite 1982; and Cullen et al., 1985).

Other more recent examples of replacement discourse can be found in the work of Christie (1977) with his notion of "conflict as property," the sociology of deviance reconceived as a "sociology of acceptance" (Bogdan and Taylor, 1987), Katz's (1988) formulation of murder as "righteous slaughter," and Pepinsky (1991) with his expansive reconstruction of crime and violence as the antithesis of democratic human interaction via his ideas of "peacemaking criminology" (Pepinsky and Quinney, 1991). However, such alternative constructions of crime are unlikely to impact the public domain of crime if they remain confined to the dormitories of academic discourse. A crucially important aspect of replacement discourse is that it should intercede in the public debate primarily, though by no means exclusively, through the news media.

One of the few criminological scholars to recognize the importance of developing an activist agenda of replacement discourse is Gregg Barak (1988) with his call for a "newsmaking criminology." Barak says that "in the post-modern era, social problems such as homelessness, sexual assault, or drug abuse are politically constructed, ideologically articulated, and media produced events" (Barak, 1991a: 5). He advocates that criminologists become credible spokespeople, make crim- inological news and participate in the popular construction of images of crime and crime control to produce crime themes "as a means of bringing about social change and social justice" (Barak, 1988: 585; see also Barak and Bohm, 1989; Barak, 1991b).

To summarize, replacement discourse is not simply critical and oppositional, but provides both a critique and an alternative vision. A direct consequence of the activist approach to replacement discourse is that "critical" criminologists deconstruct crime as a separate entity by withdrawing energy from unitary concepts of crime and by denying its status as an independent reality. Simultaneously we must write new scripts that show the intertwined connections between individuals, activities that harm, and the whole of which we are a part. Replacement discourse, therefore, involves substituting for "control talk" (Cohen, 1985), "organizational talk" (Manning, 1988), and "law talk" (Milovanovic, 1986; Thomas, 1988), a reflexive discourse which allows for the nuances of being human. Such a discourse should retain a vision of society as a recurrent and emergent outcome of human activity, but privileging neither social forces, nor individual ones. While these alternatives need to be developed outside of traditional criminological contexts in order to minimize the inadvertent contamination that comes through incorporation of existing constructions, they also must be reinserted into the public debate. Primarily this demands an activist approach whereby criminologists transfuse their alternative research-informed conceptions into journalistic constructions through "newsmaking criminology." The next section will explore several ways whereby this may be accomplished.

Styles of Newsmaking Criminology

Insofar as several constitutive agents comprise the newsmaking enterprise, each offers opportunities for intercession. Four styles of criminological intercession can be identified, although these are by no means exhaustive and have been chosen here for the purpose of illustration. I call these styles: (1) disputing data; (2) challenging journalism; (3) self-reporting; and (4) confronting media. Each relies upon expressed journalistic interest in a particular facet of crime and its reportage. Each is not, however, evenly nor equally classifiable as replacement discourse. In what follows I shall briefly outline the approach taken in each style, point out some of its advantages and disadvantages, explain what would be necessary to elevate the approach to a more active form of replacement discourse, and illustrate this with a case example.

Disputing Data: The Criminologist as Expert

This is the classic form of intercession by criminologists in the media. It is primarily reactive, involving criminologists challenging published news reports and crime stories with a dispute about their content. Typically the dispute is over a distortion in the image presented of offenders, victims, policy or crime. It may involve charges of omission but importantly, from the replacement discourse perspective, it also involves new or alternative data to correct the original image. The typical forms taken by data disputing are letters to the editor, open forums, or being known in the media as an available, criminological expert to be called on by journalists as an issue becomes a hot and ongoing story. Recent examples are the contributions of criminologists James Alan Fox of Northeastern University with his numerous media incursions on such issues as profiles of serial killers, and more recently the issue of employees who kill (Fox & Levin, 1993), and James Fyfe of Temple University in response to police brutality and the Rodney King trial and verdicts.

A problem with most forms of data disputing is that the journalist retains control over the direction of the story. As a result the criminological input, especially because it challenges other content, becomes "one side" of what may be a two- or many-sided account. In such a scenario control of the overall image or media impression is lost to the notion that "experts disagree." Take the example of a feature article in *The Toronto Star* entitled "Crime and Race: A Question of Statistics" (Sweet, 1991). The article uses the "opening hook" of various controversial public statements made by Canadian politicians and Toronto police officers about an allegedly disproportionate number of crimes committed by members of certain racial and/or ethnic groups. This is then used to carry the substantive part of the article examining the issue of whether the Canadian government should begin to gather racially based crime statistics (which is prohibited by law). Quoting experts from academia, criminology and agency representatives, Lois Sweet (the journalist), presents pro and con cases. Included is the section: "Two views on crime statistics" in which a criminologist Thomas Gabor heads a pro-race-based statistics column against a column by Wilson Head, president of the Canadian Federation of Race Relations, who is opposed to collecting statistics by race. The article does not conclude definitively and the impression left is that "the experts disagree."

Moreover, regardless of its intended objective, by following the criminologist-as-expert format, rather than deconstructing the race-crime myth, the article repeatedly ties race terms such as "Chinese" and "black" to crime, thereby reconstituting crime as a race issue. This is not to deny that such newsmaking criminology is unimportant as a contributor to informing popular culture about crime, but it does little more than reinforce the existing conception of crime. Its ability to generate alternative discourse is limited by journalistic (rather than criminological) agendas and by the criminologist's pre-cast role as one who necessarily employs the concepts contained in the initial statements, in order to "challenge" them. This leads us to the second type of newsmaking criminology: challenging journalism, in which the same type of data dispute is handled differently.

Challenging Journalism: The Criminologist as Journalist

One way to make "disputing data" into an exercise of replacement discourse is for criminologists to take over the authorship of crime news articles, rather than allowing themselves to be used as subjects or sideshows within them. Here the criminologist either becomes a freelance journalist, writing commentary or feature articles (Roberts and Gabor, 1989), or becomes the freelance reporter and writes articles for the news media on issues raised by events, or at criminology conferences (Johns, 1986a; 1986b; 1986c). Others have similarly placed themselves in the public domain by anchoring or hosting a regular radio or television slot (e.g., Ron Kramer of Western Michigan University, and Laurie Taylor of the University of York). These strategies have the advantage of shaping the total image of crime issues under consideration but the disadvantages of being subject to editorial reconstruction and are limited in their scope to the immediate listening or viewing audience (unlike, for example, educating crime reporting journalists, which I discuss below).

In the case example reprinted below, Canadian criminologists Julian Roberts and Thomas Gabor accomplish a version of replacement discourse quite deliberately to fill the silence by reticent criminologists on the same race and crime issue discussed in the preceding section. The "hook" here is Philippe Rushton's racist theories of crime. The authors achieve some considerable movement towards replacement discourse by both deconstructing the existing crime/race connection and resurrecting the displaced connections. Thus they explain how it is that crime rates vary *within* ethnic, racial, and cultural groups (deconstruction), how the simple distinction between black and white falsely assumes racial purity (deconstruction), how economic and social conditions and generations of prejudice by persons and institutions are linked to crime rate data (reconstruction), and how a global comparative perspective leads to alternative conclusions (deconstruction and reconstruction).

Case Illustration 1: Julian Roberts and Thomas Gabor on racist
theory of crime.

> **"Rushton's crime theories have no basis in fact"** by
> **Julian Roberts and Thomas Gabor. This article originally**
> **appeared in *The Toronto Star*, March 14, 1989 p. A21.**
> [Reprinted with permission from the authors and *The*
> *Toronto Star*.]
>
> Canadians have recently been exposed to the research of
> an Ontario professor, Philippe Rushton, who claims to
> have uncovered evidence of a significant relationship
> between race and crime. Although some professionals
> such as David Suzuki have challenged Rushton's views,
> criminologists have been remarkably reticent to comment.
> Rushton's opinions have achieved national prominence,
> and given that the public's primary source of information
> is the media, the potential for misinformation is
> considerable. As professional criminologists, we wish to
> respond to assertions that are at times without foundation
> or which lack qualification.
>
> Neither a geneticist nor a criminologist by training,
> Rushton asserts that there are substantial inter-racial
> differences in crime rates and that many of these
> differences are accounted for by genetic factors. He cites as
> evidence for his genetic argument data which show that
> blacks are over-represented in crime statistics. This is
> simply not evidence of a genetic component. His
> reasoning is highly flawed, on several grounds.
>
> First, his comparisons between blacks and whites are
> predicated upon the assumption of racial purity. This
> assumption is false. In North America, many blacks are
> more than half white by lineage and many whites have
> some black ancestry.
>
> Second, the over-representation in crime statistics by
> blacks only occurs in the crime rates of certain offenses.
> Crime embraces many different forms of law-breaking.
> For crimes such as fraud and embezzlement, blacks are
> under-represented, relative to their numbers in the general
> population. For many crimes there is no relation
> whatsoever between race and crime. If race is related to
> crime—even certain types of crime—why does the
> relationship appear only for some offenses? Are blacks
> genetically programmed to commit robbery rather than

fraud? The suggestion is laughable, but this is the inference from a genetic explanation of crime. The answer is that other more plausible explanations exist for Rushton's "statistic." Blacks are over-represented in the official crime statistics for certain crimes, but they are also over-represented among the poor and the urbanites, two categories of individuals that tend to be over-represented in crimes regardless of color. Rushton has not applied the meticulous statistical controls that are necessary to isolate genetic from environmental factors.

In England, it is only recently that the rates of certain crimes committed by blacks have exceeded those of the rest of the population. Such an increase cannot reflect genetic factors. But once again there is a far more plausible environmental explanation: the changing economic and social conditions in the United Kingdom.

Several well-known patterns in criminal statistics directly contradict Rushton's position. Black crime is far from uniform from one community or country to another. Substantial variation can be found in black crime rates across different cultures. Also, both black and white crime rates are higher in the southern United States than in the northeast.

Furthermore, black Americans, although racially closer to whites, have far higher levels of criminal activity than the more racially pure blacks living in the Caribbean or in Africa. As well, American whites have far higher crime rates than the black residents of many other countries. These facts do not fit Rushton's theory either.

When discussing racial differences in crime rates, it is important to remember that virtually every country has minority groups who account for more crime than would be expected, given their frequency in the population. Are we to use genetic factors to explain every case? To claim that race is a factor in explaining crime rates, one has to eliminate other factors such as class, prejudice and employment opportunities. The only way to attempt a fair comparison between racial groups is to compare blacks and whites of equal economic standing. But even this would be insufficient, for it would fail to take into account the impact of generations of prejudice— an environmental factor. The differential treatment of blacks through the criminal justice system has been well documented.

Members of the public who report crime, and the
individuals who administer the criminal justice system,
are unfortunately not always color blind.
These are but a few of the flaws in Rushton's reasoning.
They indicate that in the realm of crime, his pro-
nouncements do not meet the minimum standards of
scientific enquiry. When studying a volatile issue such as
this we expect more scholarship and less speculation from
a university professor.

In order to bring about both deconstruction and
reconstruction, then, it seems necessary for criminologists not
simply to passively respond to journalists' desire to write crime
news stories but to claim control of the crime news space
themselves. Such innovation requires more energy than simply
responding to journalists' questions. Nor is it immune from the
reproductive effects of journalistic agendas by which prevailing
stereotypes and pre-existing conceptions are purveyed. This is
because the news media retain control over the title, the nature
and placing of any accompanying photographic or illustrative
material and often, also, the opening and closing paragraphs, as
well as any extracted highlights. Such journalistic "packaging
practices" can compromise, if not completely undermine, any
critical reconstructive attempt.

Self-reporting: The Criminologist as Subject

Here criminologists overcome some of the limitations
inherent in data disputing since they are the primary initiators of
the story or are its sole subject. Typically they are involved in a
research study, program evaluation, or program implementation
and either actively publicize the results or provide the words for
local journalists to describe their work, with a view that the story
may become syndicated regionally or, preferably, nationally.
Here the criminologist relies on journalists' general interests in
covering crime stories, but also appeals to their concern for the
new, the tantalizing, and even the human interest story. The
advantage of this form of intercession is that the criminologist's
newsmaking is the prime, if not exclusive source for the story,
which allows considerable depth of discourse and the

opportunity to establish various human agency-social structure connections. As such, considerable strides can be made in creating and claiming new space about crime. A disadvantage is that, as with disputing data and challenging journalism, the journalist and editors, as well as the historically established style of the media outlet can, again, result in packaging that kills.

Case Illustration 2: Mimi Silbert beyond rehabilitation.

"Hitting bottom can be the beginning" by Hank Whittemore, *Parade Magazine*, March 15, 1992. [Extracts reprinted with permission of *Parade* © 1992.]

An excellent example of how to penetrate these limitations is Berkeley criminologist Mimi Silbert's work as founder of San Francisco's Delancey Street Project, reported nationally in numerous places such as the cover feature of *Parade* magazine (Whittemore, 1992) and ABC's "20/20." Let us examine the *Parade* article as illustrative. Described as "the world's most successful rehabilitation program for criminal offenders" (*ibid*: 1), the article reports how residents (all ex-cons) built a $30 million commercial center on San Francisco's waterfront, housing an upscale restaurant and several other businesses and housing units, turning over $3 million a year. The project is shown as the culmination of a self-supporting program that in twenty years has turned 10,000 ex-cons into productive and constructive members of society. The opening hook describes how one such resident, a former drug-dealing hustler charged with twenty-seven armed robberies and former San Quentin inmate, is now skilled in eight different construction trades and tutors other residents toward their high school diplomas. The article then turns to its primary focus, criminologist Mimi Silbert and the Delancey residents, who are revealed to be the embodiment of her self-help and mutual aid philosophy that has infused the Delancey program. The essence of her transformative approach embodies the epitome of replacement discourse, as is illustrated in her response to those inmates who felt like quitting during the building of the foundation's waterfront complex. Whittemore quotes Silbert's praxis, a combined deconstructive-reconstructive response:

> You want to quit . . . that's what you've *always* done—
> given up every time its gotten difficult. I know you're
> hammering away and thinking that this isn't worth it, but
> you're hammering away on your *lives*. . . . You're building
> your *own* foundation. If you make a mistake with that
> wall, tear it down and rebuild it! That's what we're doing
> at Delancey Street, for *ourselves*—tearing down bad things
> and making good things to replace 'em. And if you're too
> guilty and angry and hopeless to fight for yourself, then
> do it for the next guy. Because he's counting on you.
> Meanwhile you're learning new skills. You're getting
> something that nobody can take away from you. You're
> building your lives. (Whittemore, 1992: 5, quoting Mimi
> Silbert)

Throughout the interview, Silbert is quoted extensively
explaining the horrible and terrible "old lives" and how these are
now replaced by constructive and productive new ones. Instead
of confirming the popular view that criminals are a class of
losers, through journalist Whittemore she describes their former
activities as neither inevitable nor necessary and nothing if not
inefficient. Instead of resurrecting the idea that some people are
born to crime, she emphasizes how "They can be taught to help
themselves to be responsible and self-reliant" and she points out
that helping them become so is "a critical part of turning around
the rest of society" (Whittemore, 1992: 5). At the same time, in
dealing with newcomers, Silbert is shown to debunk causal
theories of crime that assume a passive offender, replacing these
with an agency-based view that acknowledges individual
responsibility and capacity to make a difference:

> I tell a person who's scowling at me with utter contempt,
> "Hey, we know you're trying to manipulate us. Our job is
> to out-manipulate you! And we're better at it than you
> are" . . . They always play the victim: "It wasn't my fault."
> We ask them to explain: "Somebody tied you down and
> injected a needle into your arm? Someone forced you to
> take a gun and bash that old lady on the head? Is that
> what happened? Who actually did those things?" Finally
> they admit, "Well yeah, it was me. I did it." We don't care
> that they don't mean what they say, just so long as they
> say it. Then we remind them of it everyday that they are
> here! (Whittemore, 1992: 5)

Silbert is not resurrecting existing constructions about crime in this interview, but consistently replacing them with the Delancey discourse. Her replacement discourse is also symbolic in that it describes a process of emulation of what is desired, a learning through doing, and becoming transformed as a result. Both projects and personal activities are organized to reflect this deconstructive/constructive approach: de-emphasis of what was negative and destructive and emphasis of what is positive: "We ask them to act as if they were upstanding citizens or successful executives, even though they feel the opposite. Through external imitation, something gets internalized" (*ibid:* 5). Transformation or personal change is shown not to be the result of external forces or treatments—indeed, the word treatment is not mentioned and "rehabilitation" is only used by the journalist—but as the outcome of an ongoing process of taking personal responsibility in the context of an extended family, based upon the principle that "people change by 'doing' for somebody else" (*ibid.*). Another form of deconstruction is "dissipation." This comprises long sessions designed to help residents "get rid of the tremendous guilt over what they did in the past" (*ibid:* 6).

Clearly, this form of newsmaking criminology is powerful in its ability to transform crime concepts held in the current popular culture. It is powerful because the criminologist being interviewed is immersed in her own discourse. In this case, it is clear that an alternative meaning is given to rehabilitation, in which it is transformed into a process of struggle for personal and social change.

One disadvantage of the criminologist-as-subject approach is that, unless there is an extended transformation of the criminologist's own discourse and an empathetic journalist (as in the above illustration), the approach risks trivialization or marginalization from the crime mainstream, even by well-intentioned sympathetic journalists. Moreover, it may be perceived by the public as "just another study" or "just another program" or "just another case of bleeding-heart liberalism." Again this may be pre-empted by criminologists reporting their own research or programs, while striving to deconstruct an existing conception of crime and replace it with a more enlightened one.

Confronting Media: The Criminologist as Educative Provocateur

Here the media are both the direct target and the medium of the newsmaking criminologist. The object of this version of replacement discourse is the media itself. The media are both the subject of the study and the object of criticism. The aim is to get the media to engage in reassessment through self-analysis, prompted by the criminologist as critical catalyst. There are several approaches to this style of newsmaking criminology. In this section I shall use two different illustrations. The first is a variation on "criminologist as expert," but in this case the subject of the dispute is the media themselves. The criminologists in the first case began with a short paper on the problems arising from the recent growth in the media's use of amateur videos in the production of crime news and the implications of this for privacy (Einstadter and Henry, 1991). This formed the basis of subsequent media contact, and became the subject of an article by a university newspaper reporter who saw mileage in the issue because of its very focus: the media. The journalistic version of the original piece was then picked up by several other news organizations and formed the subject of subsequent articles, radio and television interviews and talk show discussions. The avalanche effect is not guaranteed but, given the interest in the subject of themselves, the criminologist is able to predict a reasonable and on-going coverage, and through this is able to replace some existing discourse about crime. The following two selections comprising the third illustration indicate how this process is likely to unfold.

Case Illustration 3: Werner Einstadter and Stuart Henry on Video Vigilantes.

> **"Profs' paper looks at new trend of 'video vigilantes'" by Debra McLean, FOCUS EMU, p. 2. October 8, 1991.** [Reprinted with permission from FOCUS EMU and Eastern Michigan University.]
>
> A single picture may tell a thousand words, but a video tape can get you arrested, convicted, fired from your job

or, if you film something the local TV news wants, it can get you a lot of money.

In a trend *Newsweek* magazine recently called "the camcording of America," so many people now own video cameras that events we previously had to rely on eyewitnesses to explain, particularly street crimes, now regularly end up in vivid color on the nightly news.

Some recent examples of "video vigilantism" include: the highly publicized beating of Rodney King by Los Angeles police officers after they stopped him for speeding; the July 4 beating of a woman attending the Detroit fireworks by a group of teen-age girls; a January 1989 tape of a teen-age baby sitter repeatedly slapping an infant secretly taped by the baby's suspicious parents; and a June 1991 incident in which a gay man in California taped himself being attacked by a neighbor who had long harassed him about his lifestyle.

What all those video tapes have in common is that, unlike the infamous John DeLorean and Washington D.C. Mayor Marion Barry tapes, they weren't made by police agencies; they were made by ordinary citizens who now, seemingly, have a new weapon against crime.

They're using that weapon, however, to tattle on each other rather than to keep track of the people in power, according to two EMU sociologists.

Drs. Werner Einstadter and Stuart Henry, both of EMU's Department of Sociology, Anthropology and Criminology, recently wrote a paper titled, "The Inversion of the Invasion of Privacy." . . . In it they argue that this new video vigilantism could lead to a more repressed society as people grow more and more concerned that their every action is being watched and recorded.

"It's been described as the 'Little Brother is watching you' approach," Henry said. "The idea that these devices can be turned around to survey the people in control, the police, to watch the people watching you, has actually been turned around so that people are watching themselves . . . In societies where everyone watches each other, like Japan, there's less crime, but more repression. If everything you do is watched, you are repressed.

"Potentially, it's a better development than it not occurring at all because it does have the possibility of empowering, but at the same time it's fraught with deeper dangers."

One such danger Henry sees is that while the fear of being recorded on video tape might cut down on crime, the greater impact might be a deeper entrenchment of the notion that all crime is perpetrated by poor people in urban areas.

"These video tapes oversimplify crime. It's superficial stuff and the focus is distorted," he said. "We're not controlling crime, we're controlling the media image of what is crime, street crime, sensational crime, the already accepted stereotype of what crime is. What we're not doing is controlling all that other corporate and government crime and people need to get concerned about that because some of the fuel for that street crime is the anger and injustice as a result of the system."

Furthermore, he said, the old notion of "seeing is believing" isn't always true because video tapes provide such a narrow picture of events.

"I don't think we can believe what we see because what we see is open to interpretation and it means different things to different people . . . Whenever there's a piece of action that's so selective, it doesn't deny responsibility for the person doing that action, but we can't see the context of it. . . . You can drop people (with a camera) in the middle of a war zone and say 'Look, they're getting hit,' but it doesn't tell you why that war is going on and why those people are in the middle of it."

Some recent tapes do seem to have put a spotlight on flaws in "the system," like the March 1991 tapes of Rodney King, a black man being beaten by several white Los Angeles police officers. Henry, however, says that even that tape fails to tell the whole story.

"Things like the Rodney King case create an illusion that we're now able to police the police. But we're not controlling the controllers, just the so-called bad apples. (Video tapes) don't look at the bad system and apples can go bad not just because there's a rotten one in the barrel, but because the barrel is rotten. It's the barrel we want to put the cameras on."

While these early video tapes seem to be enjoying much credibility in the courtroom, Henry predicts that as more and more people, particularly the rich and powerful, get stung by a tape, that credibility will be questioned.

"You can have rules of evidence that are strict in terms of the admissibility of this material, so if it's going to be used in a court case we want to investigate the viability of the tape: Who took it and why? Where were they? And what's missing? We'll want to consider the whole picture," he said.

"This will lead us to the content of the visual image . . . and maybe we'll begin to question if what we see on the television news is what really happened," he added. "If those in power marshal their defense (in the courtroom) to defeat that concrete image of the video, that will have a spill-over effect. We might have a deconstruction of the media image as fact and that would be great."

"Amateur news videos criticized: Cameras distort crime, EMU professors say" by Michael Jahr, *Ann Arbor News*, November 25, 1991, pp. C1–C2. [Reprinted with permission from *Ann Arbor News*.]

The rise of video cameras as tools against crime may be a path to empowerment for the ordinary citizen, but it may distort crime and violate rights, say two Eastern Michigan University sociologists.

Professors Werner Einstadter and Stuart Henry claim that citizens are using video technology to pry into each other's lives instead of keeping tabs on the people in power.

"Technology has opened a window of opportunity for the democratization of social control," they argue in a new paper, but "control is transposed and the realm of the personal and private is transgressed as the public turns the camcorders on themselves."

The proliferation of amateur video in the news—for example, the beating of Rodney King by the Los Angeles Police Department, the beatings of suburban women by Detroit women at the Fourth of July fireworks celebration and the confrontations between police and students at a weekend party at EMU— seemed to suggest that the average person had a new weapon against crime. But closer evaluation of the trend should arouse some concern,

Henry said. "Little brother is watching you," he said. "Why is that a problem? You'd think it would be great that ordinary people are now being able to control each others' ordinary crimes by video. It looks on the surface to be superb."

But citizens taping one another can lead to invasions of privacy, emphasize street crime while de-emphasizing white collar crime and focus on crimes rather than their causes.

Henry said the invasion of privacy issue is raised not when someone breaks into a house or store, but when neighbors start "putting their cameras through their next door neighbor's window in order to control behaviors that they morally decide they don't like."

Amateur video also tends to capture "stereotypical" crime—"street offenses, violence and predatory crime," rather than that by government or corporations, he said.

"So when Channel 7 (WXYZ) asks you to become part of the news team, people are being invited to go out with their video, almost like guys are going out with their metal detectors, to see what they can turn up," he said. "And they're turning up, in the case of video, the kinds of crimes they've been sensitized to as crimes in the daily gloss news."

Bob Rowe, news director at WXYZ, disagreed.

"I think he's missing the point of what viewer video is," Rowe said. "Are we asking people to go out and do our job for us? Absolutely not."

Channel 7 only uses viewer video of newsworthy happenings that occurred where WXYZ cameras were not present, Rowe said. Only 1 or 2 percent of submitted video gets used, and those are subject to stringent guidelines.

Amateur footage of a recent student melee at Central Michigan University served as a "springboard" for a more in-depth story, he said. "We didn't just run the video, say 'That's it, thank you, good-bye.' This (the viewer video) was a minor part that helped us show the overall picture."

Rowe compared viewer video to a tool that's used once or twice in the construction of a house. "There are tremendous legal and ethical considerations that come from this kind of journalism and I think it's best left to the professionals," he said.

Author Henry encouraged citizens to take their video cameras into the board rooms and governmental meetings to try to capture a more balanced picture of crime.

Washtenaw County Sheriff Ronald Schebil said amateur video accounts of crime can be a tremendous asset to law enforcement, but he shared some of Henry's concerns about possible abuses.

"Our use (of video) can give a good accurate account—better than an eyewitness account." Schebil said.

He liked the idea of citizens using video cameras to keep track of people in power, because there needs to be an "accountability" for those who are "paid from the taxpayers' trough."

"Unless it violates someone's right to privacy, I wish someone would follow me (with a video camera) all day," Schebil said.

But in the case of neighborhoods or cities like Detroit, crime footage can lead to damaging stereotypes.

"I think the danger is we're going to get a distorted picture of crime in the U.S.," Schebil said. "We're not seeing the problem that may be at the root of the crime."

That's another problem Henry sees. "The concentration on the event itself is vivid and dramatic, but it displaces analysis of the cause," he said.

In the case of the Rodney King beating, what wasn't shown was "the systematic structuring of discrimination and racism that we don't know, but suspect is ingrained in the system of policing."

Amateur video also "individualizes" crime, Henry said. The Los Angeles Police Department tried to paint the Rodney King incident as the result of a few bad apples in the system.

"Are these police bad apples or is the barrel bad?" Henry said. "Because if you put all kinds of good apples in a bad barrel, they're going to go rotten."

News director Rowe said while amateur film may not show that, the professional media can, by using the amateur video as a starting point.

The advantage of this style of newsmaking is that the initial statement is developed outside of the media and is thereby controlled by the criminologists. The content drives the media interest and reasonably assures subsequent stages of coverage. The disadvantage is that successive stages progressively wrest control from the criminologist until the content is reduced to "the experts disagree" form.

As with our previous styles, one way of preempting the progressive deterioration of the replacement component of a newsmaking piece is for the criminologist to retain control over the content by becoming the journalist. However, unless this is done competently, it is likely that the issue will be relegated to a one time "op ed" type of commentary. This can be overcome by attempting to critically address journalists themselves, either through their conferences or through journalists' in-house journals and professional magazines. The final case illustration here is an example of such an approach. Taken from a British magazine for journalists, the article presents a critical analysis of the media coverage on employee theft. The concept of "employee theft," which in Britain is referred to as "fiddling," was virtually totally displaced (as a result of the reports by several ethnographic researchers) with discourse used by the participants. Until the 1970s no mention of "fiddling" appears in the media. When discussed, the topic was described by its legal and criminal description as "petty" theft. Primarily as a result of the ethnographic work and numerous interactions by ethnographers with the media, the criminally loaded terminology was displaced by various ethnographically derived colloquialisms which, in addition to "fiddling," included "knock-offs" and "stuff that fell off the back of a lorry."

The switch of discourse carried with it a switch of meaning. Instead of theft and dishonesty, the new language was able to convey some of the actual understanding of the activity shared by the participants as fun, exciting, and symbolic, in terms of prestige and status. In the media battle that ensued ambivalence reigned. On the one hand journalists found covering the topic highly desirable since it was tantalizing and touched everyone who had their own "little fiddle." On the other hand the assertion that many, indeed most British workers were secretly "on the fiddle"—a "Nation on the Fiddle"—disturbed many of those who held power, not least the right-wing press (led by the most popular British tabloid, *The Sun*). The article reproduced here was part of that battle, an attempt to expose the hypocrisy of the most fervent of the right-wing press and its recent attempts to use fiddling as a weapon against employees in an industrial dispute. At a broader level the article was an attempt to educate and challenge journalists to switch from moral diatribe and reproduction of existing categories of crime to taking a more philosophically consistent view of the new research data, recognizing that it dissolved the false distinction between honesty and dishonesty, and acknowledging the implications this has for the media's reproduction of criminal stereotypes.

Case Study 4: Stuart Henry on Employee Theft and the Honesty/Dishonesty Distinction.

> **"Fiddling as a media issue" by Stuart Henry, *The Media Reporter*, Winter, 1982, pp. 41–43.** [Reprinted with permission of James Brennan.]
>
> *The Sun*'s revelations earlier this year about fiddling on the trains was sensational news. This was not because fiddling had been discovered. Since 1976 news features on fiddling in all occupations have abounded. It was newsworthy because the fiddlers' crime was being used in the battle of the industrial dispute between the union ASLEF and British Rail—not by British Rail but by the media. This raises the whole question of the news media's role in crime reporting and in particular what precisely are the functions served by newspaper reports on fiddling.
>
> It has become a sociological wisdom that the stereotypes of crime used by the police are reinforced by media crime reports. The resulting moral panics lead to more focussed policing of suspect categories, which in turn produce more news stories that confirm the original "knowledge" and establish the self-fulfilling prophecy.
>
> Until recently, mugging, robbery, theft, violence, burglary and vandalism have been the familiar labels of crimes stereotypically portrayed as committed by the young, working class, urban male. But what happens to the stereotype of crime if, instead of the befriended police officer or courtroom trial, journalists find a new source of data for their crime stories? With fiddling as crime, it is only necessary to find a neighborhood fiddler, the plumber, the electrician . . . According to crime-and-the-

media theory, research data on the fiddles of "honest" citizens should direct the police to look at new areas and to develop different stereotypical categories. The explosion of tales about fiddling that has occurred in recent years, of which the railway fiddles is the latest example, threatens to bring about just such a change in the criminal stereotype, with serious consequences for us all.

Conventional crime reporting arguably serves the deterrent function once served by the stocks and public hangings. Not only does it show what happens to the miscreant who strays, but it also redefines and reaffirms society's rules, celebrating their rightness and thereby maintaining the existing social order. As Steve Box has said: "Reportage alone cannot provide the necessary potency to arouse and reaffirm public support. Only where there is a public pronouncement of the offence, drawing out its illegality and immorality, are moral boundaries reaffirmed and individually reinforced."

Paradoxically, journalists might have been partially, if inadvertently, responsible for creating the moral climate for fiddling to thrive, by their almost exclusive attention to the sensational and conventional predatory crimes of working class offenders. The more monstrous and degraded the conventional criminals, the less ordinary people can identify with them. Thus, the mass of drifting moral consciences may well be directed away from committing conventional stereotyped crime, giving the illusion of law and order, but ordinary people may simultaneously be freed from other areas of moral inhibition.

The "necessity" to decry the conventional criminal and his enterprise, which results in tales of horror and disgust, renders it virtually impossible for the "upright" citizen to see any similarity between everyday working practices and the corruption and depravity of the "small minority of criminals." They might reason, "Theft, robbing, mugging, stealing, that's what criminals do. Fiddling? I don't call that crime. How can it be? It's part of everyday life. Everyone's got a little fiddle. It's perks, something you get because you work somewhere. Like businessmen get expenses."

Nor is it easy to dismiss such reasoning as rationalization. Fiddling is an inseparable part of workers' everyday lives. The fiddler's spoils, unlike the money gained in the activities of the conventional crime, are a marginal part of one's total rewards earned for legitimate work. These rewards need not take a monetary form. The status gained from being in the know or the favors reciprocally returned, or the prestige conferred by giving away company goods that are scrap, waste, or obsolete are as unaccountable and as invisible a gain, as the sheer creative satisfaction of beating the system.

There is excitement and fun accruing to anyone who runs their own "little business" on the side, and experiences the joy of personal enterprise. As Jason Ditton has said, "Fiddling epitomizes the capitalist 'spirit'." How could it, then, be seen, let alone be labelled, as crime?

So, if in conventional crime reporting, journalists were responsible for omitting these grey areas, then the blame was not wholly theirs. It reflects a fundamental flaw in our system of social control: minimizing of ambiguity by dealing only in discrete categories of good or bad, honest or dishonest.

It is not surprising that when journalists did deal with fiddling at work, they presented a picture of a stray worker; a rather pathetic figure, a petty criminal, a rotten apple. It was also a genuine shock for the worker, who perhaps got a little carried away in his institutionalized perks or who overstepped the taken-for-granted rules of fiddling and either lost his job or was prosecuted for "employee theft." They're confused. It wasn't like *that*. But under the existing conception of crime, it has to be like that, for to accept the implications of widespread fiddling would destroy the "technology" of social control: either those convicted of ordinary property offenses are as honest as everyone else, or everyone else is to a greater or lesser degree, dishonest.

However, in 1976 fiddling became a media issue as a result of ethnographic work by sociologists such as Gerald Mars, Jason Ditton and myself. Fiddling as every person's crime became newsworthy. This was a change of tack by journalists and might prove to be as ominous in its implications for the ordinary worker as the traditional police stereotype has been for the young, male, working class city dweller.

At first, fiddling was presented under the old stereotype
of crime; either it was very big and horrible or it was so
trivial as to be funny. Thus because of the supposed
shadiness of the fiddles and their assumed similarity to
conventional crime, a colleague was asked how he slept at
night. "Don't you worry about being found in the gutter
with your throat slit?" Another was asked, "How did you
get them to tell you, let alone let you record it?"

But at first most journalists trivialized the new fiddling
research and treated it as a one-off novelty story. *The
Guardian* and the *Sunday Times* captured this mood with
come-on titles like "Fiddling with no strings" (January 30,
1976); "How bread salesmen sneak their slice of the
profits" (April 17, 1977); and "Fiddling while the roast
burns" (July 11, 1976). Even *New Society* felt that its readers
would be more attracted to my work on the hidden
economy under the title "It fell off the back of a lorry"
(February 26, 1976), whereas it had reported Ditton's
bakery study two years earlier under the big and horrible
title of "Connivance at Corruption" (February, 1974). What
was to be made of this new found "crime?"

Newspaper editors know that "left wing babble" does
not sell. We were told, "It's no use talking about the crisis
in capitalism coming home to roost. I know there are
'contradictions' but our readers just won't understand
what workers-trying-to-take-over-their-own-lives means.
It's too theoretical. Let's stick to the concrete examples.
Have you got anymore like the supermarket cashier
who. . . ?"

But like the punters, the journalists also were not quite
sure whether fiddling was *real* crime. If it was, and
everyone was fiddling, then it was no longer just "bad
apples" that workers were fingering but workmates and
colleagues, mums and dads, you and me. Only *The Sun*
was "bold" enough to take a moral stance against *all* of its
readers. In the first front-page expose, on August 9, 1976,
it screamed "Stop thief!" and indicted the British for being
a nation of fiddlers.

Its editorial blazed: "The truth is, we are all at it. Which
doesn't make it any more acceptable morally. And it
doesn't make any sense either. For in the end someone has
to pay. And who is that? US!" Contradictions indeed—
perhaps all of us judge it worth paying for, as the rewards

need not be economic but nonetheless valuable for that. However, the real sensation of accepting that the whole nation was on the fiddle had nothing to do with morality or economics but everything to do with crime control: the conventional stereotype of the criminal had been cut off at the thighs!

Now this approach of blanket moral condemnation makes for very uneasy feelings. People don't buy uneasy feelings. So how was it that by the end of 1979 features on fiddling rocketed to an average of one per week, with double-page, week-long serials not untypical? How was it that instead of mass confession and public repentance , we witnessed the rise of fiddlers' tales as the topic of conversation at all levels, from dockers (longshoremen) to doctors and from dustmen (garbage collectors) to dons? What has led to party jokes and the riddle being replaced by workers on the fiddle? "Have you heard the one about the hospital where the nurses take home a free supply of clean sheets from the linen cupboard? They don't steal them but take their dirty ones back to be laundered . . ."

A review of the mass of features on fiddling reveals a pattern that goes someway to exploring its "coming out"; articles abound, in particular, at budget time, during industrial disputes and as follow-ups to research reports. They have been used to explain everything from why holidays are up 25% in a recession (*Daily Mail*, January 13, 1982) to why, with three million unemployed, the workers haven't revolted ("Black Cash is Beautiful" *Daily Mail*, February 1, 1982). In all, four kinds of fiddlers' tale have appeared, each serving a different purpose. None antagonizes general readers; one excuses them for their infidelities, another praises them for their entrepreneurial spirit as it fights the tide of interventionism, a third pushes the pro-interventionist tax lobby, while a fourth reinforces the old crime stereotype in a new and more sinister form.

The first of these fiddlers' tales is a variation on the "nation of fiddlers" theme. Everyone is at it, but there is no moral condemnation; rather, the treatment is soft and light as in the *Daily Express*: "The joy of personal enterprise, otherwise known as fiddling" (January 30, 1982). The foundation for this perspective had been laid by the *Sunday Mirror's* double-page spread: "Britain on the fiddle" (January 30, 1977) which offered the apologia "As money gets tighter and harder to come by, more and more people are finding new ways to make ends meet. And for millions that means going on the fiddle."

The second theme went even further, suggesting that fiddling, in the form of moonlighting, actually "oiled the wheels of industry." As Jeremy Alden's *New Society* article had shown (September 23, 1976), moonlighters were anything but criminals. They were workaholics, giving up extra holidays to do other jobs and maximizing all overtime that was available. Grahame Shankland's *Guardian* article (December 23, 1977) went furthest when he said that Britain was moving toward dual economy with a personal, labor intensive, informal sector in a symbiotic, complementary relationship to the formal sector.

As the *Daily Mail*'s "No cheques please, we're British" (January 16, 1979) article explained, beneath the faltering formal economy there was "a thriving underground economy which is doing very nicely, thank you. The so-called lazy British are prepared to work extra hours from dawn to beyond sunset and on their holidays, as long as they are working for cash." This second theme was endorsed in 1981 when Prince Charles, no less, lectured businessmen on the black (underground) economy and the spirit of capitalism. It is, he said, evidence that the British worker is not work shy! The purpose of this theme is often to raise public emotions at budget time in order to persuade the Chancellor not to further over-tax the British public.

In contrast a third theme is fed by the Inland Revenue (internal revenue) and was first inspired by Sir William Pile's guesstimate of the cost of the black economy as $7\frac{1}{2}$ of the GNP. The obsession here is with macro-economic size, as in the *Financial Times*'s "Guide to Underground Economics (April 9, 1979), and the numerous other tax-evasion stories. Also appearing at budget time, these stories function to offset the anti-interventionist lobby and expand the need for the tax man.

The most sinister of the media's stereotypical responses to fiddling is the fourth approach, that of the employee-fiddler-thief expose, such as that of *The Sun*'s fiddling on the railways. This is a grand version of the fiddling-as-crime approach. It hits hard and heavy. But it resolves the aftertaste of the earlier blanket moral condemnation in a sophisticated way. The key is to select a working class service occupation with a high degree of public contact and against whom there is a long standing grudge and then bash them silly on a charge of fiddling: the minority holding the majority, *qua* consumer, to ransom. "Fiddles on the Tubes" (metro) (*Evening Standard*, February 28, 1979), "Postmen on the fiddle" (*Daily Mirror*, July 16, 1979), "Mickey Mouses on the Press" (*Evening Standard*, March 22, 1979).

It is with *The Sun*'s railway fiddlers that we can see precisely the function of this kind of stereotype. It is not so much to deter other railway fiddlers but can be invoked to exploit society's dual morality toward fiddling in order to undermine the employee's case in an industrial dispute or a wage claim, while at the same time gaining respect from a suffering public.

The day before its railway fiddles expose, *The Sun* editorial exhorted British Rail to "Shut it down!" (January 21, 1982), so as to prevent the train drivers "trying to blackmail the railways into giving them a three per cent rise." They said: "It's showdown time now! The sabotage campaign by the drivers leaves Sir Peter with no alternative. He should shut down the railways. Send the drivers home. Tell them that they will get no more wages until they are prepared to do the job."

The very next day *The Sun*'s page one exclusive exclaimed, "Taken for a ride! ASLEF (union) men paid as they drink, sleep and disco. An astonishing dossier of fiddling, cheating and lying by ASLEF train drivers can be revealed by *The Sun* today."

This new stereotypical approach to crime is not to pick off one worker as a criminal, but a whole occupational group and divisively set them against the rest. What was often used by managements inside the factory as a device to remove potential union organizers and so control a company's wage bill, is now being used, via the media, to support management's control of wage and manning levels for a whole occupational category.

Where does this leave the police's traditional stereotype of the working class urban offender? Will the crime wave and moral panic created by media reports on fiddling, guide the police away from the public, urban inner-city to the privacy of working class jobs? Will special attention be given to the new "gangs" of barter in self-help and survival economies of the "working unemployed"? Already we have an SPG of the tax inspectorate; 400 special investigators appointed in 1981 to investigate the "new" crimes of tax evasion, and the DHSS are cracking down on social security fraud.

If the labelling theorists are right, this shift in the media stereotype of crime must increase the pressure for fuller policing of the "private," while intensifying the debate about total policing in terms of feasibility with respect to human rights, manpower and costs. At present these "gaps" are being filled by a growing army of more than 100,000 private security police, equal in strength to the civil police force. But how long before the civil police see working class jobs as their beat?

In this approach to newsmaking, the criminologist directly addresses journalists. Newsmaking criminology that attempts to directly engage journalists through their own professional associations and journals has the advantage of permeating a wide variety of media as well as influencing the constitutive process whereby future crime news is constructed. The disadvantage is that unless the attempt is repeated, the weight of standard approaches will outweigh the educative attempt, and further, the very critical nature of the approach may alienate the very journalists one is seeking to court.

Conclusion

Replacement discourse, then, is not merely another package of ways to talk and make sense of the world, but a language of "transpraxis" (Milovanovic and Henry, 1991). It is a non-reificatory connecting of the way we speak with our social relations and institutions such that, through its use, we are continuously aware of the interrelatedness of our agency and the structures it reproduces through the constitutively productive work of our talking, perceiving, conceptualizing, and theorizing. A genuinely alternative, replacement discourse envelops not just crimes as popularly understood but harms that cause pain, regardless of whether these have been defined as criminal by the political process. It includes all the players in the construction of harm, the victims, the offender and the agencies of the criminal justice system. Here it captures not only the declarations of policy but the ways its practitioners and policymakers distinguish their reality from the totality that is the social order. Replacement discourse requires a "bringing back in" of the under-emphasized, informal, unofficial, marginalized practices (the unspoken) that are part of the totality of the criminological enterprise. It speaks for providing various (repressed, marginalized) discursive practices a forum for genuine consideration. Only with such a comprehension of the totality, and the contribution of these excluded parts to the reality-making process is it possible to provide an alternative understanding of the phenomena of crime and crime control in our society. Only from such an understanding of the total constitutive process is it possible to generate a replacement discourse that completes the cycle from deconstruction to reconstruction. While it is not possible for replacement discourse to be fully autonomous, it is possible for those generating it to be reflexively aware of the importance of the dialectics of control whereby their alternative structuring and conceptualization can be co-opted, weakened and contaminated. At the same time replacement discourse is capable of having transformational power over established orders. Each of the approaches to transformative newsmaking criminology illustrated here recognizes the need to generate alternative concepts and cosmologies, while realizing that there is minimal room for such activity owing to the common discourse that pervades the totality and that provides the initial medium for any alternative form.

REFERENCES

Barak, Gregg. 1988. "Newsmaking criminology: Reflections on the media, intellectuals, and crime." *Justice Quarterly*, 5: 565–87.

———. 1991a. "Homelessness and the case for community-based initiatives: The emergence of a model shelter as a short term response to the deepening crisis in housing." In Pepinsky, Harold and Richard Quinney (eds.) *Criminology as Peacemaking*. Bloomington: Indiana University Press.

———. 1991b. *Gimme Shelter*. Westport, CT: Praeger.

Barak, Gregg and Bob Bohm. 1989. "The crimes of the homeless or the crime of homelessness." *Contemporary Crises*, 13: 275–288.

Bogdan, Robert and Steven Taylor. 1987. "Towards a sociology of acceptance: The other side of the study of deviance." *Social Policy*, 18: 34–39.

Braithwaite, John. 1982. "Challenging just deserts: Punishing white-collar criminals." *Journal of Criminal Law and Criminology*, 73: 723–64.

Chibnall, Steve. 1977. *Law and Order News*. London: Tavistock.

Christie, Nils. 1977. "Conflicts as Property." *British Journal of Criminology*, 17: 1–15.

Cohen, Albert K. 1955. *Delinquent Boys: The Culture of the Gang*. New York: Free Press.

Cohen, Stanley. 1985. *Visions of Social Control*. Oxford: Polity Press.

Cohen, Stanley and Jock Young (eds.). 1981. *The Manufacture of News*. London: Constable.

Cullen, Frank et al. 1985. "Dissecting white-collar crime: Offense type and punitiveness." *International Journal of Comparative and Applied Criminal Justice*, 9 (Spring): 15–27.

Einstadter, Werner J. and Stuart Henry. 1991. "The inversion of the invasion of privacy?" *The Critical Criminologist*, 3, (Winter): 5, 7.

Foucault, Michel. 1978. *The History of Sexuality: An Introduction*. Harmondsworth: Penguin.

Fox, James Alan and Jack Levin. 1993. *How to Work with the Media*. Newbury Park, CA: Sage.

Gibbons, Don C. 1969. "Crime and punishment: A study of social attitudes." *Social Forces*, 47: 391–97.

Henry, Stuart. 1982. "Fiddling as a media issue." *The Media Reporter* (Winter) pp. 41–43.

———. 1987. "The construction and deconstruction of social control: Thoughts on the discursive production of state law and private justice." In J. Lowman, R. Menzies and T. Palys, *Transcarceration: Essays in the Sociology of Social Control.* Aldershot, England: Gower Press.

———. 1991. "Constitutive criminology: The maturation of critical criminology." *Criminology*, 29: 601–23.

Henry, Stuart and Dragan Milovanovic. (forthcoming). "The constitution of constitutive criminology." In David Nelken (ed.) *The Future of Criminology.* London: Sage.

Jahr, Michael. 1991. "Amateur news videos criticized: Cameras distort crime, EMU professors say." *Ann Arbor News* (November 25), pp. C1–C2.

Johns, Christina. 1986a. "Women and crime: Women who kill." *Southline* (November, 26).

———. 1986b. "Women and crime: The female victim." *Southline* (December, 3).

———. 1986c. "Women and crime: On the firing line." *Southline* (December, 17).

Katz, Jack. 1988. *Seductions of Crime: Moral and Sensual Attractions of Doing Evil.* New York: Basic Books.

McLean, Debra. 1991. "Profs' paper looks at new trend of 'video vigilantes.'" *FOCUS EMU*, 38, 9 (October 8), p. 2.

Manning, Peter. 1988. *Symbolic Communication: Signifying Calls and the Police Response.* Cambridge: MIT Press.

Milovanovic, Dragan. 1986. "Juridico-linguistic communicative markets: towards a semiotic analysis." *Contemporary Crises*, 10: 281–304.

Milovanovic, Dragan and Stuart Henry. 1991. "Constitutive penology." *Social Justice*, 18: 204–224.

Newman, Donald J. 1968. "Public attitudes toward a form of white collar crime" in Geis, Gilbert (ed.) *White Collar Criminal.* New York: Atherton Press.

Pepinsky, Harold. 1991. *The Geometry of Violence and Democracy.* Bloomington: Indiana University Press.

Pepinsky, Harold and Richard Quinney (eds). 1991. *Criminology as Peacemaking.* Bloomington: Indiana University Press.

Roberts, Julian and Thomas Gabor. 1989. "Rushton's crime theories have no basis in fact." *The Toronto Star*, March 14, p. A 21.

Selva, Lance and Bob Bohm. 1987. "Law and liberation: Toward an oppositional legal discourse." *Legal Studies Forum*, 113: 255–76.

Smart, Barry. 1983. *Foucault, Marxism and Critique*. London: Routledge and Kegan Paul.

Sutherland, Edwin H. 1940. "White collar criminality." American *Sociological Review*, 5: 1–12.

———. 1941. "Crime and business." *Annals of the American Academy of Political and Social Science*, 217 (September): 112–18.

———. 1945. "Is white collar crime, crime?" *American Sociological Review*, 10: 132–139.

———. 1949. "The white collar criminal." In Branham, Vernon C. and Kutash, Samuel B. (eds.), *Encyclopedia of Criminology*. New York: Philosophical Library.

Sweet, Lois. 1991. Crime and race: A question of statistics." *The Toronto Star* (October 19), pp. D1 ff.

Thomas, Jim. 1988. *Prisoner Litigation: The Paradox of the Jailhouse Lawyer*. Totowa, NJ: Rowman and Littlefield.

Whittemore, Hank. 1992. "Hitting bottom can be the beginning." *Parade Magazine* (March 15), pp. 4–6.

Willis, Paul. 1977. *Learning to Labour: How Working Class Kids Get Working Class Jobs*. Aldershot, England: Gower Press.

Contributors

Gregg Barak is professor and head of the Department of Sociology, Anthropology, and Criminology at Eastern Michigan University. He received his doctorate from the School of Criminology at U.C. Berkeley in 1974. He is the author of *In Defense of Whom? A Critique of Criminal Justice Reform* (1980) and *Gimme Shelter: A Social History of Homelessness in Contemporary America* (*Choice*'s List of Outstanding Academic Books for 1991). He is the editor of *Crimes by the Capitalist State: An Introduction to State Criminality* (1991) and *Varieties of Criminology: Readings from a Dynamic Discipline* (1994). He currently serves as a Deputy Editor of *Justice Quarterly*.

Steven Chermak is a visiting assistant professor in the Department of Criminal Justice at Indiana University in Bloomington. His research interests include crime in the mass media, victimology, and police behavior.

Werner J. Einstadter is professor emeritus of sociology and criminology, Eastern Michigan University. He is the co-author with Neal Shover of *Analyzing American Corrections* and is completing with Stuart Henry a text on criminological theory. His long-term interest is in theory development and exploring the problem of the violation of privacy. He resides in California.

Charles B. Fields is an associate professor in the Department of Political Science and Criminal Justice at Appalachian State University. He has a B.A. and M.A. in political science from Appalachian State University and received his Ph.D. in criminal justice from Sam Houston State University in 1984. His most recent articles/reviews have appeared in the *Journal of Criminal Justice*, *Criminal Justice Policy Review*, *Quarterly Journal of Ideology*, and the *Journal of Criminal Law and Criminology*, among others. He is the current president of the Southern Criminal Justice Association and is Region Two Trustee on the executive board of the Academy of Criminal Justice Sciences.

Cecil E. Greek was born in Latrobe, PA. He attended Eastern College and the New School for Social Research, earning a Ph.D. in sociology in 1983. His doctoral dissertation, *The Religious Roots of American Sociology*, was published by Garland Publishing. His long-term interest continues to be in the social construction of social problems. He became involved in newsmaking criminology as a way to combat media stereotypes. He has written on anti-pornography crusading, the use of forfeiture penalties, and juvenile justice. He is currently assistant professor of criminology at the University of South Florida, St. Petersburg.

Stuart Henry is professor of criminology in the Department of Sociology, Anthropology and Criminology at Eastern Michigan University. He received his undergraduate and doctoral degrees in sociology from the University of Kent at Canterbury. He has published eight books and more than fifty articles on aspects of crime, deviance and informal social control. His books include: *Self-help and Health* (1977); *The Hidden Economy* (1978); *Informal Institutions* (1981); *Private Justice* (1983); *The Informal Economy* (1987); *Degrees of Deviance* (1990); *Making Markets* (1992); and *The Deviance Process* (1993). His current books in progress include one with Werner Einstadter on criminological theory, one on criminal justice careers, and one from his recent NSF-funded study on the relationship between privately constructed systems of justice and state law.

Robert A. Jerin is an assistant professor in the Department of Political Science and Criminal Justice at Appalachian State University. He has a BS in criminal justice from the University of New Haven, an MS in criminology from Florida State University, and a Ph.D. in criminal justice from Sam Houston State University in 1987. He has published in the *American Journal of*

Police and his current research includes victims/witness assistance program evaluations and crime victims' rights.

Renée Goldsmith Kasinsky is associate professor of criminal justice at the University of Massachusetts at Lowell. In 1992–93 she was on sabbatical as a visiting scholar at Radcliffe College and Harvard University. She is the editor of a reader in its second edition, *Controversies in Criminology: Gender, Class and Race Considered* (1993). She also has an interest in international refugees and law. Her earlier book, *Refugees From Militarism: Draft-Age Americans in Canada* (1976), was nominated for the Sorokin Award. She has written articles on topics of crime and gender including rape, sexual harassment, and corporate violence. She is the co-editor of the series *Feminism and the Social Sciences*, Peter Lang Publishers.

Harry L. Marsh is an associate professor in the Department of Criminology, Indiana State University, Terre Haute. He received his Ph.D. from Sam Houston State University in 1988. He has published a number of articles pertaining to newspaper coverage of crime. His areas of research and publication also include the U.S. military and training for security and law enforcement officers.

Steven Stack is a professor of criminal justice at Wayne State University and the head of the criminal justice curriculum at the university. He received his Ph.D. in sociology at the University of Connecticut in 1976. He has published extensively in the areas of suicide, homicide, capital punishment and collective violence. He is currently working with Ira M. Wasserman in the development and testing of statistical models related to suicide and collective violence.

Ray Surette has published a number of articles and books on the area of media, crime, and criminal justice. His most recent work is *Media, Crime and Criminal Justice: Images and Realities* (1992). He is currently a professor in the criminal justice department at Florida International University in Miami, Florida.

Ira M. Wasserman is a professor of sociology at Eastern Michigan University. He received his Ph.D. in sociology from the University of Michigan in 1971. He has published extensively in the areas of suicide, collective violence and aging. He is currently working with Steven Stack in the development and testing of statistical models related to suicide and collective violence.